ENGLISH HERITAGE

River Thames

IN THE FOOTSTEPS OF
THE FAMOUS

Paul Goldsack

Bradt Travel Guides Ltd, UK
The Globe Pequot Press Inc, USA

First published in 2003 by Bradt Travel Guides Ltd,
19 High Street, Chalfont St Peter, Bucks SL9 9QE, England
Published in the USA by The Globe Pequot Press Inc,
246 Goose Lane, PO Box 480, Guilford, Connecticut 06437-0480

British Library Cataloguing in Publication Data
A catalogue record for this book is available from the British Library

ISBN 1 84162 044 0

Front cover Hilary Bradt (photograph), Susan Bethune (cartoon)

Illustrations Carole Vincer, Dave Colton
Maps Steve Munns, based on Ordnance Survey sources

Typeset from the author's disc by Wakewing, High Wycombe
Printed and bound in Italy by Legoprint SpA, Trento

Author/Acknowledgements

AUTHOR
Paul Goldsack, 64, says he now has trouble recognising himself in the 'elderly wrinkly who stares, wobble-eyed and weary, from the shaving mirror every morning'. He's had what he describes as a busy working life, kicking off after school as a trainee newspaper reporter, then a paratrooper, then a globe-trotting features writer scampering round the world after hot stories for a fistful of magazines. He still hankers after a bit of 'gentle adventuring' but spends most of his time travelling or boozing and eating and nattering, or researching and writing, or sailing and maintaining – with his wife Val – their 106-year-old live-aboard Dutch sailing barge.

ACKNOWLEDGEMENTS
There are so many people who have had a hand in helping my researches for this book that I don't know where to start. I am also concerned that I will mention one and forget another. So, please, everybody who has had a say in things, all those helpful souls I have met on my wanderings up and down the Thames, accept this as my sincerest, most heartfelt thanks for your help. And for the warmth of your company, of course!

DEDICATION
To my daughter Samantha, whom we all call Sam, and who died when she was just 29 but has never really left us.

Contents

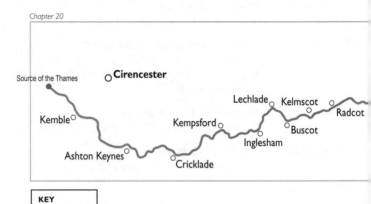

Chapter 20

Source of the Thames

○ **Cirencester**

Lechlade○ Kelmscot○
  Radcot

Kemble○

Kempsford○

Buscot○

Inglesham○

Ashton Keynes○

Cricklade○

KEY
Town maps ●

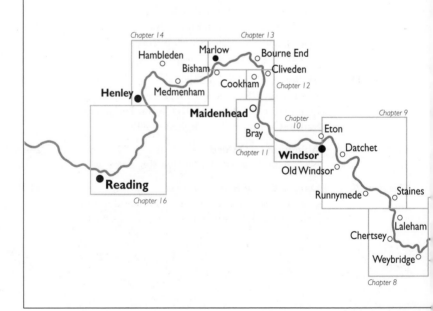

Chapter 14   Chapter 13

Hambleden○   Marlow●   ○Bourne End
      Bisham○   ○Cliveden
Henley● Medmenham○ Cookham○   Chapter 12
          Chapter 10
    Maidenhead○   Eton○   Chapter 9
        Bray○   **Windsor**● Datchet○
  Reading●   Chapter 11   Old Windsor○
    Chapter 16   Runnymede○   Staines○
                Laleham○
            Chertsey○
              Weybridge○
              Chapter 8

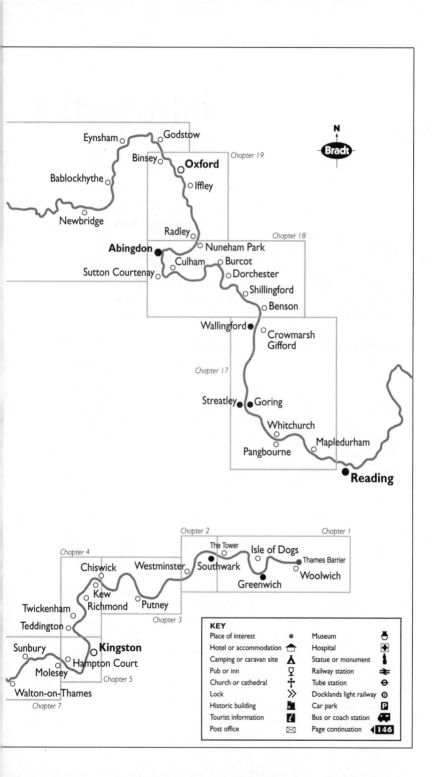

Chapter 19

Chapter 18

Chapter 17

Eynsham   Godstow
Binsey   **Oxford**
Bablockhythe   Iffley
Newbridge
Radley
Abingdon   Nuneham Park
Culham   Burcot
Sutton Courtenay   Dorchester
Shillingford
Benson
Wallingford   Crowmarsh
Gifford
Streatley   Goring
Whitchurch
Mapledurham
Pangbourne
Reading

Chapter 2   Chapter 1
The Tower   Isle of Dogs
Chapter 4   Westminster   Southwark   Thames Barrier
Chiswick   Woolwich
Kew   Greenwich
Twickenham   Richmond   Putney
Teddington   Chapter 3
Sunbury
Kingston
Molesey   Hampton Court
Walton-on-Thames   Chapter 5
Chapter 7

KEY			
Place of interest	●	Museum	🏺
Hotel or accommodation	⌂	Hospital	✚
Camping or caravan site	⋀	Statue or monument	⚲
Pub or inn	♀	Railway station	⇌
Church or cathedral	✝	Tube station	⊖
Lock	≫	Docklands light railway	Ⓓ
Historic building	⌘	Car park	P
Tourist information	𝑖	Bus or coach station	🚌
Post office	⊠	Page continuation	◀146

Introduction

You can walk it. You can pedal it, paddle it, motorboat it, or sail it. You can reach it by bus, by train, by car. You could, I suppose, even swim it from top to bottom – and someone probably has.

'It', of course, is the Thames, the wonderful, historic, beautiful River Thames. I have sailed the lower tidal reaches in majestic Thames sailing barges. I have paddled the middle and upper reaches by skiff and canoe. I've walked it, every single inch of the 180-mile (288km) Thames Path, and a good deal more if you chuck in all the riverside villages and towns and byways I have meandered through.

I have explored it not just on foot and by boat, but by car, by bus and by train, for it is a river most well (and often conveniently) served by roads and public transport. The exception, of course, is the silk-green water of the upper stripling Thames where, wonderfully, there are no roads and few dwellings close to the river – here there is little more than willow trees and buttercup meadows, where cows laze ankle deep in summer grasses and all that solitary wanderers hear is the hum of bees and the chirping of grasshoppers – but it is enough.

The Thames Path provides a wonderful opportunity for long walking or biking adventure from the Thames Barrier to the source, or, if you prefer to travel the other way round, from source to Barrier. Ideally, if you ever have the opportunity, then make the journey by boat, slowly, from the tidal waters of the 'London River' to the infant Thames and the more-or-less end of river navigation at Lechlade's Ha'penny Bridge. If you'd rather, of course, there is nothing to stop you and yours exploring the river's banks and villages and towns in smaller nibbles, arriving by car or public transport in order to 'do' the Thames and its path bit by bit, day's-out style.

This book is for walkers or bikers or boaters who yearn to discover something new and beautiful and fascinating. Or for armchair travellers in search of history. The Thames is a magnificent river, a 'noble' one of incredible history. You will be amazed, as I was, at how many of history's 'greats' have left their footprints on the banks of the Thames … the splendid reminders of England's yesterdays.

Note on maps Read the linear Thames Path maps from right to left in order to follow the direction of the Thames from the Barrier to its source. The arrows indicate the relevant page numbers of the preceding and subsequent maps.

The Thames Barrier to Tower Bridge

THE STARTING POINT

The Thames walk starts beside the Thames Barrier, downstream of historic Greenwich on the south bank of the River Thames. The Blackwall Tunnel upstream and the Woolwich Ferry downstream. Access by road is via the A206 Woolwich Road; take Eastmoor Street leading to Unity Way and park beside the Thames Barrier Visitor Centre. The nearest bus stop is on the A206, about half a mile from the Thames Barrier (Nos 177 and 180). Charlton railway station is 15 minutes' walk away, and there are trains every 30 minutes from Charing Cross, Waterloo East, London Bridge and Dartford. North Greenwich Underground station is two miles from the Thames Barrier. For further information, tel: 020 8305 4188; fax: 020 8855 2146; web: www.environment-agency.gov.uk.

Distances From Thames Barrier: Millennium Dome Thames Path Diversion (liable to change) 1.98 miles (3.16km), end of Millennium Dome Diversion at Blackwall Reach (liable to change) 3.75 miles (5.04km), Trinity Hospital Almshouses 4.97 miles (7.95km), *Cutty Sark* and Greenwich Pier 6.47 miles (10.35km).
From Greenwich Pier (north-bank route/south-bank route): Tower Bridge 5.74/7.16 miles (9.18/11.45km).

THE THAMES BARRIER

The town of Woolwich grew up alongside its Dockyard, its Arsenal, its Royal Military Academy and its free ferry. The Dockyard and Arsenal have gone, the Royal Military Academy is a shadow of its glory-days, and though the ferry still connects south bank with north, as it has done since 1889, this bustling London borough is nowadays best known for the Thames Barrier.

The Thames Path begins here, on the south bank, overlooking the seven silver

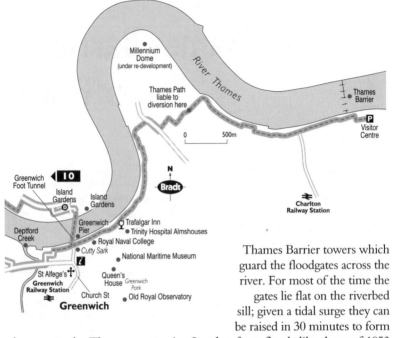

Thames Barrier towers which guard the floodgates across the river. For most of the time the gates lie flat on the riverbed sill; given a tidal surge they can be raised in 30 minutes to form a dam across the Thames, protecting London from floods like those of 1953 which swept the east coast of England, killing 300 people, or those of 1663, which put fright in **Samuel Pepys**. He wrote that it was 'the greatest tide that ever was remembered in England to have been in this river: all White Hall having been drowned'.

Visitor information There is a cafeteria adjoining the visitor centre and an exhibition that is meant to explain all about the barrier's doings, but it is a tatty thing and a sore disappointment, and hardly worth the entrance cost of £1 for adults, £0.75 for senior citizens and £0.50 for children.

GREENWICH

All in all, this is a depressingly concrete place to begin the Thames walk. The river hereabouts are is dull as pewter and empty as a pigeon's head save for the rare cruiser or river bus. Push on, that's my advice, to the delights of Greenwich, three-and-a-bit miles (5.2km) up-river. On the way you will pass the translucent, 'squashed-mushroom' **Millennium Dome**. Its impressive (320m) diameter is suspended from 12 steel masts, each one 328ft (100m) high, held in place by more than 43 miles (68.8km) of high-strength cables. As many as 40,000 people could comfortably be fitted inside – if anyone could ever get that many people to visit at one time; certainly,

nothing like that number ever turned up on a single session during millennium year.

The riverside walk northwest alongside Bugsby's Reach, past the dome then south down Blackwall Reach to the skirts of Greenwich, is a bleak and desolate stretch comprising abandoned wharves and pipes belching steam and peculiar smells. Sometimes, although increasingly less often these days, the monotony is relieved by ships unloading mysterious cargoes.

Opposite the dome, on the north bank, is the modernist **Reuters Building**, British headquarters of Reuters's international business and financial news organisation, which started life as a Continental pigeon post in 1849. The yellow cranes and exposed steel girders on the building's roof are supposed to make it look unfinished, which they do. Ahead, dominating the north shore, is **Canary Wharf Tower** which we shall visit after Greenwich (see page 10) if we choose to take the northern-bank route of the Thames Path (there are two optional paths between Greenwich and Teddington, one on the south shore, the other on the north).

Once past the Millennium Dome, the Royal Naval College (see page 5) at Greenwich comes into sight for the first time. It is not the best of views, which are from the other side of the river or, best of all, from the deck of an excursion boat as it scurries past. However, the prospect is good enough to echo the words of **H J Massingham**: '. . .the sight of the Royal Naval College set like a jewel of unexampled lustre in that drab scenario between the Surrey Commercial Docks and Blackwall Reach' (from *London Scene*, published in 1934).

Greenwich

You will like Greenwich, a bustle of markets and people, of sumptuous buildings and, of course, the magnificent *Cutty Sark* clipper ship. One day is not enough to see everything worth seeing – the park is large and mesmerising, the **Royal Observatory** a whizz, the **National Maritime Museum** a stunner . . . and as for the village, the market stalls, the riverside walks. . . Someone said that 'Greenwich and its palaces are the nearest equivalent to the Versailles of Paris that England has'. He, or she, was right.

The path passes first through a small open space of grass and flower-beds, near the front of the **Trinity Hospital almshouses**, overshadowed and overburdened by the flaky-white slab of a power station which, until the 1930s, supplied electricity for Greenwich's trams and trolley buses. The almshouses, built in 1613, represent the oldest building in Greenwich; it's like a toy fort with crenellated battlements. Twenty pensioners live here and it is closed to the public, which is a pity for it means we cannot see the mummified rat on display in a glass cabinet, one of the actual rodents which brought the Great Plague to London in 1665. Hundreds of Londoners sought refuge from the disease on board boats moored between Greenwich and Rotherhithe. **Daniel Defoe** described the scene from the top of Greenwich Hill:

> There must be several Hundreds of Sail, and I could not but applaud
> the Contrivance, for ten thousand people, and more, who . . . were
> certainly sheltered here from the Violence of the Contagion, and liv'd
> very safe and very easy. . . As the richer Sort got into Ships, so the
> lower Rank got into Hoys, Smacks, Lighters and Fishing Boats. . .

The 17th-century **Yacht** public house, homely, comfortable and unpretentious (its walls covered with photographs of famous yachts and Thames maps), rubs shoulders with the more famous **Trafalgar Inn** on the paved alleyway (Crane Street) of the Thames Path. The Trafalgar, with pretty canopied balconies overlooking the river's Greenwich Reach, was built in 1837, the year Victoria came to the throne, although it looks for all the world more clean-cut Regency than ornate Victorian. From the day its doors opened it was a wow with the high-born, the done-good and the well-heeled. Cabinet ministers and Fellows of the Royal Society came by barge to eat the inn's celebrated whitebait caught in the Thames, and get merry on champagne or a mulled wine called 'Badminton'. So did **Charles Dickens** and his writer-chums **William Harrison Ainsworth** and **Wilkie Collins**. On more than one occasion Dickens walked ten miles from his home near Gravesend to meet and dine here. The inn appears in *Our Mutual Friend* when Bella Wilfer and John Rokesmith eat their wedding feast: 'What a dinner! Specimens of all the fishes that swim in the sea surely had swum their way to it'. Whitebait dinners are still served in the Inn.

F0r further information on Greenwich call at the Visitor Information Centre, 2 Cutty Sark Gardens (next to the Cutty Sark), Greenwich, London SE10 9LW; tel: 0870 608 2000

The Royal Naval College

Next to the Trafalgar Inn is Christopher Wren's baroque Royal Naval College, built on the site of **Henry VIII**'s Placentia Palace, where his daughter, who became Elizabeth I, was born. Henry thought Placentia a 'pleasant, perfect and princely palace'. He enjoyed hunting and hawking in the wooded surrounds, and took part in jousts and tournaments in Placentia's tilting yard with 'ye spere of 8 fote long'. **Queen Anne Boleyn** was carried up-river to her coronation celebrations from Placentia. Visualise the scene. An awed bystander wrote:

> There were so many boats and barges, filled to cramming with ladies and gentlemen, it was a thing to be wondered at, and although it was four English miles from Greenwich to London, and the river was so wide, nothing else could be seen all the way but boats and barges draped with awnings.

Now the Thames is a sad and abandoned highway, used sometimes by a lone pleasure boat and occasional water-buses; poet-philosopher **Peter Levi** saw it as 'a glittering sheet of water, a huge, romantic dancing floor almost empty of shipping'. Yet, only seventy-something years ago, the leading writer on London shipping, **H M Tomlinson**, wrote in *London River* about Greenwich's,

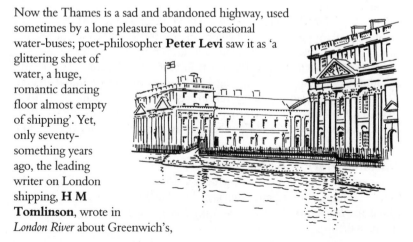

DICKENS AND THE THAMES

Great chunks of Charles Dickens's dark novel *Our Mutual Friend* are set on the Thames. Much of the book focuses on Greenwich Reach where the book's hero – the river – travels 'in and out among vessels that seemed to have got ashore, and houses that seem to have got afloat – among bowsprits staring into windows, and windows staring into ships'. Dickens's description of the ship-crowded Thames, its 'slime and ooze' mudlarked and scavenged by the 'accumulated scum of humanity', is hard, almost impossible, to recognise in the Thames today.

coasters and nearby Continental traders . . . timbermen and big transatlantic liners. . . Thousands of people stand on the bank there for hours. . .

But where were we? Ah, yes, at the Royal Naval College, built on the site of King Hal's Palace of Placentia. The college buildings were commissioned by **Charles II**, and subsequently by **Mary** and **William**, mainly to the designs of **Christopher Wren** (1632–1723), but with bits by his clerk, **Nicholas Hawksmoor** (1661–1736), and **John Vanbrugh** (1664–1716) thrown in. Wren used to cross the river to gaze at the masterpiece from the Island Gardens on the far side of the Thames. So should you, if you have the time, the way Italian artist **Giovanni Antonio Canal** (**Canaletto**) (1697–1768) did, in 1751, shortly after the college was completed in 1751; his painting of the scene is in the Greenwich National Maritime Museum – evening sunlight, a silk-placid Thames, great doings of barges and wherries, and a serenely elegant Royal Naval College on the opposite bank. Apart from the scurry of boats, the scene from the north bank of the Thames is very little different from the way it was some 250 years ago. Wonderful, eh?

The Royal Naval College building was used for a time (1813–1873) as a naval hospital for pensioners and sailors, then as the Royal Naval College, and is now part of Greenwich University and the Trinity College of Music. The **Painted Hall**, where Nelson lay in state in 1806 beneath **James Thornhill**'s extraordinary trompe l'oeil paintings, and **James Stuart's Chapel** (rebuilt 1718–25), decorated in neo-Grecian style, are open daily (Mon–Sat 10.00–17.00, Sun 12.30–17.00; free admission; for details, freephone: 0800 389 3341, or tel: 020 8269 4747; website: www.greenwichfoundation.org.uk).

National Maritime Museum

Some say the best bit of Greenwich is the Royal Naval College, others the Queen's House, the sublimely elegant heart of the two-winged **National Maritime Museum**. In fact, one is as good as the other and only a fool would compare them.

Inigo Jones (1573–1652) built the Queen's House as 'a house of delights' for **Queen Anne of Denmark**; it has been described by Richard Ormond, the museum's director, as 'the jewel in the museum's many-faceted crown'. Founded in 1934, the museum tells the story of Britain and the sea: its navy, its merchants, its explorers. There are boats, navigational instruments and model ships galore. There is an ancient and ornate royal barge built for **Frederick, Prince of Wales** in 1732 (it was called 'a floating coach' by its creator, William Kent), there are some rooms devoted to Cook and Nelson, and others to whichever seamen/explorer are the flavour of the time.

Visitor information National Maritime Museum is open daily May–Sep 10.00–17.00, and Oct–Apr 10.30–15.30. Admission free.

Greenwich Park and the Royal Observatory

Greenwich Park, behind the National Maritime Museum, is the oldest of London's royal parks. **James I** walled it in 1619, **Charles II** commissioned the formal, tree-lined walks in the 1660s, together with the giant 'steps' which run down the hillside and where dandies used to 'roll' their ladies. This was a traditional, sometimes dangerous, pastime in the 17th century when gentlemen rolled their sweet-hearts down the hill of Greenwich Park, 'creating disorder in the dress' of pretty girls, wrote an obscure poet called **William Mountfort** in 1691, who continued in verse:

> At Greenwich lies the scene, where many a lass
> Has been green-gowned upon the tender grass.

At the top of the escarpment is the old Royal Observatory, offering the best views of historic Greenwich across the river to the Isle of Dogs and Canary Wharf Tower with the dome of St Paul's and other buildings of the City of London beyond.

The observatory was set up by **Charles II** in 1675, primarily to resolve the problem of establishing longitude at sea. Built specifically for **John Flamstead**, first Astronomer Royal, it was used by his successors until 1948 when they moved to Hurstmonceaux Castle, Sussex, and subsequently to Cambridge in the 1990s. The Royal Observatory buildings include the **Meridian Line House**, where visitors straddle eastern and western hemispheres. Since 1833, a 'time ball' on the eastern turret has provided a time check every afternoon at 13.00 GMT (Greenwich Mean Time); the ball is wound to the top of its pole two minutes before the hour and drops at precisely 13.00.

On the hill close by the Observatory is a statue to **General James Wolfe** (1717–59) with the inscription 'a gift of the Canadian people'. Wolfe lived in Greenwich and is buried in the parish church, St Alfege's. He won fame for a great victory against the French at Quebec.

> *Visitor information* Greenwich Park and Royal Observatory are open
> daily 10.00–17.00. Admission free.

Cutty Sark

The last of the tea-clippers, *Cutty Sark*, slumbers in a vast dry-dock a minute's
walk from **Greenwich Pier**. On the swooping V-shaped bows is the fierce-
faced wooden figurehead of a woman flimsily wrapped in a 'cutty sark', the old
name for a short chemise.

This great clipper, the speediest of her kind, was the last of the
windjammers to carry tea from India and China, and grain and wool from
Australia. She made the fastest-ever clipper voyage in 1871, racing rival
clippers from China, sometimes neck and neck, in 107 days. **H M
Tomlinson**, prince among tidal Thames writers, recorded how, as a young
shipping clerk in the 1870s, he was instructed to send two consignments to
Australia that had to arrive two weeks apart. The cargo intended to arrive first
went by steamship, the other by *Cutty Sark* which, of course, arrived first, two
weeks ahead of the supposedly faster steamship.

The *Cutty Sark* is now a museum, complete with models, photographs,
charts, and the largest collection of figureheads in the world.

Near by is another, much smaller vessel, the 54-foot (16m) *Gypsy Moth IV*.
This is the boat in which **Sir Francis Chichester** sailed around the world
single-handed in 1967, at speeds equal to the average run of the *Cutty Sark*. Sir
Francis was knighted by Queen Elizabeth II right here, at the entrance to
Greenwich Pier. Another Sir Francis, **Drake**, was knighted close by, on
Deptford Creek, which we shall visit soon (see page 11).

> *Visitor information* The *Cutty Sark* is open Apr–Sep (Mon–Sat
> 10.00–18.00, Sun 12.00–18.00), Oct–Mar (Mon–Sat 10.00–17.00, Sun
> 12.00–17.00). Admission adult £3.90, concessions £2.90.

From the pier it is only a short walk to the tourist shops, the covered market,
and the cafés of Church Street, or to the tourist information centre hard by the
Cutty Sark. The church of **St Alfege**, street markets and secondhand book
shops are all just a stroll away.

A DECISION

It is at this point that you must make a decision. Do you cross beneath the river
via the Greenwich Foot Tunnel to the Island Gardens on the Isle of Dogs and
walk the north-bank Thames Path route through London to Teddington
where the freshwater stream begins, or do you take the original southern-bank
Thames Path from here to Teddington Lock?

The entrance to the foot tunnel is marked by a glass-topped dome not far

St Alfege's
Church

from the pier where water-buses from and to Westminster and the Tower of London embark and disembark passengers several times daily; the tunnel can be walked in four or five minutes. The views of Greenwich's **Royal Naval College** from the north bank's lawns and the shady trees of **Island Gardens** (there's a cheerful café here, open 09.00–17.30, with a steaming teapot sprouting from the brickwork) are superlative, providing one of the best riverside prospects in all of London. The double-routed Thames Path through London provides both you and I with a dilemma; you because it means deciding which route to take, me because I need to make my mind up how best to describe, concisely, both walks at the same time. Each bank of the river has singular fascinations. So I'm going to cheat by travelling the 30½ miles (49.9km) from Greenwich Pier to Teddington Lock by water-bus, leap-frogging from shore to shore, missing out the boring bits and pointing out the interesting ones, omitting the dull and visiting the famous. That way we will reach Teddington and the non-tidal Thames (where, in my opinion, the real Thames Path begins) as blissfully as we can. You, of course, could travel by water-bus, as well; I've walked the Thames Path twice, travelled by water-bus once (and by Thames Sailing Barge twice), and still can't decide which is the better way to go. If you choose the water-bus, depending on which service you use, there are opportunities to jump ship at the pier-side 'hop-on, hop-off' stops (see below).

Visitor information Summer-time tidal Thames river bus services may be liable to timetable changes, but broadly speaking it should be possible to depend on the following:

It's a 60-minute journey between Greenwich Pier and Westminster Pier, or a 50-minute journey to or from the Embankment Pier at Charing Cross. Some services call at Tower Bridge, Embankment, Waterloo, Bankside and Greenwich (to check all 'hop-on, hop'off' river bus services, tel: 020 7987 1185). Sailings from Greenwich leave every 30 minutes. From Greenwich Pier there are also regular river excursions sailing to the Thames Barrier; for information, telephone Greenwich TIC on 0870 608 2000.

In addition, there are 11 bus services criss-crossing the Thames from pier to pier, roughly every 20 minutes. They call at Greenwich, Canary Wharf for City Airport, St Katherine's Dock Pier, London Bridge, Festival Pier for South Bank, Charing Cross, Cadogan Pier for Chelsea, Lambeth and Westminster, and Chelsea Harbour. For information, contact London Travel Information on 020 7222 1234.

THE ISLE OF DOGS

The Isle of Dogs is a peninsula – changed to an island in 1800–2, when the great West India Docks were built with a canal sliced across the top. It is at the heart of 'docklands' development, converting the unused and unusable London docks into a barren wasteland of high-rise, high-tech buildings from which workers flee west to the soul of London when the sun sets. There is, as yet, little evidence of Maggie Thatcher's 'exciting new community changing tomorrow's world'. The 812ft (244m) **Canary Wharf Tower**, the tallest skyscraper in the UK and the second-tallest in Europe, winks a cold red light from the tip of its pyramid roof. Visitors used to be able to ride by lift to the roof, for a price, but not even a bag of gold will buy a ride these days; when I recently made enquiries, a gloomy and threatening member of the Tower's security staff informed me, in no uncertain manner, that the complex is an office block and NO LONGER open to the public.

Some say the Isle of Dogs got its name because **Henry VIII** kept kennels there so that the barking did not disturb his royal slumbers; others that it was once the 'Isle of Ducks' and the name became corrupted. There are two worthwhile modern things to see and visit there: the London Docklands Visitor Centre and **Billingsgate Fish Market**.

The **London Docklands Visitor Centre** has an exhibition of photographs and documents tracing the history of London's docks up to and beyond the creation in the 1980s of the London Docklands Development Corporation (LDDC). There are regular guided tours. The centre is at 3 Limeharbour on the Isle of Dogs (tel: 020 7512 1111; fax 020 7537 2549; open Mon–Fri 08.30–18.00, Sat and Sun 09.30–17.00).

Billingsgate Market, at the east end of the northernmost strip of West India Dock, is marked and recognisable from a goodly distance by a glowing fish-shaped weather vane on the roof. The market was moved here in 1986 from its original riverside site in the City, close to the Tower of London. To my mind it's the best and most colourful free-entry visitor venue in London – although not as colourful, perhaps, as old Billingsgate. There, fish boxes were manhandled – high, tottering stacks – by porters wearing tar-blacked bowlers-cum-mortar-boards specially made to save their heads being crushed by the weight of fish and boxes. But the Billingsgate of the Isle of Dogs is still as exotic a cockney floor show as could be wished this side of the West End. Here are strange-shaped and multi-coloured fishes trundled in from the

Coral Seas, and cockney 'bummarees' haggling with bruising good humour over prices. Fishes by the score are carried away to restaurants and fish shops throughout the land. Mind you, one needs to be up before first sparrow cheep because the market is over and done by 07.00. 'Billingsgate', by the way, is a synonym for foul language, although the 'bummarees' and 'fish porters' of today don't seem especially foul-mouthed to me.

DEPTFORD

Back to the southern shore. Immediately upstream of Greenwich is Deptford Creek then Deptford merging seamlessly into Rotherhithe, Bermondsey, Southwark and Bankside, and so on.

Elizabeth I knighted **Francis Drake** on board the *Golden Hinde* when it was anchored in Deptford Creek after his round-the-world voyage of discovery, pillage and plunder.

Deptford is typical of many South London suburbs – a high street crammed with cars, red double-decker buses, vans unloading plastic-wrapped mysteries, people of all races and colours, steamy-windowed cafés, shops with strange, sometimes exotic, contents, others shuttered, and mysterious, with heavy iron grids. The diarist **John Evelyn** (1620–1706) used to live here, at Sayes Court, now a public park through which the Thames Path scurries as if it has no place here. Evelyn moved into the court in 1652 and created a garden famed for beauty throughout the Western world. **Peter the Great** rented Sayes Court from Evelyn in 1698, and stayed here, incognito, while he was studying British ship design and construction in order to go back home and build a decent Russian fleet. The royal guest left the house and garden in 'a deplorable state', moaned Evelyn; the Tsar much enjoyed being pushed through Evelyn's trim hedges in a wheelbarrow, usually after a tipple of his favourite brew – hot brandy and pepper – in one of the 'locals' over the way. The Tsar's stay is commemorated by Czar Street, along which The Thames Path runs towards the Strand where there is a boundary stone between Deptford and Rotherhithe parishes and little else to indicate you are passing from one to the other.

The graveyard of Deptford's old parish church, **St Nicholas** (tower built around 1500, the remainder at the end of the 17th century), contains the grave of playwright and poet **Christopher Marlowe** (1564–93). Marlowe was killed in a Deptford brawl either because he refused to pay his bill or because he was a government agent – nobody knows the real reason why.

The Georgian riverfront buildings on Deptford Strand, immediately northwest of the creek and upstream of the high-rise flats on the site of what was Deptford Dockyard, are former rum warehouses belonging to the Royal Victoria Victualling Yard.

Historically, Deptford was important as the birthplace of the Royal Navy, for **Henry VIII** set up the first Royal Naval Dockyard here in 1513. Deptford ships played a vital part in the defeat of the Spanish Armada in 1588 and the yard was the starting point for many voyages of discovery. In 1576, for instance, **Martin Frobisher** sailed from this very spot to seek a northeast passage to China, and the following year **Francis Drake** left on his voyage round the world.

Established in 1742, the yard was filled to the rafters with bedding, salted meat, hard tack, medicines, baccy and booze, including the famous vats of navy rum. One rum vat alone contained 32,000 gallons of spirit, almost enough, but probably not quite, for the entire navy's morning 'sippers'. In addition, there were slaughterhouses, pickling houses, manufactories, brewhouses, sail-lofts, wheelwrights' shops, a cooper's shop, and sawmills, all crammed into the yard's 35 acres (14ha). Most of these buildings were demolished in 1961 and replaced by high-rise flats.

MILLWALL

On the opposite bank, downstream of the apartment blocks on **Burrell's Wharf**, is **Millwall**, where **Isambard Brunel** (1806–59) built the huge *SS Great Eastern*. There are marks on the wharf, until some moron of a developer obliterates them, showing the great ship's length: 680ft (206m). **Brunel** had already built the 236ft (72m) SS *Great Western*, the first steamship to make regular ocean crossings between England and America, with a record time of 15 days. The *Great Eastern* was three times the size, so big that Isambard had to devise ways for it to be launched, in 1858 – sideways (there is a picture and model in the Greenwich National Maritime Museum, see pages 6–7).

LIMEHOUSE

Up-river from Millwall, on the north side of the Thames, is **Limehouse**, once the Chinatown of Charles Dickens, once the place of opium dens, once the home of 'the scum of the world's worst countries', according to Thomas Burke in his *Limehouse Nights*. **Oscar Wilde**'s hero in *The Picture of Dorian Gray*, and perhaps Wilde himself, came to Limehouse to smoke opium. Here were 'rookeries', Fagin-style warrens of ramshackle streets, of drains and putrid creeks, of taverns, brothels and gaming houses; the notorious Ratcliffe Highway – haunt of prostitutes and cut-throats – ran between Limehouse and the Tower of London, through Wapping and Shadwell. In 1872 the French journalist **Jerrold** wrote scathingly of the area's

> squalid recklessness. By day and night it is the same interminable
> scene of heedless, shiftless money-squandering of Jack ashore, in the
> company of his sweetheart.

The American **Nathaniel Hawthorne** was no more impressed in the early days of the 20th century:

> The [Limehouse] shore is lined with the shabbiest, blackest and
> ugliest buildings that can be imagined, decayed warehouses with blind
> windows, and wharves that look ruinous . . . and the muddy tide of
> the Thames, reflecting nothing and holding a million of unclean
> streets within its breast . . . is just the dismal stream to glide by such a
> city.

Hmmmm! Now, the disused warehouses have been converted into up-market flats and Limehouse has become wonderfully respectable; even its Chinatown has become almost boringly middle class. It was much more sordid, more wicked and a lot more down-at-heel when I was a young man in the 1960s and ventured into Limehouse to seek out whatever remained of its seamier side. Chinamen, whores, and drunken sailors is what I remember best, and the flickering shadows which street lights cast across the narrow lanes of docklands. Oh yes, and of course the sounds of singing and pianos from corner pubs.

Charlie Brown's pub, a well-known and rowdy sailors' haunt no more than some forty years ago, is still in West India Dock Road; there are no longer fights most nights of the week to disturb the pub's intriguing collection of East-End memorabilia.

I hope you like pubs, historic ones anyway; we're going to visit a lot of them. The famous **Grapes**, formerly the 'Bunch of Grapes', is in Limehouse – in Narrow Street, overlooking Rotherhithe's Surrey Commercial Docks. Dickens knew the pub well, calling it the 'Six Jolly Fellowship Porters' in *Our Mutual Friend*. The book describes it as

> a narrow lop-sided wooden jumble of corpulent windows . . . with a crazy wooden veranda impending over the water; indeed the whole house, inclusive of the complaining flagstaff on the roof, impended over the water, but seemed to have got into the condition of a faint-hearted diver who has paused so long on the brink that he will never go in at all.

Dickens's pub was popular for three mulled drinks, 'Purl, Flip, and Dog's Nose'.

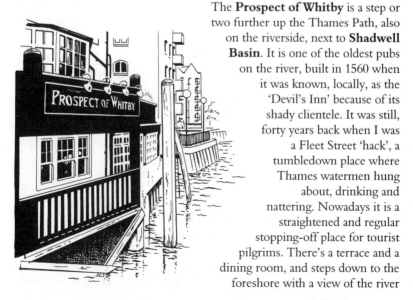

The **Prospect of Whitby** is a step or two further up the Thames Path, also on the riverside, next to **Shadwell Basin**. It is one of the oldest pubs on the river, built in 1560 when it was known, locally, as the 'Devil's Inn' because of its shady clientele. It was still, forty years back when I was a Fleet Street 'hack', a tumbledown place where Thames watermen hung about, drinking and nattering. Nowadays it is a straightened and regular stopping-off place for tourist pilgrims. There's a terrace and a dining room, and steps down to the foreshore with a view of the river reaches, the West India Dock and, in the middle distance, the white tower of St Anne's Church in cobbled St Anne's Passage.

Hawksmoor's magnificent **St Anne's** (built in 1714–30) is a docklands landmark and one of its glories. Another architect, **Philip Hardwick** (1792–1870), rebuilt the interior after a disastrous fire in 1851 and equipped it with a beautiful organ.

> *Visitor information* St Anne's is open for services Sun 10.30–18.00 and Thu lunchtimes. Outside these times permission to visit should be sought from the Rectory in St Anne's Passage (tel: 020 7987 1502).

Close by St Anne's, on the other side of Commercial Road, is a remnant of old Limehouse's Chinatown and a handful of yesterday's streets between the north side of India Dock Road and Saracen Street. Simple, and genuine, Chinese restaurants are in Nankin, Pekin and Canton streets. The historic **Town of Ramsgate** pub is up-river a little, on the Thames Path at Wapping on the north shore, where the infamous '**Hanging Judge Jeffreys**' was arrested and thrown into the Tower of London in 1688. He was James II's hated chancellor, responsible for hanging 300 supporters of the Monmouth Rebellion during the Bloody Assizes. The pub's proprietors seem to think that Jeffreys was always boozing and carousing here, but that I doubt.

Beside the pub, on the edge of the river, is the site of **Execution Dock**, where miscreants were hanged in chains. The chronicler **John Stow** (1525–1605) called it

> the usual place for hanging of pirates and sea-rovers, at the low water mark, and there to remain until three tides had overflowed them.

One of the most notorious villains to end his days here was **Captain Kidd**, hanged before an enormous festive audience in 1701. On the scaffold he spotted one of his mistresses in the crowd of onlookers. 'I have lain with that bitch three times, and now she has come to see me hanged,' he said. Style, that's what Kidd had in aces. Public hangings, like public holidays, were attended by throngs of spectators, minstrels and orange-sellers.

Not far downstream of Tower Bridge, still on the northern shore, is the entrance to **St Katherine's Dock**, the first of London's big dock expansions. It was built in 1825, and closed and converted for yachts and yuppies in 1968; many, but not all, of its fine warehouses are gone. The Scottish civil engineer **Thomas Telford** (1757–1834) built the docks between 1824 and 1828. The dockmaster's house by the dock lock entrance, and the austere and elegant **Ivory House** in the heart of the docks (where ivory tusks from Africa and

India really were once stored), are the best survivors of the docks' late-20th-century rehabilitation. Fine vessels, including, usually, magnificent tall-masted Thames Barges, are moored here, and the quays are lined with restaurants, shops, and a pub, **The Dickens Inn**.

ROTHERHITHE

Now we must leap-frog back, downstream, to the southern bank-side Thames walk. The Rotherhithe peninsula, stretching from Greenlands Dock to Cherry Pier, faces Limehouse and Wapping.

Rotherhithe was once a village called 'Redriff', the name **John Gay** gave to it in his *Beggar's Opera*. **Christopher Jones**, captain of the Plymouth Pilgrims' ship, *Mayflower*, is buried where he was christened, in Rotherhithe's St Mary's Church. His grave is unmarked, but there is a plaque commemorating the Pilgrim Fathers' voyage to America in 1620 in *Mayflower*, which departed from the jetty behind the riverside **Mayflower** public house, a street away in Mayflower Road. Also buried in the church is 'Prince Lee Boo, son of Abba Thule, Rupark or King of Island of Coo-roo-ram, one of the Pelew Islands' who died of smallpox in the 1780s after being brought, like Pocahontas, to England for people to gawp at. Carvings in the church sanctuary are by the famous Dutch-born English sculptor and woodcarver, **Grinling Gibbons** (1648–1721).

At the side of the church is a small building shaped like a sentry box, which is exactly what it was. Called a 'watch house', it was a lodging place for warders guarding the churchyard against body snatchers.

Following the curve of Rotherhithe peninsula, past **Cuckold's Point** (so named because King John made love to another man's wife on this spot; for years it was marked by horns hung from the river wall), is the **Thames Tunnel**. This is the world's first underwater bore, and it took the Brunels, father and son, 20 years to build, completing it in 1843.

Marc Brunel (1769–1849) started it and **Isambard** (1806–59) took over the work in 1827. Marc devised a brand-new system for tunnel construction after he had watched a wood-boring mollusc gnawing through wood and lining the tunnel with its extruded droppings of wood pulp. He designed a tunnelling shield that imitated the mollusc's behaviour. Even so, construction was slow and laborious, hundreds of labourers died, and the river broke through on five occasions. When at last it was finished, the Victorians loved it, held street fairs beneath its brick arches, paraded there on holidays and high days. But as a road tunnel it was a flop and got taken over as a railway tunnel in the 1860s; it still carries the London Underground from Rotherhithe to Wapping. All this is told in a museum at **Brunel's Engine House**, in Tunnel Road, close to the Thames Path, behind Rotherhithe tube station.

Visitor information The museum at Brunel's Engine House is open Sundays only (13.00–15.00). For information, tel: 020 7231 3840.

Rotherhithe Street, which runs parallel to the Thames Path all the way to Bermondsey, is the longest street in London. Today it is genteel housing and respectability. And boring. It wasn't in the 1930s, when **A G Linney** wandered Rotherhithe in search of copy for *Lure and Lore of London's River* (published in about 1932):

> [N]o houses appear and a length of street is given over to trade, rickety overhead bridges joining different parts of warehouses and mills. . . [The inhabitants were] typical riverside Londoners, quite a number of people of Scandinavian blood, dark-skinned southerners, negroes.

BERMONDSEY

To the west of Rotherhithe, on the south bank, is Bermondsey, where the quaintly named **Cherry Garden Pier** refers to a pleasure garden and orchards visited by **Samuel Pepys** to buy cherries for his wife. In the days before the introduction of ship-to-shore radio, incoming vessels sounded their horns as they passed the pier as a warning that Tower Bridge should be opened for their passing. It was from this vantage point that **J M W Turner** (1775–1851) made sketches for his painting *The Fighting Temeraire* showing that veteran ship from the Battle of Trafalgar arriving in a Rotherhithe sunset to be broken up in yards here. On the edge of the Thames walk is a bench shared by a life-size statue of a reclining entrepreneur and politician, **Dr Alfred Salter**, who was much loved locally as a Member of Parliament and for his slum-clearance policies.

The river-bank **Angel** pub, dating from at least 1682, was visited by **Samuel Pepys** and **Captain Cook**. The American painter **James Whistler** (1834–1903) sketched Rotherhithe from the pub balcony.

THE POOL OF LONDON

We are now entering the Pool of London, stretching three miles from Bermondsey to Tower Bridge (the 'Lower Pool') and then to London Bridge (the 'Upper Pool'). The Pool was, until ships became too large to use it in the 1960s, London's larder; bustling and picturesque, alive with shipping rafted one to the other in the river or moored to either bank. The growth in the size of ships, a dwindling tea trade, poor labour relations, and 'containerisation' meant that business was gradually and eventually lost to more specialised terminals closer to the sea – for instance, Tilbury, down-river opposite Gravesend, and Felixstowe at the mouth of Harwich Harbour on the southeast coast.

Change, when it came, was shocking and sudden. Within just a decade of the London Docklands Development Corporation being set up in 1981 the banks of the Thames below London Bridge had been transformed. Old warehouses were ripped down or converted, new and face-lifted buildings – residential, commercial and leisure – sprung up in their place. It is easy to regret the sudden transformation and romanticise about the bustling wonders of the old Pool. **Virginia Woolf** (1882–1941), in her 1930s evocative essay *The Docks of London*, helps, perhaps, to put a saner perspective on things:

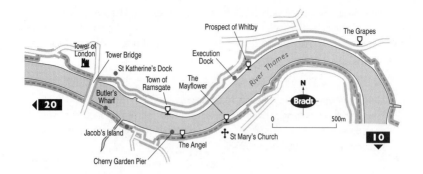

If we turn and go past the anchored ships . . . we surely see the most dismal prospect in the world. The banks of the river are lined with dingy, decrepit-looking warehouses. They huddle on land that has become flat and slimy mud. . . Behind masts and funnels lies a sinister dwarf city of workmen's houses. In the foreground cranes and warehouses, scaffolding and gasometers line the banks with a skeleton architecture.

In Dickens's day, the area just west of Cherry Garden Pier was known as 'Jacob's Island'. Here Bill Sikes, in *Oliver Twist*, fell from a roof to his death in

> the filthiest, the strangest, the most extraordinary of the many localities that are hidden in London . . . its dirt-besmeared walls and decaying foundations; every repulsive lineament of poverty, every loathsome indication of filth, rot and garbage . . . unemployed labourers . . . ballast heavers, coal-whippers, brazen women, ragged children, and the raff and refuse of the river.

Things have improved. For example, the re-shaping of China Wharf has turned **Saviour's Dock** – the area bordering the upstream side of Jacob's Island – into a distinctive, exuberant, red river-front façade of the 1980s, likened to a Chinese dragon or pagoda. Windows punch half-moon holes through the red-pink concrete walls and from the lowest window the stern of a boat juts out over the water to form a balcony.

Next to China Wharf is **Shad Thames**, where the essence of old docklands and the Pool of London is best preserved; the tall walls of warehouses rise sheer on either side, footbridges cross high overhead. Even today, the spice-soaked beams of the great warehouses still perfume these surrounds with the mixed scents of aniseed, cardamom and cinnamon. A workman who worked at Butler's Wharf on the riverside wrote in 1937:

> We had just about everything coming through . . . rubber, cocoa, coffee, cassia, cardamoms, canned salmon, ginger, dates, nutmegs, wines, spirits.

The riverside Butler's Wharf has become the **Design Museum**, founded by Terence Conran as a 'broker of ideas, not a collection of curios'. Opened in 1989, it provides a mix of exhibitions of the old, and not so old, and the most recent and speculative of design.

Visitor information The Design Museum is open Tue–Sun 11.30–17.30. There are regularly changing programmes of films, lectures and seminars. There is a design shop, a café and a restaurant. For information, tel: 020 7403 6933.

Tucked behind the Design Museum is the **Bramah Tea and Coffee Museum**, where the story of these beverages is told. About 6,000 tea chests a day were once a normal consignment off-loaded at Butler's Wharf.

Visitor information The Bramah Tea and Coffee Museum (The Clove Building, Maguire Street, Butler's Wharf, SE1; tel: 020 7403 5650) is open daily 10.00–18.00. There is an admission charge: £4 adults, £3.50 children & concessions.

Dead ahead is Tower Bridge, beyond that on the north bank is the Tower of London, and on the opposite side of the river is Southwark and Bankside. How many people, I wonder, visit Southwark or Bankside when there's the famous Tower to prowl about? Not many. But they should. In fact, so much has been written about the Tower and so many guidebooks are available about it, that I feel able to ignore it. Instead, let's break the mould and visit the people and times of historic Southwark. It will be an eye-opener, I promise.

Tower Bridge to Westminster

Distances From Tower Bridge: London Bridge 0.73 miles (1.16km), Blackfriar's Bridge 1.25 miles (2km), Waterloo Bridge 2.9 miles (4.65 km), Westminster Bridge 3.9 miles (6.24km)

Between Tower Bridge and London Bridge is the austere but breathtakingly impressive former Royal Navy cruiser, **HMS *Belfast***, moored in the river off the south bank. *Belfast* helped sink *Scharnhorst* in World War II. Visitors can walk the decks, visit the bridges, climb up ladders, climb down ladders, and huddle into turrets where the guns are maintained in gleaming order. There are exhibitions, maps and photographs.

Visitor information Access to HMS *Belfast* is from Symons Wharf on the river frontage of Hay's Galleria (tel: 020 7407 6434), once the Victorian warehouses of the Pool of London's Hay's Wharf. Here nowadays, beneath a remarkable snake-curved glazed roof, wealthy folk shop till they drop, and eat and drink till they balloon. There are offices, shops, restaurants, cafés, and pubs and entertainers. HMS *Belfast* is open daily Mar–Oct 10.00–18.00, Nov–Feb 10.00–17.00. There is a shop and café. Admission to visit the ship is adult £5.40, concessions £4.40, child (under 15) free. For further information, tel: 020 7940 6300. A ferry runs from the ship to Tower Pier daily Mar–Nov.

Opposite, on the northern bank, is old **Billingsgate Fish Market**, where fish was sold since Saxon times until the market moved down-river on to the Isle of Dogs in 1982 (see page 10). The building, with glinting goldfish weather vanes, dates from 1875. It was bought in 1987, for stacks of money, and converted into a securities dealing room, for stacks more, until the stock market crashed and the building was immediately abandoned.

SOUTHWARK

The south bank's Southwark, behind Hay's Galleria, runs into Bankside so seamlessly that there is no knowing where one ends and the other begins.

This was the place of Victorian fish-smokers and bone-boilers, of 'all disagreeable-smelling trades', of tumbledown back-to-back houses with rag-patched windows, airless courts where urchins wallowed in vice and wretchedness, and of fever-wrought alleyways where prostitutes sought business. It's respectable today, but a hidden place, full of delights that many tourists rarely see. There's the cathedral where **William Shakespeare** worshipped; there's an inn with a galleried coaching yard, like the one, also in Southwark, where Pickwick met Sam Weller; there's the site of Marshalsea Prison, where **Charles Dickens**'s father was imprisoned for debt along with his mother, who went to prison of her own accord in order to be with her husband; there's the nearby Lant Street, were 12-year-old Charles lodged while his parents were locked away in the Marshalsea; there's the Anchor Inn, where **Pepys** watched the Great Fire of London; and, of course, there's the famous Globe Theatre.

Where to start, there's the rub? Southwark Cathedral is, I suppose, as good a place as any.

Southwark Cathedral

Unlikely as it might seem, Southwark Cathedral once stood in the grottiest, seediest, most exciting part of London. From the Tudors to the 16th and 17th centuries, it was a dreadful, wonderful place – a noisy, jostling, revelling, sex-pot of a place, a sort of unsanitised Soho; not the crummy, boring Soho of today, but the naughty, seedy, lovely one of the 1950s and '60s, which, even so, was a seemly sort of place compared with the gorgeously vile Southwark of Henry, Elizabeth and the Charleses.

By the end of the 16th century there were four theatres, three rings for baiting bulls, two-dozen cockpits for fighting cocks, and 20 brothels. The whores of Bankside were nicknamed 'Winchester geese' because the bishops of Winchester owned them, herded them into brothels where the girls laid their trade; they pocketed their rents, and who can tell what other favours, with a 'taa, very much', and 'now trot along and don't expect us to bury you in consecrated ground, because we won't'. And they didn't.

The cathedral is close to the Thames Path, in Borough High Street, a church that, at one time, was so down-at-heel that there was a bakery instead

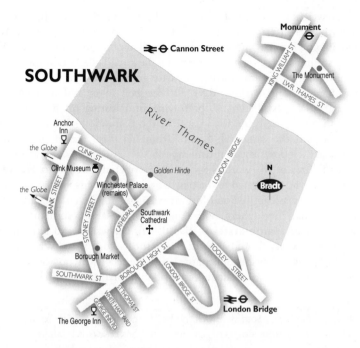

of pews and the altar was shared with a pigsty. It was restored in the 19th century, and elevated to cathedral status in the 20th century. There is a remarkable Gothic choir, chancel, chapels and some stupendous monuments, including one to William Shakespeare who worshipped here. In fact, Southwark Cathedral is home to the most extraordinary collection of tombs and epitaphs outside of Westminster Abbey.

Apart from anything else, Southwark is a must for 'Dickensians'. It was on the steps of **Charles Dickens**'s 'St George the Martyr' church that Little Dorrit, born in the borough's Marshalsea Prison, was found asleep and taken by the verger to the vestry. She can be seen in the modern, stained-glass east window,

> pale transparent face . . . a
> delicate bent head, a tiny form, a
> quick little pair of
> busy hands, and a
> shabby dress. . .

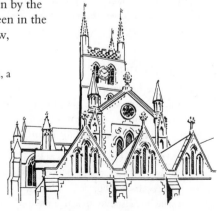

The cathedral used to be St Mary Overie, and then St Saviour's, which was its name when used by **William Shakespeare** and his family.

The playwright's brother, Edmund, is buried in the church; he died, prematurely, in 1607. The register states 'Edmond Shakespeare, player, buried in ye church, with a forenoon knell of the great bell XXs.' XXs (twenty shillings) was the price for ringing the knell bell. As Edmund was an actor and poor, some unknown benefactor must have paid the XXs, a not inconsiderable sum in those days, for the bell to be tolled. There is a memorial to the bard himself, portraying him resting on his side, head cupped in one hand; behind is a frieze of the Bankside he knew, including the Globe and the cathedral. Scenes from his plays are in the modern stained-glass windows above the memorial.

Other figures of the world stage are remembered here. **John Harvard**, for instance, who emigrated to the new world and gave his name to Harvard University; he was baptised on November 29 1607 in the chapel which now bears his name. Two others, both Americans, are also commemorated. A plaque to **Oscar Hammerstein** (1895–1960), playwright and lyricist, is in the Harvard Chapel and another, to the actor **Sam Wanamaker** (1919–1993), whose vision and energy led to the reconstruction of the Globe Theatre not far from the cathedral, is beside the memorial to Shakespeare.

Visitor information Southwark Cathedral is open daily, 09.00–18.00. There are no admission charges, but donations towards its upkeep are invited. Nearest tube and railway station: London Bridge.

Permanently moored in the Thames near the cathedral is a replica of *The Golden Hinde*. The original carried **Sir Francis Drake** on his 1580 circumnavigation of the world. This perfect replica, built in Devon in the 1970s, sailed round the world, too, before becoming a museum in 1996.

Visitor information The *Golden Hinde* is open daily 09.00–sunset. Tea and coffee available. Admission adult £2.50, concessions £2.10, child £1.50. For further details, tel: 020 7403 0123.

Marshalsea Prison

The infamous and grim Marshalsea Prison used to stand next to Southwark Cathedral. **Dickens** wrote about it in *Pickwick Papers* and described it again in *Little Dorrit*. There are scant remains in the form of tablets on the wall adjoining the graveyard of *Little Dorrit*'s 'church of St George's':

> [Marshalsea Prison was] an oblong pile of barrack buildings,
> partitioned into squalid houses standing back to back, so that there
> were no back rooms; environed by a narrow paved yard, hemmed in
> by high walls, duly spiked at the top. Itself a close and confided prison

for debtors, it contained within it a much closer and more refined jail for smugglers, offenders against revenue laws, and defaulters to excise and customs, who had incurred fines which they were unable to pay, were supposed to be incarcerated behind an iron-plated door, and a blind alley some yard and a half wide, which formed the mysterious termination of the very limited skittle-ground, in which the Marshalsea debtors bowled down their troubles.

Charles's father John was arrested for debt in 1824, and imprisoned initially in King's Bench and later in the Marshalsea. Mrs Dickens and her younger children joined him, voluntarily, in Marshalsea. Charles, aged 12, found lodgings in nearby Lant Street and each day walked to and from Warren's Blacking Warehouse near Charing Cross, where he was woefully employed. The entire district surrounding the location of the prison is ringed with associations of Dickens: Marshalsea Road, Dorrit Street, Quilp Street and, of course, Lant Street.

Winchester Palace

A single wall of the once fabulous **Winchester Palace** is at Pickford's Wharf in Clink Street, dark and gloomy, running under Cannon Street Railway Bridge. Its magnificent rose window, 13 feet (3.96m) across, provides a hint of the wealth enjoyed by the bishops of Winchester who resided in regal grandeur there. For more than five centuries, the palace and its 70 acres (28ha) of parkland dominated London's south bank. A royal love story began in the palace when **Henry VIII** met **Catherine Howard** here in 1540. Having got the hots for her, he divorced Anne of Cleves, married Catherine the same year, and sent her to the block two years later.

The Clink

Adjacent to what is left of the bishops' palace is **The Clink**, a gaol once so feared that its name became slang for 'prison'. By the 16th century it was being used to imprison anyone whose religious views countered those of the State. **Henry Barrowe**, **John Greenwood** and **John Penry**, founders of the Puritan movement that led to the emigration of the Pilgrim Fathers, were imprisoned and put to death at The Clink. The prison was burned down in the Gordon Riots of 1780 and never rebuilt.

Visitor information There's an exhibition at The Clink (1 Clink Street; tel: 020 7403 6515), revealing things you probably didn't know about the ancient brothel area of Bankside. Open daily 10.00–21.00. Admission adult £4, concessions £3.

Southwark taverns

The **Anchor Inn** is on the corner of Bankside, beside the river, facing the entrance to Clink Street. It occupies the site of two stews, the Castle on the

Hoop and the Gonne, both renowned 'for the entertainment of lewd persons'. **Doctor Johnson** came to the Anchor to be entertained by Mr Thrale, but mostly by Mrs Thrale, whom he fancied. **Samuel Pepys** came by boat, then moved to the shelter of the Anchor during the Great Fire:

> [A]ll over the Thames, with one's face in the wind, you were almost burned with a shower of fire drops. . . [W]hen we could endure no more upon the water, we to a little ale-house on the Bankside . . . and saw the fire grow, and as it grew darker, appeared more and more, and in corners and upon steeples, and between churches and houses, as far as we could see up the hill of the City, in a most horrid malicious bloody flame.

The Anchor is now a restaurant and pub, with five bars (some on the ground floor, some upstairs), plus three delightful 18th-century dining rooms on the first floor with views over the river. A little quay projects over the river and is used as an open-air bar in fine weather.

Even in Dickens's day, London was changing fast. The great coach-rumbling inns about which he lovingly wrote were already falling into decline, killed by the railways. The **White Hart** in Borough High Street, where Pickwick meets Sam Weller in *Pickwick Papers*, and where Jingle and Rachael are discovered after their elopement, was demolished in 1889. But there is a surviving look-alike: the **George Inn**, at No 77 in the same street, the last of London's great galleried inns. The George is one of those treasures of London which add spice to their discovery by hiding away in the most unpromising places, this one just a short stone's throw from London Bridge and about the same distance from London Bridge railway station.

The most famous of the Southwark taverns was the **Tabard**, where **Chaucer**'s Canterbury pilgrims started their pilgrimage to the tomb of Thomas à Becket. Like all the borough inns, it was built round a large courtyard with galleries on three sides, more or less as the George remains to this day, and the White Hart – setting for Jack Cade's final plea to his deserting followers in Shakespeare's *Henry VI Part II* – was in *Pickwick Papers*:

> In the Borough especially, there still remain some half dozen old inns, which have preserved their external features unchanged, and which have escaped alike the rage for public improvement, and the encroachments of private speculation. Great, rambling, queer, old places they are, with galleries, and passages, and staircases, wide enough and antiquated enough to furnish materials for a hundred ghost stories. . .
>
> A double tier of bed-room galleries, with old clumsy balustrades, ran round two sides of the straggling area, and a double row of bells to correspond, sheltered from the weather by a little sloping roof, hung over the door leading to the bar and coffee-room. Two or three gigs and chaise-carts were wheeled up under different little sheds and pent-houses; and the occasional heavy tread of a cart-horse, or rattling

of a chain at the further end of the yard, announced to anybody who cared about the matter, that the stable lay in that direction. When we add that a few boys in smock frocks were lying asleep on heavy packages, woolpacks, and other articles that were scattered about on heaps of straw, we have described as fully as need be the general appearance of the yard of the White Hart Inn, High Street, Borough, on the particular morning in question.

Plays were performed from the wide double-tiered balconies of the George during the 16th century before there were any formal theatres, and so the inn's keepers can justifiably boast that **Shakespeare** was sometimes a visitor when he lived and worked in this area. The playwright not only had lodgings close by, near Southwark Cathedral, but almost certainly came to watch, and perhaps perform in, his own plays. Two of the inn's galleries have since been destroyed, but the remaining third is enough to provide a shadowy picture of a bustling past within the now quiet courtyard.

Visitor information The George (tel: 020 7407 1056), restored by the National Trust, still functions as a pub and a restaurant and sometimes, in the summer, as a stage for Shakespeare's plays. Viewing from the outside is free and the courtyard gates are normally left open. The pub and restaurant opening hours are variable.

The Globe Theatre

The name of The Globe Theatre is synonymous with Shakespeare and an enduring symbol – 'this wooden 'O', a round, thatched turret with raised stage – of Elizabethan England. It is wonderful that such a faithful reconstruction of the theatre has risen on Bankside, on the south side of Park Street, all trace of the original having long gone. The first Bankside Globe opened in 1599 and a string of new plays by Shakespeare was performed there: *Richard II*, *Romeo and Juliet*, *King Lear*, *Othello*, *Henry VIII*, *Love's Labour's Lost*, *The Winter's Tale*, *The Taming of the Shrew* and *Macbeth*.

Teasingly little is known of Shakespeare's life. We don't know where he lived or what his life was like, but can presume it was much the way of everybody else's in Bankside: crowded, revelling, noisy, dangerous, a round of pleasure, poverty and crime. And very, very smelly, of course. We don't know whether it is true, as legend has it, that The Globe was burned to the ground in 1613 when cannon fire during a performance of

Henry VIII caught the thatch of the theatre. But it's a nice story and so I shall go on believing it.

The theatre was rebuilt and survived until 1642, then demolished two years later. By the mid-20th century there was no trace left, other than a grimed plaque erected by a long-gone Shakespeare Reading Society. That's how the American actor and director **Sam Wanamaker** found the site in 1949 while filming *Give Us This Day* (released in the US as *Christ in Concrete*). It took him nearly 40 years (work finally began in 1987) to reconstruct the new 'Shakespeare's Globe'.

Visitor information The Globe can be seen from the outside at any time in New Globe Walk, Bankside. The complex includes an open-air auditorium where plays are presented from May to August, whatever the weather, rain or shine, and an exhibition and tour which explores Shakespeare's theatre and the London in which he lived and worked. The exhibition and tour lasts about 1½ hours. Admission to the exhibition plus tour costs adult £5, concessions £4; tickets for performances start at £5. For general information, tel: 020 7902 1407; for the box office, tel: 020 7401 9919.

Bear Gardens

A few paces from The Globe is **Bear Gardens**, marking the site of the last bear-baiting ring on Bankside. Both monarchs and subjects considered bull- and bear-baiting no end of a hoot. **Henry VIII** and **Elizabeth I** visited Bankside baiting rings, the queen regarding it as such excellent entertainment that she took the French and Spanish ambassadors with her. It remained a jolly way for the upper crust to spend their leisure hours up to and into the reign of Charles II. The diarist **Samuel Pepys** and his contemporary **John Evelyn** came to watch the show. Pepys even brought his wife, and wrote on August 14 1666 of it as a place

> where I had not been, I think, of many years, and saw some good sport of the bull's tossing the dogs – one into the very boxes. . .

A few years later Evelyn recorded a Bankside visit:

> I went with friends to the bear garden, where was cock fighting, dog fighting, beare and bull baiting, it being a famous day for all these butcherly sports . . . the Irish wolfe-dog exceeded . . . who beate a cruell mastiff . . . all ended with the ape on horseback. . .

The Old Operating Theatre Museum

In Southwark's St Thomas Street, at No 9A, is an extraordinary time capsule unearthed in 1957 when **Raymond Russell**, an inquisitive historian, squeezed through a hole in the belfry of old **St Thomas Hospital**'s chapel to discover an intact operating theatre dating from 1822. It is now a museum, complete with blood-stained floor, and mop and bucket, left over from the days when patients were doped by ale or opiates, and held down by six brawny assistants while their limbs were amputated by saw and knife.

Visitor information The Old Operating Theatre Museum is open daily 10.30–17.00. Admission adult £2.90, child £1.50, concessions £2.

Lant Street

Bob Sawyer, from *Pickwick Papers*, lived in Southwark's Lant Street. David Copperfield lodged there too. So did their creator, **Charles Dickens**, who in April 1824, when he was just 12, found himself occupying 'a back attic . . . at the house of an insolvent court agent' in Lant Street not far from the Marshalsea Prison where his father and mother were imprisoned:

> The little window had a pleasant prospect of a timber yard, and when
> I took possession of my new abode I thought it was Paradise.

No-one knows at which house in Lant Street Dickens lodged, but we do know that his route to work at Warren's Blacking Warehouse took him over London Bridge, which was to become the setting for Nancy's fateful rendezvous in *Oliver Twist*.

> The church clocks chimed three quarters past eleven, as two figures
> emerged on London Bridge. One, which advanced with a swift and
> rapid step, was that of a woman who looked eagerly about her as
> though in quest of some expected object; the other figure was that of
> a man, who slunk along in the deepest shadow he could find, and, at
> some distance, accommodated his pace to hers; stopping when she
> stopped; and as she moved again, creeping stealthily on: but never
> allowing himself, in the ardour of his pursuit, to gain upon her
> footsteps. Thus, they crossed the bridge, from the Middlesex to the
> Surrey shore, when the woman, apparently disappointed in her
> anxious scrutiny of the foot passengers, turned back. The movement
> was sudden: but he who watched her, was not thrown off his guard
> by it; for, shrinking into one of the recesses which surmount the piers
> of the bridge, and leaning over the parapet the better to conceal his
> figure, he suffered her to pass on the opposite pavement . . .

The Fire of London

On the far side of London Bridge, all but obscured by the bulk of neo-Egyptian **Adelaide House** (built in 1926, shortly after the discovery of Tutankhamun's tomb), is the 202-foot (61m) **Monument to the Fire of London**. This fluted column, topped by the gold flames of a burning urn, was designed in 1677 by **Robert Hooke**, a friend of Christopher Wren. It stands precisely 202 feet (the same as its height) east of the bakery in Pudding Lane where the fire broke out on September 2 1666.

'Pish! A woman might piss it out!,' the incompetent and blustering Mayor of London boasted when he was woken during the night. But the fire blazed for three days. **Samuel Pepys** watched in horror, and described how he had seen

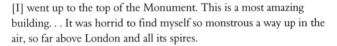

> poor people staying in their houses . . . till the very
> fire touched them, and then running into boats or
> clambering from one pair of stairs by the waterside to
> another.

These days – for a price (adult £1.50, child £0.50; tel: 020 7626 2717) – visitors can climb to the top of the monument; those who manage the 311 steps are awarded a fitness certificate! Charles Dickens (and David Copperfield) gazed at the Monument's golden flame from London Bridge, while his character John Willet's (*Barnaby Rudge*) idea of a pleasant day out was to go to the top of the Monument and sit there. Dr Johnson's biographer, **James Boswell**, made the climb to the top in 1763:

> [I] went up to the top of the Monument. This is a most amazing
> building. . . It was horrid to find myself so monstrous a way up in the
> air, so far above London and all its spires.

London Bridge

London Bridge may be the capital's most famous bridge, but it is a disappointment for all that. 'London Bridge is falling down, falling down, falling down' is a huge understatement. It has fallen down at least seven times since the Romans built the first one.

Knocked down again, and rebuilt in 1973, today's bridge is wide, flat, balustraded, and plain. The building-crammed medieval London Bridge – the sole crossing place, other than by boat or wherry, until Westminster and Putney bridges were erected in the 1720s – was a much more exciting affair, lined with houses, shops and warehouses, some seven storeys high, and the heads of traitors, boiled and dipped in tar displayed on spikes on the southern approach. Sometimes, as in the reign of **Queen Elizabeth I**, there were as many as 30 heads spiked there at one time – 'As thick as pins on a milliner's cushion,' observed a 1578 visitor. The head of **Sir Thomas More** (1478–1535), chopped off for refusing to recognise Henry VIII as head of the English Church, and that of **William Wallace** (c1270–1305), champion of independence for Scotland in the reign of Edward I, were impaled here.

David Copperfield 'was wont to sit in one of the recesses [of the pre-1831 London Bridge], watching the people go by; it was here that Copperfield met "the Orfling"'. The bridge features again . . . in *Pickwick Papers* (over which the Pickwickians return to London) . . . in *Great Expectations* (crossed by Pip after opening Miss Hailsham's eyes to the wreck she has made of his and Estella's lives) . . . in *Oliver Twist* (when Nancy has her fatal conversation with Rose Maylie on the steps of the bridge on the Surrey bank – don't bother to search, the steps are no longer there) . . . in *Martin Chuzzlewit* (as the place where Jonas Chuzzlewit sinks bloodstained clothes after murdering Tigg).

Downstream, Lizzie and her father, in the opening scenes of Dickens's *Our Mutual Friend*, fished for dead bodies in the river. If you think I am devoting too much time and space to Dickens then you are probably right, but just wait until we get to the non-tidal river and meet with Jerome K Jerome and his *Three Men in a Boat!*

Tate Modern

East and up-river of London Bridge, followed by the equally undistinguished **Southwark Bridge**, is south bank's **Bankside Power Station**, now the **Tate Gallery of Modern Art**, linked to the north bank by Sir Norman Foster's **Millennium pedestrian bridge**. After its initial opening, the bridge had to be closed because it wobbled too much; it was eventually opened once more in 2001. Tate Modern's dour power station fortress was designed by **Sir Giles Gilbert Bridge**, opened in 1963 and closed just 33 years later.

Gutted and flooded with natural light via a great glass canopy roof designed by Swiss architects **Herzog** and **de Meuron**, the new Tate Modern is a sensation. It has 100,000 square feet of galleries housing ever-changing loan exhibitions, together with Tate's modern art collection in its entirety: Picasso, Matisse, Bonnard, Brancusi, Dali, Krasner, Pollock, Beuchamp, Moore, Gabo, Giacometti, Warhol, Hockney and many, many others.

Blackfriars Bridge

Blackfriars Bridge is at the boundary between Bankside and the South Bank Complex, which includes the **Royal Festival Hall**, the only permanent building to come out of the 1951 Festival of Britain. (There are excellent free concerts in the Festival Hall foyer Wed–Thu 12.30–14.00.) It has since been joined by the **Hayward Gallery**, the **Queen Elizabeth Hall**, the **Purcell Room**, and the **National Theatre**.

Blackfriars Bridge is pillared stout in granite with bases and capitals carved with swans and herons in Portland stone. Most of today's people like it, but when it was built, between 1865 and 1869, Victorian critics attacked it violently as

> a wonder of depravity. . . the parapet is a fiddle-faddle of pretty cast-
> iron archading, a propos of nothing, a well-known evidence of
> desperate imbecility.

Ho-hum, extraordinary!

Anyway, Blackfriars Bridge has witnessed some gruesome doings. The Italian banker with intriguing connections to the papacy, **Robert Calvi**, was

found hanged here in June
1982. In 1989, 50 party-goers
were drowned when their
pleasure boat, *The Marchioness*,
was run down in the dark by
a dredger. Nor was this the
first Thames disaster
involving a pleasure craft and
working boat; a century
earlier, in 1878, 640 day-
trippers perished when their
pleasure steamer, *Princess
Alice*, was struck by a collier,
The Bywell Castle, in Gallion's
Reach, 11 miles (17.6km) downstream of Blackfriars Bridge.

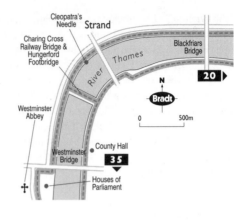

THE VICTORIA EMBANKMENT

Our next stop is the Victoria Embankment, starting at Somerset House, close
by the southern side of Waterloo Bridge (three swoopingly graceful arches by
Sir Giles Scott, completed in 1945 despite the blitz), and ending at
Westminster Bridge. Waterloo Bridge, bye the bye, inspired the Kinks's
'Waterloo Sunset' hit of 1967. From a flight of steps leading to the bridge from
the embankment there are good views (usually windy ones) of the south bank,
with the South Bank Complex to the east providing living proof that concrete
can be brutal stuff in the hands of architects.

Somerset House

Bulky Somerset House (opened in 1786) was architect **William Chambers**'s
some-what ponderous Georgian response to the elegance of Robert Adam's
Adelphi buildings at Charing Cross. It's a pity the old Somerset House, a royal
palace built in 1547, was pulled down; **Inigo Jones** decorated it for James I's

---

CLEOPATRA'S NEEDLE

Cleopatra's Needle has nothing to do with Cleopatra. It's a circa
1450BC granite obelisk presented to Britain by Egypt's Turkish rulers in
gratitude for Nelson's victory at the 1798 Battle of the Nile, and
brought from Alexandria in 1878. It was nearly lost in a gale in the Bay
of Biscay, when several sailors drowned, but was eventually rescued
and brought to London. It dates from the reign of Pharaoh Thothmes
III, a great warrior according to the hieroglyphics down its side which
recorded his victories. There are two sealed time capsules buried
beneath it, containing a picture of Queen Victoria, a bundle of
newspapers, four bibles, hairpins, *Bradshaw's Railway Guide*, a box of
cigars and photographs of 12 pretty girls.

Queen Anne of Denmark, who liked it so much that for a while it was renamed 'Denmark House'. Another queen, Charles's Henrietta Maria, liked it as well; her rooms, according to Pepys, were 'most stately and nobly furnished'. From the 18th until the 20th centuries, Chambers's building became Somerset House and the place where births, marriages and deaths were registered. Now it is the home of the dreaded Inland Revenue and the excellent Courtauld Institute's galleries housed in a string of Louis XV-inspired rooms. There are paintings by Manet, Renoir, and dozens of other French impressionists and post-impressionists, plus canvasses by Rubens, Van Dyck and more.

> *Visitor information* The triple-arched entrance to Somerset House is in the Strand, surmounted by Jove-like heads with plaited beards. The galleries open Mon–Sat 10.00–18.00, Sun 14.00–18.00. There are guided tours, lectures, workshops, special exhibitions, an art bookshop and a café. There is an admission charge of £4 for adults (£3 for senior citizens) but not for students and children. For further information, tel: 020 7872 0220.

The big stink

Victoria Embankment forms one of London's most attractive riverside promenades. It was built not as a walkway, but as part of a plan to rid London of the 'big stink'. By 1855, the river had become an open sewer. The scientist Michael Faraday, in a letter to *The Times*, described its appearance as

> an opaque brown liquid . . . near the bridges the feculence rolled up
> in clouds so dense that they were visible at the surface.

By 1856, the stench had become so overpowering that it became known as the 'year of the big stink'. Business in the Houses of Parliament could not go on until the windows where curtained with sheets soaked in disinfectant and tonnes upon tonnes of lime were dumped in the river. The chief engineer of the new Board of Works, Joseph Bazalgette (1819–91), was commissioned to draw up a comprehensive sewage system which was immediately put into practice. The Victoria Embankment, lit by elegant lamps decorated with sea creatures, dolphins twined round their bases, and seats supported by kneeling camels, was constructed as part of Bazalgette's programme to hide one of the giant pipes carrying London's sewage along the north bank to outfalls at Barking and Crossness.

Between the junction of Waterloo Bridge and the Victoria Embankment is the site of the former Savoy Palace, owned first by the Count of Savoy and then by John of Gaunt (1340–99), the Black Prince's brother, when the building was attacked and ransacked by Wat Tyler (?–1381) and his peasant revolters in 1381. They threw a locked chest into the fire, thinking it contained gold which would melt and make them rich, but it was full of gunpowder which blew the roof off the Great Hall and entombed Tyler's followers; they were left to starve to death. The building's name survives in the Savoy Hotel, built in the 1880s, overlooking the Embankment. Here the chef **Auguste Escoffier** (1847–1935) created peach Melba for the Australian-born soprano **Dame Nellie Melba** (1861–1931) and tournedos Rossini for the Italian composer **Gioacchino Rossini** (1792–1868). When **Richard D'Oyly Carte** decided to build the new Savoy Hotel in 1880, he demanded it should have 70 bathrooms – such an unheard of number in those days that the builder asked if the guests were to be amphibians.

The Adelphi

The Adelphi, a series of romantically elegant terraces of houses running from The Strand to the riverside next to the present Victoria Embankment Gardens, was knocked down in the 1930s. It was built in typical neo-classical style over a series of arched openings giving on to the river. The architects were the **Adam brothers**, Robert (1728–92) and James (1730–94). They designed their buildings to have a harmonious relation between the exterior, the interior, and the furniture. Their light, elegant, and essentially decorative style was a free, personal reconstitution of antique motifs. But the elegantly simple Adelphi (Greek for 'brothers') was bitterly criticised in its day. The writer **Horace Walpole** (1717–97), whose stuccoed and battlemented Gothic home in Twickenham we shall visit (see page 58), remarked 'Scotchmen, by the name of Adam . . . have stole the river from us'. Others loved it, especially the paved archways redolent of Venice. Anyway, the Aldelphi was so generally disliked that it was demolished in 1936, but there are traces of the Adams' work close by. In Robert Street, for instance, a blue plaque marks the charming house where first Robert lived, and then, at separate times, the writers **John Galsworthy** (1867–1933) and **James Barrie** (1860–1937).

Victoria Embankment Gardens

Behind Charing Cross Underground station, off Villiers Street, are the pleasant and restful **Victoria Embankment Gardens**, where there are lawns, a fish pool, and bands that play in the summer. There are numerous statues and memorials here, including a little one to the Imperial Camel Corps (1921), and statues of the poet **Robert Burns** (1759–96), **Robert Raikes** (the founder – in 1780 – of Sunday schools) and the composer **Arthur Sullivan** (1894–1900). The gardens were once in the grounds of York House, belonging first to the Tudor **Archbishop of York** and then, in the reign of Charles I, to the first **Duke of Buckingham** (1592–1628). Buckingham, said the king, 'excelled all courtiers for wit and debauchery'. He knocked down the old house and had a magnificent mansion erected in its place, but couldn't actually afford it because the cost – let alone the price of his debaucheries – forced him eventually to sell the house and the land surrounding it. All that is left of his great riverside estate is a stone arch, **York House Watergate**, decorated with sculpted shells and two dismal looking lions. This was the river gateway from Buckingham's garden to a flight of river steps. In old engravings, it stands in the river, swans and reeds surrounding it. As the present-day riverbank is some 150 yards/137m away, it is difficult to believe that this was where 17th-century toffs and their ladies climbed ashore when visiting Buckingham's York House. But they did, which just goes to show how far the Thames was pushed from the land when the Embankment was built.

Hungerford Stairs, near what was Hungerford Market – demolished in 1861 – is now covered by Charing Cross railway station. It was here that the boy **Dickens** was put to work in Warren's Blacking Warehouse, washing and sorting bottles amidst dirt and rats and loneliness and despair, as he later recorded in *David Copperfield*. **Rudyard Kipling** lived for a time in a first-floor apartment in Villiers Street, next door to Charing Cross station, marked by a blue plaque.

Also close to Charing Cross, just off the Strand, is **Craven Street**, a quiet backwater where the foundations of the United States of America were forged by the statesman **Benjamin Franklin** (1906–90). He lived here, for five years (1757–62), on a mission which was to lead to the American War of Independence. He returned to Craven Street (this time living at No 7, which has been demolished) for a further eight years (1767–1775). He was visited by most of the great political leaders of the day, including **William Pitt the Elder** and the **Earl of Chatham**. Franklin left England in 1775, certain that the two nations would soon be at war. And they were. As this book was being made ready for the printer, work was being completed on turning No 36 Craven Street into a museum dedicated to Franklin's life and work.

Victoria Embankment continues all the way to Westminster Bridge, Big Ben, the Houses of Parliament, Thorneycroft's statue of Queen Boudicca, and Westminster Pier (on the downstream side of the bridge), which is one of the principal starting places for trips up and down the river.

Westminster Bridge to Strand-on-the-Green

Distances From Westminster Bridge (north-bank route/south-bank route): Vauxhall Bridge 0.9 miles/1.1 miles (1.44km/1.76km), Chelsea Bridge 2 miles/2.35 miles (3.2km/3.76km), Putney Bridge 4.2 miles/6.8 miles (6.72km/10.88km) Strand-on-the-Green (south route) 8.9 miles (14.24km), Kew Bridge 9.7 miles/11.6 miles (15.5km/18.56km)

WESTMINSTER BRIDGE TO CHELSEA BRIDGE

This isn't the same Westminster Bridge from where **William Wordsworth** (1770–1850) sang his clumsy verse of praise to London's river in 1802 – it was the same place, but an older bridge:

> Earth has not anything to show more fair:
> Dull would he be of soul who could pass by
> A sight so touching in its majesty. . .
> Ships, towers, domes, theatres and temples lie
> Open unto fields, and to the sky;
> All bright and glittering in the smokeless air.

It wasn't the bridge where **James Boswell** (1740–95) pulled a whore, either:

> [I] picked up a strong jolly young damsel and taking her under the arm I conducted her to Westminster Bridge, and there in amour complete did I engage up in this noble edifice. The whim of doing it there with the Thames rolling below us amused me much.

Boswell's bridge had 15 arches, and a recess in each one covered with a half-circular turret where people could shelter. Before the bridge was opened, in 1750, people wanting to cross the river had to use London Bridge, or Putney Bridge, or take the horse ferry at Lambeth, or hire a waterman to row them across.

Apart from the handsome stone lions guarding its approaches, today's version of Westminster Bridge doesn't have a lot going for it. It was built between 1854 and 1862 by one **Thomas Page**. Other bridges, upstream, are nicer. Lambeth Bridge isn't especially stunning, but it is painted red and gold and sometimes at night is wonderfully floodlit. The next, Vauxhall, is

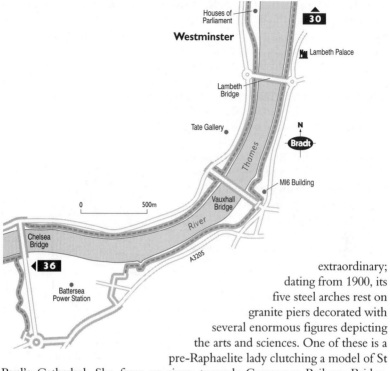

extraordinary; dating from 1900, its five steel arches rest on granite piers decorated with several enormous figures depicting the arts and sciences. One of these is a pre-Raphaelite lady clutching a model of St Paul's Cathedral. She faces up-river, towards Grosvenor Railway Bridge, which carries trains to and from Victoria railway station.

Just downstream of Vauxhall Bridge, on the north-bank Thames Path, is **Tate Britain**, housing two major collections, one of British modern art, the other related to British art (but not necessarily British artists) and based on **J M W Turner**'s bequest of a large number of his own paintings. The Tate building stands on the site of what was Millbank Penitentiary, or the 'Tench', the most hated of London's prisons. The riverside was ideal for loading prisoners into ships and transporting them overseas, mostly to Australia. On the embankment near the Tate is a fountain-washed bronze by **Henry Moore** called *The Locking Piece* commemorating those incarcerated in the 'Tench'.

On the opposite bank is **64 Vauxhall Road**, a self-consciously futuristic headquarters building for James Bond, 1,999 other spies, and the rest of MI6. This building is close to the site of what was Vauxhall Pleasure Gardens from before the time of Samuel Pepys until 1855, when 'the place seemed literally worn out; the very trees grew scribby and shabby, and looked as if they were singed; and it was high time to say ... "Farewell"', according to a contemporary newspaper comment.

Pepys described his 1666 visit there as 'pretty merry'. There was a chap who did bird impressions, another who imitated dogs and pigs, and with whom Sam was so 'mighty pleasant' he 'stayed there all night'. The gardens were laid out in avenues with pretty pavilions and secluded arbours popular with the fashionable and the randy. **Boswell** commented on its 'mixture of curious shew, gay exhibition, music, vocal and instrumental, not too refined for the general ear'. Boswell and **Doctor Johnson** came often, sometimes with **Joshua Reynolds**, 'dressed in velvet, of course'.

In **William Thackeray**'s *Vanity Fair*, Rebecca Sharp and Amelia go to a party at Vauxhall where Jos Sedley, who accompanies them, gets exceeding drunk on rack punch. **Dickens** and **Landseer** came to the gardens together and watched the **Duke of Wellington** attend an entertainment called 'The Battle of Waterloo'.

Beyond Vauxhall Bridge and Grosvenor Bridge are Chelsea, Albert and Battersea bridges. **Albert Bridge** is something special, London's prettiest, designed by a **Rowland Ordish** in 1873. It is a cantilever-and-suspension structure resembling a gigantic iron cobweb, or a sailing ship, depending on how you see it. It's a bouncy affair that moves up and down as traffic passes over it; notices on the toll kiosks at either end advise soldiers to break step when marching over.

There are good westward views looking towards **Battersea Bridge** and the sky-kissing **Chelsea Harbour Tower** beyond the north bank's Chelsea houseboats and creek. There are footpaths over **Chelsea Bridge**, walled off from the road down the middle, so if this is your crossing point choose, first, if you want to look eastwards (Pimlico and Battersea Power Station) or westwards (Chelsea Royal Hospital and Battersea Park).

CHELSEA

One way or another you must allow time to spend in Chelsea, especially if you intend to walk in the footsteps of the famous. You don't have to stray from the north-bank Thames Path, for it runs along the embankment's handsome, although traffic-thundered, **Cheyne Walk**. Here, and in adjoining streets, an astonishing number of brilliant people lived at one time or other.

Sir Thomas More had a palace here. Hans Sloane, the

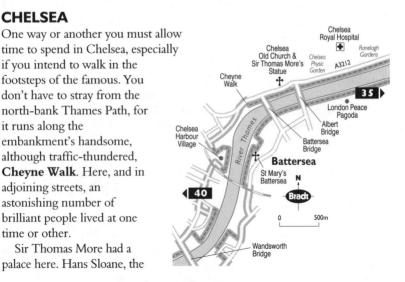

Irish physician whose collection formed the nucleus of
the British Museum, lived here. So did Oscar Wilde,
George Eliot, Thomas Carlyle, and the painters
Dante Gabriel Rossetti, Joseph Mallard William
Turner, James Abbott McNeill Whistler and
John Singer Sargent.

Cheyne Walk

The impressive statue of a black-robed
figure, Henry VIII's statesman and Lord
Chancellor, **Sir Thomas More**, stands
close to his one-time house and ground –
'the greatest in Chelsey' – which sprawled
across the countryside from Beaufort Street
to the river. More's friend **Erasmus**
(1466–1536), the Dutch-born humanist who
became professor of divinity at Cambridge,
called the house 'comodious [*sic*] . . . neither
mean nor subject to envy, yet magnificent
enough'.

It must have been enormous, a fine Tudor mansion, surrounded by vast
grounds, occupying about a third of the entire manor of Chelsea, and including
even a home farm. It is teasing to discover that there isn't a real trace of it left –
not a wall, not even a foundation. But we do know it was on land which is now
Cheyne Walk and that by the riverside was a flight of steps where More kept
his ornate barge and eight watermen ever ready to row him to Westminster.
After More was beheaded, **King Henry VIII** knocked the mansion down, built
another and gave it to **Katherine Parr** as part of her dowry.

Hans Sloane, then in his 80s, moved into whatever was left of the
More/Henry VIII/Katherine Parr mansion in 1712. He intended to leave it to
the nation as a place to stow and show his gold, silver, porcelain, natural history
collection of fish, insects, snakes and lizards, and library of 50,000 priceless
books. When he died in 1753, however, the government was not a bit interested
in preserving Henry VIII's manor and razed it down. The collection was moved
to Bloomsbury Place to become the beginnings of the British Museum.

Thomas Carlyle (1795–1881), a Scottish historian, philosopher and
author, and one of the most influential writers in the UK in the 19th century,
lived at No 24 Cheyne Row from 1834 until his death. Of all the houses on
the Chelsea riverside inhabited by the famous, this is, perhaps, the most
satisfying because it stands more or less exactly as the Carlyles left it.

When Thomas first discovered the house, and decided to rent it, he wrote
to his wife that it was

> on the whole a most massive, roomy, sufficient old house; with
> places, for example, to hang say three dozen hats or cloaks on. . . Our
> row runs out upon a parade running along the shore of the river . . . a
> broad highway with huge shady trees, boats lying moored and a smell
> of shipping and tar. Battersea Bridge is a few yards off; the broad river

with white-trousered, white-shirted Cockneys dashing about like arrows in their long canoes of boats and beyond the green beautiful knolls of Surrey with their villages.

He considered it a 'genteel neighbourhood, two ladies on one side, unknown character on the other, but with pianos'. **Coleridge**, **Dickens**, **Tennyson**, **Browning**, **Hazlitt**, **William Thackeray**, and **Whistler** visited Carlyle here, and all have left footprints. Carlyle's portrait was painted by Whistler (see below), who lived just round the corner in Cheyne Walk. The house is now a National Trust property. A bronze statue of Carlyle, seated and contemplating the river, is in a small riverside garden near the end of Cheyne Walk.

Visitor information The Carlyle house (tel: 020 7352 7087) is open to the public Apr–Oct (Wed–Sun 11.00–16.30); closed throughout the winter months. Admission adult £3.60, child £1.80.

A blue plaque commemorates the fact that **Sir Marc Isambard Brunel** (1769–1849) and his son **Isambard Kingdom** (1806–59) lived here, at Lindsey House, No 98 Cheyne Walk, from 1808 to 1824 except when Sir Marc was in debtors' prison between 1821 and 1824.

At the junction of Cremorne Road and Cheyne Walk is a small house, once No 6 Davis Place, where a Mrs Booth from Margate took a 21-year lease in 1846 and moved in with Mr Booth who, in reality, was the artist **Joseph Mallord William Turner** (1775–1851).

The Chelsea watermen took a shine to Turner, called him 'the Admiral' because of his obsession with the river and water, and his sailor-like appearance. One of the watercolours Turner painted while living in Chelsea was *The Artist and the Thames*, presently exhibited as part of the Courtauld collection in Somerset House (see page 31); it shows a typical Turner sunset behind the Chelsea embankment. According to legend, a Chelsea neighbour, the American artist Whistler, added the dog with its front paws on the embankment parapet.

In 1891, the American **James Abbott McNeill Whistler** (1834–1903) sold his portrait of Thomas Carlyle, which had at one time been in pawn, to the Glasgow Corporation for 1,000 guineas. Whistler spent much of his life in Chelsea – 'this wonderful village', he called it – before and after his mother's arrival from the USA in 1863 when she was escaping the American Civil War. They lived at No 96 Cheyne Walk, where Mrs W so disapproved of her son having a live-in mistress that she threatened to leave unless he threw her out – the mistress, not the mother, and thank goodness she did, or we might not have had the painting we call 'Whistler's Mother' (but which the artist entitled *An Arrangement in Grey and Black*).

The odd-shaped corner house, No 104 Cheyne Walk, was the home of **Hilaire Belloc** (1870–1953). No 93 has a plaque on the wall celebrating the birth here of **Mrs Gaskell** (1810–65), the Victorian authoress. Mrs Gaskell's mother died when the child was a baby and she was sent off to an aunt in Cheshire, so her stay in Chelsea was only a short one.

Cheyne Walk has some fine Georgian houses. The dissolute poet and pre-Raphaelite artist **Dante Gabriel Rossetti** (1828–82) lived in the best of them, No 16, with its paved courtyard. There is a painting in the National Portrait Gallery of Rosetti in the drawing room of the house, a beautiful festival of colour, crammed with paintings, papered with turquoise and gold Morris wallpaper. Rossetti gave wild parties, and collected animals which he kept in the garden and in the house. There were kangaroos, peacocks and a fat wombat which was said to be the original dormouse in *Alice's Adventures in Wonderland* after **Lewis Carroll** came to photograph Rossetti at home in Cheyne Walk. Other visitors included the actress **Ellen Terry**, and the artist-craftsman **William Morris** and his exotically beautiful wife Janey, for whom Rossetti had an obsessive passion (see page 216). The poet and critic **Algernon Charles Swinburne** (1837–1909) came to live for a while but couldn't stand the animals and the smell. Rosetti died of mercury poisoning – not here, but at Birchington in Kent where he is buried.

At another of Cheyne Walk's handsome houses, No 4, **George Eliot** (1819–80) died. She had moved there, after returning from a honeymoon with her second husband in 1880, and died of a chill 19 days later.

Leigh Hunt (1784–1859) – poet, essayist, but mostly journalist – arrived with his family at No 22 Upper Cheyne Row in 1833. His seven-year stay is commemorated by a blue plaque . Hunt recorded in his autobiography:

> My family moved to a corner of Chelsea where the air was so
> refreshing, and the quiet of the thoroughfares so full of repose, that
> although our fortunes were at their worst and my health almost a
> piece of them, I felt for some weeks as if I could sit for ever,
> embalmed in the silence.

It is doubtful if their neighbours found their coming 'full of repose' or 'embalmed in silence'; the Hunts' seven children were 'dirtier and more mischievous than Yahoos' according to poets **Shelley** and **Byron**.

Leigh and his wife Marianne befriended **Thomas** and **Jane Carlyle**, a friendship more enjoyed by Thomas than by Jane because Marianne was a perpetual borrower of domestic items and usually more tipsy than sober.

Another great American artist lived in Chelsea, **John Singer Sargent** (1856–1925), who had his home in Tite Street. One of Sargent's portraits is of fellow American, the writer **Henry James**, then living not far away in Carlyle Mansions. James subsequently recalled his delight at the sittings:

> J S S being so genial and delightful a nature de grand maitre to have
> to do with, and his beautiful high cool studio, opening upon a
> balcony that overhangs a charming Chelsea green garden, adding
> charm to everything. . .

Oscar Wilde lived on the opposite side of Tite Street and wrote, when Ellen Terry was sitting for Sargent:

> The street that on a wet and dreary morning has vouchsafed the
> vision of Lady Macbeth in full regalia magnificently seated in a four-
> wheeler can never again be as other streets: it must always be full of
> wonderful possibilities.

There is confusion concerning the blue plaque on No 34 Tite Street, which
commemorates Wilde's two-year residence here, because it was then No 16.
He arrived with his beautiful bride Constance in 1883, and left in 1895 after
the libel trial of the 'Screaming Scarlet Marquis' in April and the first
unsuccessful attempt to prosecute him. During his stay he wrote three
domestic comedies – 'drawing-room plays with pink lampshades', he called
them – *Lady Windermere's Fan* (1892), *A Woman of No Importance* (1893), and *An
Ideal Husband* (1894). They took the London stage by storm and Wilde was
fêted for his witty, epigrammatic style, insolent ease of utterance, and suave
urbanity.

On the opposite bank in Battersea, beside the north-bank Thames Path, is
London's only riverside church, often called 'Blake's Church' because it was
here in 1782 that the poet **William Blake** married Catherine Boucher,
daughter of a local market gardener. The pillared Georgian **St Mary's** started
life in 1777, replacing an earlier church. **Turner** used to study the moving
waters of the Thames from the bay window, perched on a high-legged chair
that is still there.

The iron **Battersea Bridge**, built by the engineer of the Thames
embankments, **Sir Joseph Bazalgette**, is a nice one – decorated gold and
green with turquoise scrollwork, and lit by Victorian gaslights – but it's not as
picturesque as its predecessor was. That one, built in 1772, was slender,
timber, lit by a string of lamps, and painted with love by Whistler (in *Nocturne
in Blue and Silver*, now in the Tate) and Turner.

Along Chelsea's Royal Hospital Road there's a gateway leading into the
Royal Hospital (originally built in 1681–6, with later additions), which
Charles II founded for retired soldiers and Christopher Wren designed. It's
one of Chelsea's showpieces, where about 420 Chelsea Pensioners have their

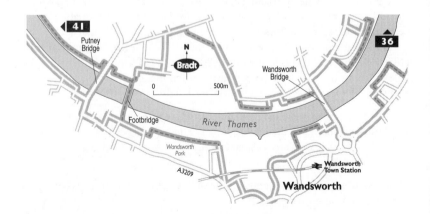

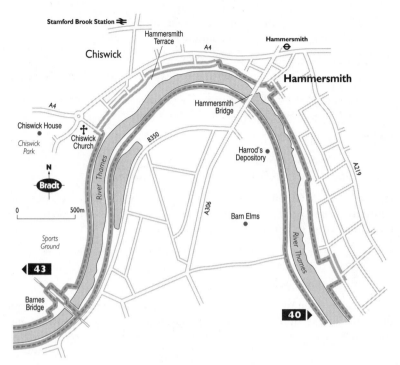

Stamford Brook Station
Hammersmith Terrace
A4
Hammersmith
Chiswick
Hammersmith
A4
Hammersmith Bridge
Chiswick House
Chiswick Park
Chiswick Church
B350
River Thames
Harrod's Depository
A219
N
Bradt
0   500m
A306
Barn Elms
River Thames
Sports Ground
◀ 43
Barnes Bridge
40 ▶

home, their winter blue uniform coats and their summer scarlet ones, cutting a dash in Chelsea's streets. For a few days in May the grounds of the hospital are taken over by the Chelsea Flower Show.

> *Visitor information* Chelsea Royal Hospital is open Mon–Sat 10.00–12.00 and 14.00–16.00, Sun 14.00–16.00. Admission free. For further information, tel: 020 7730 0161.

Next to the Royal Hospital is the 66-acre tree-filled **Ranelagh Gardens**, all that is left of a one-time pleasure ground as famous as Vauxhall's but more seemly. The Earl of Ranelagh was King Charles's Paymaster General and Treasurer to the Royal Hospital, from which he stole a third of its land and embezzled enough money to build himself a posh house east of the hospital. On the waters of the Thames, just off the gardens of Ranelagh's house, **George Frederic Handel** (1685–1759) gave the first public performance of his 'Water Music' in the summer of 1717. A contemporary account describes how the king and several ladies 'took Water at Whitehall in an open Barge'. There was a second barge

> wherein were 50 instruments of all sorts, who play'd all the Way from
> Lambeth . . . the finest Symphonies, compos'd express for this

> Occasion by Mr Handel which his Majesty liked so well, that he
> caus'd it to be plaid over three times in going and returning.

Ranelagh Gardens went public after the earl's death in 1742. They were an
instant success. By 1744, the writer and bon viveur **Horace Walpole** went

> every night, constantly, to Ranelagh, which had totally beat Vauxhall.
> Nobody goes anywhere else, everybody goes there.

Dr Johnson concurred:

> Yes, Sir, there are many happy people here who are watching
> hundreds, and who think hundreds are watching them.

Ranelagh became famous for its music, reaching its height when the composer
Thomas Arne was in charge during the 1760s. As an entrepreneur, he
brought **Mozart** to London to play at Ranelagh:

> The celebrated and astonishing Master MOZART . . . child of 7 years
> of age . . . justly esteemed the most extraordinary Prodigy, and most
> amazing Genius that has appeared in any Age.

Come, time is pressing. Let's scamper on towards Teddington, passing
through Hammersmith, Chiswick, Strand-on-the-Green, Kew, Richmond,
and Twickenham on the way, leaving time to discover more 'greats' as we go.

HAMMERSMITH

Hammersmith Suspension Bridge is loved by Londoners for its fanciful
decoration and its pinnacles. It was designed in 1887 by **Sir Joseph
Bazalgette**, who changed the face of London's Thames with his Victoria
Embankment (see page 31). In the centre of the bridge is a bronze plate

---

A P H AND THE DOVE

I don't expect you are old enough to remember the playwright, essayist,
novelist, wit, sailor and politician, **Alan Patrick Herbert** (1890–1971) –
few people are. You won't, therefore, recall his genially mesmeric television
presentations, nor his books, not even the best of them, *The Water Gipsies*
(1930), set on the Thames and turned into a film (with music and dancing
chucked in) which had a sort of simple black-and-white charm. He was
better known as 'A P H' and was a great Thames man and character, an
eloquent lover of the river who lived beside it at Hammersmith for more
than 50 years. His boat was moored at the bottom of the garden, Nos 12
and 13 Hammersmith Terrace, which was built (or so it is said, as it is said
about lots of houses along the Thames) for royal whores.

A P H often held quiet court at the olde-world **Dove** in Hammersmith's
Upper Mall beside the river. In the 18th century it was the Dove Coffee
House and 'wits and citizens resorted to it . . . to sip their coffee, enjoy the

commemorating a South African-born RAF lieutenant, **Charles Campbell Wood**, who dived into the Thames at this spot to save a drowning woman at midnight in September 1919. He died later of his injuries.

Thomas Faulkner, a Victorian and forgotten local historian, wrote affectionately of the river stretches between Hammersmith and Kew bridges:

> From Kew Bridge the river flows majestically on in sweeping courses between shores skirted with villages and fine seats, passing Mortlake, Barnes, Chiswick and Hammersmith, where it is enlivened and embellished with one of the most magnificent works of art that modern skill and ingenuity have produced – the suspension bridge.

The Hammersmith home of arts and crafts champion **William Morris** (1834–96), **Kelmscott House** (built in 1790) is at the end of Upper Mall. There is a plaque to Morris, hidden by a large magnolia (unless someone has drastically pruned the tree since I last visited). He lived here for the last 18 years of his life, delighted by its peace and proximity to the Thames. 'The

sweet prospect of the river and talk over the literature and politics of the day'. **Charles II** and **Nell Gwyn** are said to have met here – but then they are said to have met in just about every 'olde' meeting house and pub on the river from Whitehall to Staines. The poet **James Thomson** (1700–48) did compose 'Rule Britannia' at the Dove, in one of the upstairs rooms. **Doctor Arne** set the words to music and they were first sung for the Prince of Wales, which I shall tell you about when we reach lovely Cliveden on the middle Thames (see page 132).

Meanwhile, craftsman, writer and political activist **William Morris** (1834–96) lived just down the road (we visit above, and on page 44) and often entertained his pre-Raphaelite friends and patrons at the Dove, which is described in *The Water Gipsies* (where A P H called it 'the Pigeons'). There are three low-ceilinged bars, and a vine-covered terrace overlooking the river. It is a lovely, lively spot, crowded with sailors and rowing-men, and I once ate a delicious hors d'oeuvres there.

situation is certainly the prettiest in London,' he wrote. He called it 'Kelmscott' after his country riverside home in Oxfordshire, which we shall visit between Oxford and the source (see page 214). While Morris's Oxfordshire home is open to visitors, the Hammersmith one isn't.

CHISWICK

The walk from Hammersmith Bridge to Chiswick is a beautiful one at any time of the year, passing centuries-old houses, gardens, Chiswick Eyot, piers, and many a pleasant pub. There is the 16th–18th-century **Walpole House** on Chiswick Mall, where 'the fairest and the lewdest of the Royal concubines' – **Barbara Villiers**, Countess of Castlemaine and Duchess of Cleveland – spent the last years of her life. **Charles II** was devoted to her and impregnated her (thrice), **Dryden** wrote poems to her, **William Wycherley** fell in love with her, and **Samuel Pepys** leched over her dark auburn-haired beauty and melting eyes.

Walpole House became a school in the early 19th century and **William Thackeray** (1811–63) was taught there and is said to have used it as Miss Pinkerton's Academy in *Vanity Fair* (where Miss Becky Sharp threw away her dictionary as she drove away in dudgeon). Boston House, near Hogarth's in Chiswick (see opposite), also claims to have been Becky Sharp's school.

The imposing **Bedford House** at the end of Chiswick Mall was for years the home of the **Redgrave family**, Sir Michael, his wife Rachael, and their children, Vanessa, Lynne and Corin.

Five minutes from the quiet riverside of Chiswick Mall are the walled grounds of **Chiswick House**, with an entrance in Burlington Lane providing the best of views of the mansion and its tree-lined avenue. The house is cool, classical Palladian, a work of art created by the infinitely refined third Earl of Burlington, **Richard Boyle** (1694–1753), and landscape-gardener-cum-interior-designer, **William Kent** (1685–1748). Burlington built the house, his country villa, so as to have somewhere to show off his arts and entertain his cultured chums. It is modelled on the Villa Capra, near Vicenza in Italy. A neighbour, the poet **Alexander Pope**, advised royal gardener **Charles Bridgeman** on the layout and exotic planting of the grounds. The house's exterior is exquisite, the interior near perfect, from vaulted basements to painted top-floor ceilings; **Horace Walpole** said that Burlington was a man who 'possessed every quality of a genius and an artist except envy'. There are portraits of **Inigo Jones** (Burlington's patron saint of design) and William Kent (the plump, self-confident, Yorkshire-born man who became the oracle on 'furniture, frames of pictures, glasses, tables, chairs . . . for a barge, for a cradle'). Alexander Pope liked and admired Kent, calling him 'the Signor'. Near the ceiling of Chiswick House's 'Blue Room' is a cherub-circled portrait of a haggard-looking Pope, who was crippled, often in pain, funny, brilliant – 'a lively little creature, with long arms and legs . . . a spider is no ill emblem of him,' according to Pope himself.

The echoes of many famous footsteps can be heard at Chiswick House if you listen hard enough. Pope and Gay, Swift and James Thomson, wits and philosophers, considered by the gentry to have 'taste', came to admire. One-time foreign secretary, **Charles James Fox** (1749–1806), came to die. He was brought by the dazzling **Georgiana**, Duchess of Devonshire, when she ruled over the house at the end of the 18th century. Fox, brilliant, learned, hopelessly extravagant statesman, much loved by his friends and hated by his opponents, was seriously ill when Georgiana fetched him away in September 1806. There was a mountain ash growing by the window of his bedroom, a small plain room called, simply, the 'Bedchamber'. The ash has gone, but Fox peered longingly at it every morning during his illness. 'His last look at that mountain ash was his last look on nature,' wrote a biographer. Twenty years later his parliamentary successor **George Canning** (1770–1827) died in the same room.

Edward VII used to spend summers at Chiswick House; there's a watercolour of him and his children playing in the garden in a little room called the 'Red Closet'. Two of the children are the future George V and Queen Mary.

You will need to decide if it is worth shuffling round Chiswick's thundering

Visitor information Chiswick House is open and closed at such weird times that it would be best if you checked by telephone (020 8995 0508) before visiting. Roughly speaking, as of autumn 2002, the house is closed throughout the winter from November 1 to March 30, and open from April 1 to Oct 31 (Wed–Fri and Sun). In other words, Chiswick House, for reasons not clear to me, isn't open very often these days.

M4 roundabout to see **Hogarth's House**, on the edge of the Great West Road in Hogarth Lane, close to Chiswick House. It's cottage-sized and of the period of Queen Anne. 'My little Country Box', Hogarth called it when it was surrounded by open fields. It's no longer that, but struggles to cling to its solitude, surrounded by a crumbling wall, shadowed by the beauty of an ancient mulberry tree and the ugliness of modernity.

William Hogarth (1697–1764), sometimes called 'the father of English painting', who held up a caricaturist's mirror to the lunacies of the 18th century, bought his 'box' in 1749. By then he was famous and had completed his series of 'modern moral subjects', which included *A Rake's Progress* (1733–5), and his masterpiece *Marriage à la Mode* (1743–5). Short and pugnacious, with an expression described by Leigh Hunt as 'a sort of knowing jockey look', Hogarth lived a virtuous and decorous life at Chiswick, and a roguish one in the taverns and brothels of London to which he not infrequently escaped with his friends.

Today's Hogarth House is neat, snug, the rooms furnished with 18th-century mood, with furniture and with Hogarth's engravings. The garden has shrunk since Hogarth's day but the mulberry tree is the same one from which local children used to pick the fruit and under which they ate Jane Hogarth's homemade mulberry tarts.

Visitor information Hogarth's House (tel: 020 8994 6757) is open Apr 1–Oct 31 (Tue–Fri 13.00–17.00, Sat and Sun 13.00–18.00; closed Mon), and Nov 1–Mar 31 (Tue–Fri 13.00–16.00, Sat and Sun 13.00–17.00; closed Mon, whole of Jan, Christmas Day and Boxing Day). Admission free but donations invited.

Chiswick's river frontage, retaining something of what it looked like when it was tiny and independent of big-brother London, stretches from Hammersmith Bridge to Strand-on-the-Green. The concrete **Chiswick Bridge** was built in 1933, and looks it, to the designs of architect **Sir Herbert Baker**. Just downstream, opposite the **Ship Inn**, is the finish line of the Oxford and Cambridge Boat Race. The Ship Inn is popular and cheerful, and serves inexpensive meals that can be enjoyed with views of the long curving river.

STRAND-ON-THE-GREEN

Try to ignore the railway crossing the river on its way to Richmond for then Strand-on-the-Green on the Middlesex (northern) shore becomes again an unspoiled fragment of Georgian England, a huddle of balconied houses with Dutch gables and coloured shutters, smothered in roses and wisteria. There are many old fishermen's cottages, dating from the 18th century, which only extremely rich Londoners can now afford. Their gardens are fine. At the top-most of the biggest spring and autumn tides, the river invades the village, ducks and moorhens swim round the lampposts, and the Thames Path disappears under water.

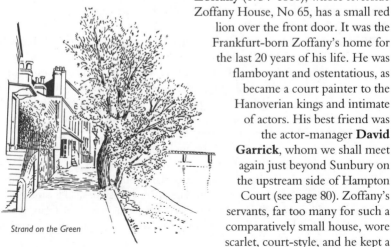

Strand on the Green

Those who have not minded running the risk of having their sitting-rooms flooded thigh-high by the Thames include the painter **Johann Zoffany** (1734–1810), whose riverside Zoffany House, No 65, has a small red lion over the front door. It was the Frankfurt-born Zoffany's home for the last 20 years of his life. He was flamboyant and ostentatious, as became a court painter to the Hanoverian kings and intimate of actors. His best friend was the actor-manager **David Garrick**, whom we shall meet again just beyond Sunbury on the upstream side of Hampton Court (see page 80). Zoffany's servants, far too many for such a comparatively small house, wore scarlet, court-style, and he kept a garish pink-and-green sloop in the river outside his house. The prince regent came to musical evenings, sitting in Zoffany's treehouse listening to the music. There is a Zoffany painting in St Paul's Church at **Brentford**. It portrays fishermen apostles, and the faces are those of Zoffany's fishermen neighbours and their wives; the artist is portrayed as St Peter, his child-wife is St John, and a local lawyer, with whom he had quarrelled, is Judas. Zoffany House isn't open to the public.

There have been other distinguished residents of Strand-on-the-Green. For example, the writer **Nancy Mitford** (1904–73), arbiter of 'U' (upper-class) and 'non-U' behaviour, lived here in the 1930s. Judging by her sister's description of her as 'an elegant pirate's moll', she should have fitted well into riverside living. Another was the Welsh poet **Dylan Thomas** (1913–53), who much enjoyed the booze and chatter in the local historic pubs. These include the **City Barge** (dating from 1497), upstream of the railway bridge, where the Lord Mayor's barge used to be moored in winter, and the **Bull's Head**, downstream of the railway bridge, from where, it is said, **Oliver Cromwell** escaped to the island in the river, since called **Oliver's Ait**, during the English Civil War.

Pretty Strand-on-the-Green should be entirely safe from developers, but possibly isn't. In 1968 it was declared a conservation area. Would that, I wonder, mean anything should the powers-that-be see profits and votes in driving a four-lane highway through it?

Strand-on-the-Green and Kew to Teddington Lock

Distances From Strand-on-the-Green and Kew (north-bank route/south-bank route): Syon House and Park (south-bank) 2.98 miles (4.7 km), Richmond Lock 5.01/3.94 miles (8/6.3km), Marble Hill Park (south-bank) 6.94 miles (11.1km), Teddington Lock and footbridge 14.9/6.99 miles (23.84/11.2km)

It's no more than an ambling stroll from Strand-on-the-Green to Kew Bridge, upstream of which, on the northern (Middlesex) bank, is Syon House. On the other side of the river is Kew itself, the palace, and the Royal Botanic Gardens, the world's most exotic gardens that occupy the Surrey bank for the next couple of miles. The bridge is glowered over by tall office blocks and growled at by traffic jams at one end or the other, often both at the same time. Yet just a breath of fresh air away is Kew, still retaining a few of its ancient charms. At the centre is the 'green', wall-to-wall shaved grass on which cricket has been played for over 200 years, watched over by splendid Georgian houses and the yellow-bricked St Anne's Church.

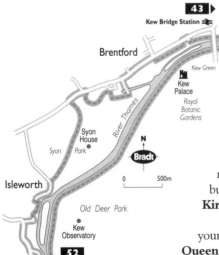

St Anne's has had all sorts of top-knots and whatnots added on since it was built in the 18th century, yet it remains stylish and is wonderfully maintained. Two painters are buried in the churchyard: **Zoffany** (see page 46), and **Thomas Gainsborough** (1727–88; see page 165), who was not a Kew man but requested to be buried here beside his friend **Joshua Kirby** who had worked at Kew Palace teaching 'perspective drawing' to a young George III.

Queen Elizabeth I visited her Keeper of the Great Seal at Kew in 1594 and, in return, was buttered up with a diamond-decorated fan, a diamond pendant, a pair of virginals, a dress and petticoat, and a spoon and fork made of agate. She thought he was a very nice man.

The gardens and the palace

The entrance to the **Royal Botanic Gardens** is just off the green. The gardens began as a royal riverside plaything for **Princess Augustus**, wife of **Frederick, Prince of Wales**. The latter was disliked by his parents, George II and Caroline, as 'the greatest ass and the greatest liar . . . the greatest beast in the whole world', but loved by the people; 'My God,' said Queen Caroline, 'his popularity makes me vomit'.

Frederick, 'Fritz' to his friends, loved life, art, music, village cricket, fishing, rowing races on the Thames, and Kew. He and Augusta – ungracious, stupid and plain, with a long nose and double chin – planned the palace gardens as a pleasure ground and commissioned the orangery (now a good shop and restaurant) and the Chinese pagoda. Augusta had green fingers, and collected rare and foreign plants and trees. During her lifetime she made Kew famous. Her son, the poor, mad, ill-treated **George III**, nicknamed 'Farmer George', enlarged it from Augusta's nine acres (3.5ha) to eleven (4.5ha). He loved Kew well, and used it as his country home. Once a week 'Farmer and Missus George', countrified gentlefolk with simple, homely tastes and pleasures, shepherded their vast family through Kew Gardens in twos, like a school crocodile. In 1772, George built wife Charlotte the small thatched 'Queen's Cottage' on the edge of the gardens, to be used as a family summerhouse. The cottage is open to the public (for details of opening times, see *Visitor information* below).

After George and Charlotte, the royals quit Kew and put the gardens into the public domain. During Victoria's reign they were enlarged from 11 acres (4.5ha) to 75 (30ha), and later to today's stupendous 300. Now they provide wonderful open-air pleasure, which used to cost visitors nothing, or next to nothing, and nowadays a lot. There are green lawns, rare trees, glass hothouses full of orchids, huge lily pads, lakes, woodlands full of flowers . . . and the Thames flows placidly by, offering an entrancing view across the river to lion-topped Syon House.

Kew Palace

Kew Palace, within the Royal Botanic Gardens, is the name for what was the 'Dutch House' when it was built by a Dutch merchant in 1631. The smallest of the royal palaces, it remains much as George III knew it when he and his family lived there.

Visitor information Royal Botanic Gardens and the palace (tel: 020 8940 1171) are open daily 09.30–18.00 (last admission 17.30; glass houses and gallery close at 17.30). Admission adult £6.50, concessions £4.50, under 16s free.

SYON HOUSE

After **Kew Bridge**, the river is split by islands, three of them, **Brentford Ait**, **Hog Hole**, and the smallest, **Lot's Ait**, immediately upstream of the Brentford entrance to the Grand Union Canal linking London and Birmingham. Beyond the canal is Syon House in Isleworth. The house remains what it has been since the Stuarts – one of the most spectacular of all the palaces beside the Thames. The surrounding park, landscaped by the great **'Capability' Lancelot Brown (1716–83)**, is now a small, cheerful and not entirely unlovely theme park complete with trout fishery, adventure playground, miniature steam railway, and similar delights. It is all difficult to ignore.

Originally a convent (hence the name from the place called Syon in Palestine), the estate was purloined by **Henry VIII**, who imprisoned his fifth wife, **Catherine Howard**, here shortly before her execution. It was predicted that dogs would drink the king's blood in revenge, and they did; when Henry's body was left in the house overnight on its way to burial in London, the household's dogs were discovered next morning chewing over his bones.

The place is full of history and aristocratic footprints. **Edward VI** gave it to his uncle, **Somerset**, who turned it into the Tudor mansion it is today (with later bits and pieces added here and there, and the inside and outside remodelled), before getting himself accused of treason and sent to the block. His great enemy **Dudley**, Earl of Warwick, who became Duke of Northumberland, took Syon over. He, and a group of his noble chums, offered the English crown (on the death of Henry VIII) to a forlorn and grim-faced **Lady Jane Grey** (there is a portrait of her in the 'Print Room') at Syon. Quiet, religious, innocent Lady Jane was proclaimed queen in the Tower of London, but nine days later was imprisoned there for high treason and subsequently beheaded. Elizabeth acquired the mansion and grounds on her accession and she stored Drake's treasure from the *Golden Hinde* – 'enough to pay for seven years' war' – at Syon while she looked around for a permanent safe place for the loot.

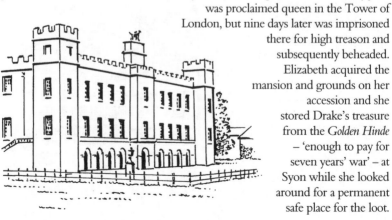

The **Percys**, dukes of Northumberland, have owned the estate ever since James I gave it to them. If you can wangle it, arrive at Syon by water. It's the way the **Percys** originally came after the king gave them the place; their boathouse – more a posh summerhouse than a boat-park – is still on the river in front of the house which stands in a park and water meadows. It is a quadrangular building with battlements like a child's sandcastle. On the roof is a lion that came from the Percys' mansion in the Strand, demolished in 1874.

John Evelyn visited Syon in the 1660s:

> I viewed that seat . . . builte out of an old Nunnerie, of stone, and
> faire enough; but more celebrated for the garden than it deserves; yet
> there is excellent wall fruit [there still is – *Ed*] and a pretty fountaine,
> yet nothing extraordinarie.

Ah, Mr Evelyn, that's where you're wrong! There are several 'extraordinarie' things, and one in particular, built since your day: the Great Conservatory, designed in the 1820s by **Charles Fowler**. It was the inspiration for Joseph Paxton's Crystal Palace.

Visitor information Syon House (tel: 020 8560 0881) is open Wed, Thu & Sun only, Apri–Nov, 11.00–17.00; admission £6.95 adults, £6.50 concessions, £50 children (5–16 years).

The gardens and Great Conservatory open daily closed Christmas Day), 10.30–dusk; admission £3.50 adults, £2.50 concessions and children.

There is a recently opened Butterfly House (tel: 020 8560 7272) open daily 10.00–15.30 winter, 10.00–17.30 summer, admission £4.85 adults, £4.25 concessions, £3.95 children (5–16 years).

Leaving Syon, the river heads due south, passing the **London Apprentice**, a famous riverside pub looking out on to **Isleworth Ait**. It is pleasant, old and stylish, with beautiful 17th-century plasterwork in the upstairs restaurant where there is a bow window overlooking the river.

The pub was popular with artists like **Zoffany**, **Constable** and **Turner**; Zoffany painted a portrait of his fellow artist **Richard Wilson** (1714–82) in the pub. Tourist

Isleworth

books, which insist that history's royals couldn't stay away from Thames pubs, claim that the London Apprentice was a regular for dissolute crowned heads, especially **Henry VIII** and **Charles II**. As its name indicates, however, it was the favourite port of call for the apprentices of the livery companies of the City of London, who rowed up-river to their favourite inn on rare holidays.

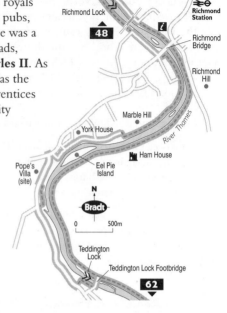

For the next few miles the river continues its generally southerly course, dramatically and suddenly changing character as we approach **Richmond Lock** and weir. The lock is half-tidal, meaning that boats can pass over the weirs on high tides, or through the lock gates when the water is low. Over the lock is a pair of restored elegant Victorian ironwork footbridges. Above the lock it is clear that we are passing towards the more placid, more tranquil, non-tidal reaches of the Thames; near Richmond Bridge rowing boats are for hire, with elaborate mouldings and tiller ropes to control the steering, the first since we left the Barrier at Woolwich.

Expect from now on – and contribute to – a slower, more lingering pace of life than that below the Thames's locks.

In a short distance comes Twickenham Bridge, next to Richmond Railway Bridge, where Isleworth gives way to Twickenham on the Middlesex bank (route of the north-bank Thames Path), and Kew to Richmond on the Surrey (south-bank Thames Path) side of the Thames.

RICHMOND

Immediately on the left is **Asgill House**, built on what was the river frontage of Richmond Palace in 1758 for a wealthy banker who became Lord Mayor of London, **Sir Charles Asgill**. Here he riotously entertained City friends, bringing them up-river in a fleet of barges, accompanied by musicians. His son, another Charles, was taken prisoner during the American War of Independence and chosen by lot to die as a reprisal. The King of France, **Louis XVI**, and **Marie Antoinette** interceded on his behalf (I don't know how they came into the affair, but they did) and an Act of Congress was passed to save young Asgill's life; he was allowed home on permanent parole. **Richmond Bridge** is London's oldest surviving bridge across the Thames, built 1774–5 on the site of an old ferry crossing, an enchanting five-spanned structure with semi-circular arches, increasing in size towards the centre as the bridge curves upwards. The river here is 300 feet (90m) wide.

MARBLE HILL HOUSE

Upstream of the Surrey-side Thames Path, beyond the meadows of Petersham, is a coffee-and-cream doll's house, Marble Hill, a spaciously elegant mansion and park overlooking the Thames, with views towards Richmond Park. It was built for a royal mistress, **Henrietta Howard**, and later lived in by another, **Mrs Fitzherbert**. Intimate rather than grand, its floors shine like dark pools, its carved staircase a reminder of the days when kings could order naval ships to bring back stacks of Honduras mahogany purely for the delight of their mistresses.

George II gave his 'exceedingly respectable and respected mistress', Mrs Henrietta Howard, £11,500 to build the Palladian villa in 1723, an astonishing sum of shove-off-and-shut-up money for such a mean man. Poet, friend and Twickenham neighbour, **Alexander Pope**, designed the garden, and **Jonathan Swift** stocked the cellar. There's a story that all the weeping-willow trees which line the Thames, and indeed all those in the whole of the British Isles, came from a single twig pulled from a Spanish hamper by Pope who plunged it into the earth of Marble Hill where it flourished and grew.

Henrietta Howard (1681–1767) was George II's mistress for a decade or so prior to the building of Marble House. Her husband, Charles, moaned so much about her royal romps that George said, 'Oh, alright, you can be Groom of the Bedchamber and here's £1,500 a year to spend on booze and gals if you push off and I can have the use of your missus'. So Charles went, leaving Henrietta and Georgie to get on with their thing – whatever that was, because some people insisted the affair was purely platonic. **Horace Walpole**, another of Henrietta's close acquaintances, scoffed, observing that she was so deaf, and the king's passions 'so indelicate', that the pleasures of their get-togethers could never have risen above the belt.

There's a portrait of Henrietta in the National Portrait Gallery: smoky blonde hair, almond eyes, double chin, and a wow of a bosom. Walpole, forever the bitch, described her as 'of a just height, well made, extremely fair, with the finest light brown hair', but added that her 'mental qualifications were by no means shining'. Other people, though, thought her clever.

Another famous friend, Jonathan Swift, wrote that

A FEW FAMOUS FACES

People have always been attracted to Richmond. Irish essayist and playwright **Richard Steele** (1672–1729) came to pick apricots. **Horace Walpole** came to watch a boat race, writing afterwards:

> The crowds on those green velvet meadows ... the yachts, barges, pleasures and small boats, and the windows and gardens lined with spectators, were so delightful when I came home from that vivid show, I thought Strawberry Hill [where we are off to soon; see page 58 – Ed] as dull and solitary as a hermitage.

William Wordsworth composed a poem from Richmond Bridge:

> Glide gently, thus for ever glide,
> O Thames! That other bards may see
> As lovely visions by thy side
> As now fair river! come to me.

Charles Dickens was dotty about Richmond. He liked it so much, especially the early-morning dips in the Thames, that he begged a friend to join him:

> I myself have risen at 6 and plunged head foremost into the water to the astonishment and admiration of all beholders.

In the near distance, perched above the woods of Surrey's famous **Richmond Hill**, is the looming and colossal red-bricked **Star and Garter Home** for disabled servicemen. It was built in 1824 on the site of a famous inn, which was much loved by Dickens and **J W M Turner** and goodness knows how many others besides until it burned down in the 1920s. Somebody described the hotel as:

she was 'an excellent companion for men of the best accomplishments who have nothing to ask', whatever that may imply. She enjoyed at Marble Hill 'more happiness ... than I have yet had prospect of'. Pope continued to 'dangle' after her, said Swift. But so, too, did Swift and Walpole and a jolly little fat man who wrote the *Beggar's Opera* and whom everyone loved to spoil, **John Gay**. Henrietta died on July 26 1767.

The twice-widowed Mrs Fitzherbert, who was clandestinely and illegally married in 1785 to the Prince of Wales, later **George IV**, lived briefly at Marble Hill House when the prince went off to wed Princess Caroline in 1795. Astonishingly, during the 20th century **William Cunard**, of the Atlantic liner family, purchased the entire estate and announced his intention of building on it. Prompt action by several local councils saved the house and its grounds, which are now safe with **English Heritage**.

Marble Hill was a favourite of the English film actor who became an autobiographical best-seller, **Dirk Bogarde**. He used to visit when he was a more like a mansion of a nobleman than a receptacle for the public; looking down with stately aspect from the adjoining valley, and seen to advantage from every point of the horizon.

Kings dined and stayed there. Dickens gave a yearly supper to celebrate his wedding anniversary.

The hotel's fame owed much to the famous view of the Thames from the top of Richmond Hill which inspired one of Turner's finest landscapes, *Thomson's Aeolian Harp*, itself, in turn, inspired by **James Thomson**'s (1700–48) poem, 'The Seasons':

> Heavens, what a goodly Prospect spreads around,
> Of Hills, and Dales, and Woods, and Lawns, and Spires,
> And glittering Towns, and golded streams, till all
> The stretching Landskip into smoke decays.

A **Walter Scott** (1771–1832) heroine, in his 1818 *The Heart of Midlothian*, came to the hill and admired the:

> huge sea of verdure, with crossing and intersection promontories of massive and tufted trees . . . tenanted by numberless flocks and herds, which seemed to wander unrestrained and unbounded through the rich pastures. The Thames, here turreted with villas and there garlanded with forests, moved on slowly and placidly.

It is all so stunning that when the American **William Byrd** returned to Virginia, after a visit in 1733, he founded the city overlooking the James River and called it 'Richmond'.

A final word and we shall move on: in 1902 the view from Richmond Hill was the first to be protected by an Act of Parliament, which probably protects it not at all but, I suppose, can do no harm to it either.

boy. In *A Postillion Struck by Lightning* (the first volume of Bogarde's autobiographical recollections) published in 1977, he records:

> It was a big white house, not as big as Hampton Court, but white and gleaming in the sun. There was a great park all about it, and real hills which you could run up, and trees and, best of all, a lake-thing full of lilies and goldfish. . .

Visitor information Marble Hill (tel: 020 8892 5115) is open daily Apr 1–Sep 30 10.00–18.00, Oct 1–31 10.00–17.00; Nov 1–Mar 28 10.00–16.00 (Wed–Sun). There are audio tours and videos available, a gift shop and café, and picnicking is permitted. Admission adult £3.30, concessions £2.50, child (aged 5–16) £1.70, under 5s free.

TWICKENHAM
Eel Pie Island

Horace Walpole and **Alexander Pope** lived just upstream, neighbours, in Twickenham, beyond Ham House and Ham Lands Nature Reserve on the Surrey bank, beyond York House on the Middlesex side, and beyond Eel Pie Island which is linked to the Twickenham shore by a hump-backed footbridge.

Today's **Eel Pie Island**, at two-acres one of the largest islands in the Thames, is a scrambling of bungalows, shacks, corrugated roofs, patchy gardens, remnants of old orchards, house boats and eccentric residents. The inventor **Trevor Baylis**, who dreamed up the clockwork radio, lives here in a house he built himself some 30 years ago. His latest invention is a pair of shoes generating enough electricity to power a mobile phone.

Yesterdays' Eel Pie Island was a noisy and raffish one, a place of high jinks and pleasure, seemingly far out of place in these reaches of suburban and polite Thames folk. During the 1950s and '60s it was famed for the Eel Pie Hotel, a venue for jazz and pop groups. **George Melly** worked here, as did **Mick Jagger** and the Rolling Stones. Then, mostly because it was such a loud place that kept Twickenham awake, the hotel lost its drinks licence, most of its members, and was closed and demolished.

The island gained its name in the 18th century after the dishes of eels and lampreys that were served to boating parties and anglers at Eel Pie House. **Henry VIII**, on more than one occasion, sent from Hampton Court to Eel Pie Island for lampreys or eels baked in a pie with a squeeze of lemon juice, mixed herbs, fish stock and pepper. Eel Pie Island was a resort for pleasure excursions through the 18th and 19th centuries; **Charles Dickens** came, and in *Nicholas Nickleby* took the Kenwigs family there for picnics on 'bottle beer, shrub and shrimps'.

Old Twickenham, which Pope and Walpole called 'Twitnam', as today's rugby footballers call it 'Twickers', is just about discernible amid the contemporary suburban sprawl of stockbroker Twickenham where the rich and the hopeful rub shoulders. Today, Twickenham and Teddington, linked by Walpole's Strawberry Hill, are almost indistinguishable except in what remains, just, of their 'villages'.

The 18th-century Twickenham was remarkable for its vast numbers of artists, authors, and actors, drawn there either by the beauty of the river or by the kudos of having royal neighbours, or ones that were regarded as 'noble', or even ones who were just plain rich. It is not so different from attitudes to day, where people love to rub close to those with stacks of cash and dash.

Behind a high brick wall on the edge of the river next to Eel Pie Island is the 1848 church of **St Mary the Virgin** where Pope is buried. There's a plaque on the wall, placed there by the poet before he died, 'in grateful thanks to a faithful old servant'.

The church is 'a sufficiently plain, not to say morose, building of red brick, with a redeeming point in the shape of its ivy-embattled tower' – not my words, but those of Charles Dickens's son, another Charles, in his *Dictionary of the Thames*.

Pope's Villa

Further along the Middlesex shore is a long balustrade in front of the landmark tower and gardens of **St Catherine's Convent**, site of Pope's Villa, between the road called Cross Deep and the river. It was, according to Pope,

> high enough to attract the eye and curiosity of the passenger from the
> river, when, upon beholding a mixture of beauty and ruin, he
> inquires what house is falling, or what church is rising.

The present 'Pope's Villa' is not the house on which the poet spent so much love from 1719 onwards. His was a small Palladian villa, with a crowning glory 'grotto' beneath the road dividing the villa from the garden of 'dusky groves, tiny lawns and cypresses leading to mother's tomb'. **Alexander Pope** (1688–1744) described the grotto as 'a kind of temple' in 1725 when he had finished the 'subterraneous way and grotto':

> I there formed a spring of the clearest water, which falls in a perpetual
> rill that echoes through the cavern day and night. From the River
> Thames you see through my arch up a walk of the wilderness to a
> kind of open temple, wholly composed of shells in a rustic manner,
> and from that distance under the temple you look down through a
> sloping arcade of trees, and the sails on the river passing suddenly and
> vanishing, as though through a perspective glass. When you shut the
> doors of this grotto, it becomes on the instant . . . a camera obscura;
> on the walls of which all objects of the river – hills, woods, and boats
> – are forming a moving picture in their visible radiations.

To modern tastes it all seems as ornamental as Pope's language. Sadly everything, villa and grotto, have all but gone – just an empty subway under the Teddington road remains. It was all pulled down and broken up in 1807 when its new owner, **Baroness Sophia Howe**, got fed up with rubber-necking Pope-worshippers and rid herself of the attractions which drew literary pilgrims to her gates. For her vandalism she became known as the 'Queen of the Goths'. She wouldn't have had to go to such lengths these days because barely anyone, other than academics, reads Pope's poems or cares much for him the way people did 200 years ago. Following publication of *The Rape of the Lock* he was fêted (worshipped, almost) as the successor to Milton and Shakespeare, which he wasn't; he might, perhaps, in another age, have rivalled Wordsworth.

Pope was frail, stunted by illness, and suffered blinding headaches and pain, but neither his poetry nor his sex life were affected. He did all right with the girls, especially the well-known society hostess, **Lady Mary Wortley Montagu**, with whom he had a long-term affair, and two more who lived up-river whom we shall visit when we go to Mapledurham House (see page 174).

Pope adored all three, and called Mary Montagu 'the second Eve'. She was married with two children and her relationship with Pope was the big society scandal of the day. By 1723, however, it had all ended in tears, and Pope called her lascivious, mean, and told everybody she suffered from the pox; but on the day he died there was still a portrait of her in his drawing room.

Strawberry Hill

Upstream and next door to the site of Pope's Villa stands Strawberry Hill. This is the ridiculous neo-Gothic castle creation, and life's work, of **Horace Walpole** (1717–97), youngest son of Prime Minister **Robert Walpole** (1676–1745). Walpole was the great gossip of his age, a dilettante, a wit, and one of the world's greatest-ever catty writer of letters which, to this day, provide wonderful political scandal and social historical accounts of 18th-century nobby England.

He moved to Twickenham in 1747, when he was 30, and bought the house that was to become his obsession:

> It is a little plaything-house that I got out of Mrs Chenevix's shop [a fashionable London toy-shop – *Ed*] and the prettiest bauble you ever saw. It is set in enamelled meadows, with filigree hedges. . .
>
> Two delightful roads, that you would call dusty, supply me continually with coaches and chaises: barges as solemn as Barons of the Exchequer move under my window; Richmond Hill and Ham Walks bound my prospect. . . Dowagers as plenty as flounders inhabit all around, and Pope's ghost is just now skimming under my window by the most poetical moonlight.

For the next 30 years Walpole converted his 'little plaything' into a castle in what he referred to as 'charming, venerable Gothic' and 'venerable barbarism'. He unearthed the name of the site, Strawberry Hill, from old deeds and accordingly gave the house its now historic title. Some say it is the earliest example of Gothic revival in English domestic architecture. It's not, but it is the most notorious and the first to have any real influence over contemporary architects who, until then, had regarded classicism as the be all and end all. The world famous historian of English architecture **Nikolaus Pevsner** (1902–83) described the house as 'both amusing and awful, both rococo and romantic'. Not surprisingly, it was within Strawberry Hill's batty atmosphere that Walpole wrote his Gothic novel *The Castle of Otranto* (1764), complete with haunted castle, damsel in distress, and spooky murders. The novel was inspired by a dream – 'I thought myself in an ancient castle . . . and that on the upper bannister of the staircase I saw a gigantic hand in armour'. Walpole's public loved it, but to today's taste it is poor stuff.

The exterior of the house can be seen from the river. Because the house is used as a training college, the interior can only be viewed on pre-booked private tours (tel: 020 8892 0051 for information), but Walpole has left a vivid description:

Now you shall walk into the house. The bow-window below leads into a little parlour hung with a stone-colour Gothic paper and Jackson's Venetian prints [chiaroscuro-style prints revived by John Jackson, who died c1780 – *Ed*] which I could never endure while they pretended, infamous as they are, to be after Titian, etc, but when I gave them this air of barbarous bas-reliefs, they succeeded to a miracle . . .

From hence, under two gloomy arches, you come to the hall and staircase, which it is impossible to describe to you, as it is the most particular and chief beauty of the castle. Imagine the walls covered with . . . Gothic fretwork: the lightest Gothic balustrade to the staircase, adorned with antelopes . . . bearing shields; lean windows fattened with rich saints in painted glass, and a vestibule open with three arches on the landing-place, and niches full of trophies of old coats of mail, Indian shields made of rhinoceros's hides, broadswords, quivers, long bows, arrows, and spears . . .

Yes, it was, I am sure, quite as daft as it sounds.

TEDDINGTON

And so to the final stretches of the tidal Thames. About 300 yards (270m) downstream of **Teddington Lock**, where salt water finally changes to fresh, is an obelisk on the Surrey bank marking the official boundary between the tidal river controlled by the Port of London Authority and the non-tidal under the care of the Environment Agency (formerly Thames Conservancy). Teddington Lock is the largest on the river, capable of taking a tug and a string of lighters, which it rarely, if ever, is called upon to do these days. The large building on the Teddington, Middlesex-bank, side of the river is a television and film studio.

It is such a relief to be done with the tidal, London, urban Thames, to leave behind the Thames Path of the tideway, which, for the most part, is for walkers unbothered by concrete paths, noise, grot and traffic. It is only upstream from Teddington – perhaps from Kew – that the Thames Path is entitled to qualify as a great long-distance trail. From here on most of the land between the river's towns and villages is natural, luscious and leafy, and the best of the remainder contains old church towers, houses glimpsed beyond rust-red walls, amazing and varied villages, market towns, lichened bridges punctuating the path, and good, ancient inns. Beyond the lock at Teddington, the Thames Path becomes a true water-path where river-flow reflections are as fleeting as the clouds. The very thought of pushing on makes my mouth water.

First, though, there are some long-ago people I'd like you to meet in Teddington Village, on the Middlesex side of the bridge. It was at Teddington, I should mention in passing, where **Barnes Wallis** (1887–1979) developed his bouncing bomb at the National Physical Laboratory.

Beneath the floor of **Teddington Church** porch lie the remains of **Dr**

Stephen Hales (1677–1761), a quite brilliant and much-forgotten man. As well as being the vicar from 1708 until 1761 – more accurately the 'perpetual curate' – he was Clerk to the Closet of the Princess of Wales. Goodness knows what the position requires, but Hales was obviously good at it because when he died the Princess of Wales had a monument to him put up in Westminster Abbey. He would, almost certainly, have been entitled to one anyway, for he was one of those talented amateur-scientist clerics, a physicist-cum-botanist-cum-biologist typical of the 18th and 19th centuries.

Hales was the first to demonstrate that plants take nourishment from the air. He worked on the circulation of the blood. He pioneered sanitation and ventilation; he was responsible for pioneering the ventilation of 18th-century hospitals, naval vessels and the cells of Newgate Prison. He was instrumental in giving Teddington Village a clean and plentiful supply of water, recording in meticulous detail (when the first village water pump was installed) that the outflow filled a two-quart vessel in 'three swings of the pendulum, beating seconds'. Before the new water supply reached the village, Hales's parishioners had been dying before they were 40; afterwards they began to live to 70 or 80.

He was an active parish priest, brow-beating his female parishioners into doing public penance for 'irregular behaviour' (the mind boggles; perhaps he was referring to 'Peg' Woofington – see below), enlarging the churchyard, and helping to construct a sound-box affair within the then-wooden tower so that the church bells could be better heard from miles away. The timber tower was pulled down in 1754 and the present brick one put in its place; his bones were laid to rest beneath this tower which now serves as a porch.

Alexander Pope, one of Hales's parishioners, said of him, 'I shall be glad to see Dr Hales, and always love to see him; he is so worthy and good a man'. **Horace Walpole**, another neighbour, called him 'a poor, good, primitive creature'. Others spoke of his 'native innocence and simplicity of manners'. Outside the church, as near as possible to the grave of Dr Hales, is the tomb of **Isabella**, **Countess of Denbigh**, who romantically insisted she be buried close to him. Her inscription describes her 'lively talents and open heart', and adds:

> Like Hales, the gen'rous friend of mankind
> With love of philosophie learning fraught
> She wisely practis'd what his virtues taught
> Then seal'd his praises with her dying breath
> And grateful courts his last remains in death.

Another of Hales's parishioners was **Margaret Woofington** (1714–60), the celebrated 18th-century 'Peg' – 'most vivacious and coquettish lay in London' – who lived in Teddington. She was born in Dublin, came to the London stage when she was 26, and 'carried all hearts and loins by storm'. Once established as an 'actress beyond compare' on the London stage, she played opposite **David Garrick**. They were lovers, initially as a three-in-a-bed affair with another actor, **Charles Macklin**. When that didn't work out, however, they chucked Macklin out and Garrick bought a wedding ring and would have married her, except they quarrelled 'beyond reconciliation'.

Peg is said to have been the handsomest woman ever to appear on the stage. A number of portraits are in existence: three – by Hogarth, Mercier and Wilson – hang in the Garrick Club, London, while another, an engraving, is in the National Portrait Gallery. She was certainly one of the most courted, most caressed,  women in all of 18th-century London and loved men – many and often. History records her as vivacious, generous to a fault, fascinating, but subject to 'tantrums'.

She died on March 28 1760 and is buried in Teddington Church, where there is a decorated tablet to her memory on the east wall of the northern aisle. In her will she left money to build the charming almshouses in a row by the church; one is named after her.

Kingston to Hampton Court

Distances From Kingston Bridge: Ravens Ait 1.27 miles (1.6km), Thames Ditton 2.07 miles (3.3km), Hampton Court Bridge 3 miles (4.8km)

KINGSTON-UPON-THAMES

Don't expect very much of Kingston-on-Thames and you might even like it. It's not grotty, merely tedious and mundane. Stick to the river, that's the thing: rowing and sailing clubs, riverside cottages on stilts, yacht-club gardens, chromium-plated gin-palaces, flower-potted houseboats, people-watching pubs, upstream views of trees and meadows and spaciousness. Lovely!

Beyond the river, Kingston is a brick-and-glass clone of other motor-smirched towns and townships. It wasn't always. **Jerome K Jerome** considered it 'picturesque in the flashing sunlight', and **Ernest Ryan** a 'dear town' in his 1938 *Thames from the Towpath*. Nowadays, only the dottiest of dotty Kingstonians call their town 'picturesque' or 'dear'.

It is, however, historical, the one-time coronation

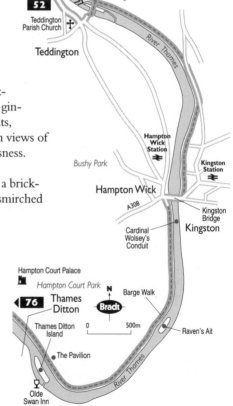

place of England's Saxon kings. Their reputed coronation stone is displayed outside the Guildhall, an uncomfortable seat of weathered, lumpish sandstone, not a metre high, which supported the bottoms of **Edward 'the Martyr' II** (AD975), **Aethelred 'the Unready'** (AD979), and others. The best bits of Kingston's past are in the ancient **Market Place**, where there are splendid carvings and mouldings on the façade of Boots the Chemist, and statues of kings and queens stare down on the market stalls and the growling traffic.

Jerome's staircase

Jerome K Jerome's 'magnificent carved oak staircase' in *Three Men in a Boat* is still in Market Place, at the back of what was Chieseman's department store and is now Border's Bookshop, carrying shoppers from books and magazines on the ground floor to more books and the Starbuck coffee bar on the first. Lovingly renovated in 2001, and lifted back on-site in 2002, it has giant banisters, superb scrolls and curlicues, carvings of birds and fruit. People rarely give it a second glance. Sadly, the oak panelling described in *Three Men in a Boat* – 'all carved oak, right up to the ceiling' – isn't there, and never was; I wonder why Jerome ever made out it was?

Three writers

John Galsworthy (1867–1933) was born to 'Forsyte' parents (typical of the starched and upright citizens portrayed in Galsworthy's *Forsyte Saga*, his most famous novel) at Kingston, in a villa called Parkfield on Kingston Hill in the town's northeastern corner. He went to school at Coombe Leigh (now called Coombe Ridge) in George Road.

Edward Gibbon (1737–94), who was to write the extraordinary and massive *Decline and Fall of the Roman Empire* (whose pessimistic errors of history in no way detract from the literary greatness of the book), went to Kingston Grammar School:

in my ninth year . . . by the common methods of discipline, at the expense of . . . tears and . . . blood, I purchased the knowledge of Latin syntax.

The playwright **Robert Cedric Sherriff** (1896–1975) went to the same school. He went on to write the smash-hit, anti-World-War-I trench drama, *Journey's End*, which was switched to the skies, with airmen replacing trenchers, in Jack Gold's 1976 film, *Aces High*.

Visitor information The Kingston Tourist Information Centre can be contacted on 020 8547 5592.

HAMPTON WICK: WEBBED FEET

There's not much of Hampton Wick, on the other side of Kingston Bridge. What there is retains the airs and graces of a riverside village, of old cottages, hollyhock gardens, residents with webbed feet, and yachtie-types who know a man who sells rope and blocks and Stockholm tar and all manner of other nautical bits. I like the place – people bid you 'good morning' and 'good afternoon'.

Wolsey: a mistress and a pipe

Facing Hampton Wick's much-renovated Tudor Swan pub is a house called **Wolsey's Cottage**, just up the road from the Thames Path, which crosses over the bridge, switching from right bank to left. **Cardinal Thomas Wolsey** hid a mistress in the cottage while he was living it up in Hampton Court. He would pop down river to scramble ashore for feminine comforts. The cottage isn't open to the public, but someone who has been inside tells me that it has a Tudor fireplace with twinned initials chiselled into it, one letter of which is 'T' for Thomas.

A short way above Kingston Bridge – level with a depressingly crude, seven-storey block of redbrick flats on the opposite bank (near where the Hogsmill River enters the Thames) – Cardinal Wolsey sunk a **lead pipe conduit** into the river to carry fresh water from Coombe Hill in Kingston (a fall of 160 feet) to his Court at Hampton. The water was conveyed three-and-a-half miles by gravity, under the Thames and through Hampton Park to the palace bathrooms and lavatories. The water, according to Wolsey, was 'efficacious, excellent for drinking and washing' – although unfit for culinary use because it turned vegetables black!

I'm not sure if the conduit is still there, but during the 1950s skippers of barges working this reach used to complain when their keels grated on 'sumat' as they passed over this spot. The Kingston Society (tel: 020 7222

1234) maintains two small Wolsey Conduit buildings on Coombe Hill which are open to visitors. Open Apr–Aug, every second Sun. Admission free.

For the next three miles, the Thames Path follows a great stately swoop of the river between the elegant arches of Kingston Bridge and the clean but uninspiring lines of Hampton Court Bridge, which carries the dreaded and dreadful A309.

QUEEN'S REACH AND A FROTH OF HAWTHORN

This reach of the river (called Queen's) is country all the way: alders, willows and cedar trees, and a froth of flowering hawthorn in the spring. The Thames Path riverside walk, called 'the Barge Walk', accompanies the perimeter wall of Hampton Court Park to the riverside gates of the great palace. It was one of Jerome's favourite walls:

> What a dear old wall that is that runs along the river there! I never
> pass it without feeling better for the sight of it. Such a mellow, bright,
> sweet old wall. . . There are fifty shades and tints and hues of every
> ten yards of that old wall. . .

It's an attractive reach. **Raven's Ait**, the island 1.27 miles (1.6km) upstream of Kingston Bridge, used to be an osier ground in the 19th century where willows were lopped, pollarded, bundled, soaked and worked into baskets and chair seats; the island is now a residential watersport centre.

Immediately upstream, tucked into the wall surrounding Hampton Court Park, is an iron gateway leading to the pastoral palace grounds. Go through this gate to the palace, if you will, but by doing so you won't enjoy what is one of the nicest stretches of the river so far.

Approximately half a mile (1km) – and a tiny bit more – up-river from Raven's Ait, on the southern-side right bank, opposite the Thames Path, is **Thames Ditton Marina**, created in what was an old reservoir. Around the bight of the great bend is another island, shaped like an orange quarter, squashed with bungalows and heavy with the scent of scarlet geraniums.

A charming suspension bridge links the island with Thames Ditton on the opposite bank, its spiky-spired **St Raphael's Church** and popular 13th-century riverside **Olde Swan Inn** (three bars, log fires, an interesting dining-room, accommodation, private moorings for craft drawing no more than three feet, or 0.9m). It's nice, just as it was when **Theodore Hook** (1788–1841) – man of letters, maker of puns, practical joker, and crook jailed for fiddling accounts – dined here in 1834 and wrote a poem about the pub:

> The Swan snug inn, good fare affords
> At table e'er was put on
> And worthier quite of loftier boards
> Its poultry, fish and mutton
> And whilst sound wine mine host supplies
> With beer of Meux or Tutton
> Mine hostess with her bright eyes
> Invites to stay at Ditton.

(Thames Path walkers can often visit the Olde Swan at Thames Ditton without doubling back to Kingston Bridge in order to cross the river and rejoin the Thames Path. They use, instead, the foot-passenger **Hart's Ferry**, which operates intermittently – sometimes Sundays only, sometimes weekdays and weekends, sometimes not at all – from the Thames Sailing Club, located on the left bank, just down-river from Thames Ditton Marina in Portsmouth Road. Check that the ferry is running by telephoning Thames Sailing Club on 020 8399 2164.)

The Pavilion

Between the Thames Path and the grounds of Hampton Court, abreast of Thames Ditton Island, is the Pavilion, built by **Christopher Wren** so that **William of Orange** had somewhere comfortable and dry for water-watching and entertaining visitors. **Queen Victoria**, then 'a pretty little princess, plump as a partridge', spent some of her childhood here while it was the off/on home of her father, George III's fourth son, Edward, who never really knew what to do with the place. Nor did **Cecil King** (1901–87), who lived here in the 1930s, '40s and '50s when he was chairman of the Daily Mirror Group (and that newspaper was a powerful force to be reckoned with). The great and the not so great, including **Charlie Chaplin** and the **Duke** and **Duchess of Windsor**, were sometimes house guests.

The Mole

The river which enters the Thames a quarter of a mile (0.4km) below Hampton Court Bridge is the Mole – the poet **John Milton**'s 'sullen Mole, that runneth underneath'. For some reason, Milton (1608–74) put it about that the river disappeared into Box Hill in Surrey, which it doesn't. Apparently, although I haven't done it (and won't), nor do I know anybody who has, the Mole can be navigated by canoe for over 30 miles (48km), nearly to its wild origins in the forest of St Leonard's, close by Turner's Hill in Sussex. It flows through the wilderness of Crawley, past the roar of Gatwick Airport, into the sharp heights of the North Downs by Dorking, through Leatherhead's fine brick bridge of 14 spans, before meandering through Cobham, coming within a mile of the River Wey near Esher Common, uniting with the River Ember before joining the Thames – a long and difficult adventure and hardly anyone even knows the poor thing is there.

HAMPTON COURT: MUDDLED, ERRATIC, ECCENTRIC

And so to Hampton Court Palace, England's muddled, erratic, eccentric version of Versailles, embodying in rich-red brick some five centuries of history.

If you have any choice, voyage to Hampton Court by water rather than by road. Go on a Sunday, when Londoners are abed with newspapers, or on a summer weekday when there is less of a crush in the palace's tiny Tudor rooms and the queues to the **King's Apartments** – painstakingly and brilliantly restored after a devastating fire in 1986 – are shorter.

Arriving by boat is the regal way to come. It is how **Henry VIII** and **Anne Boleyn** came, lots of times, accompanied by a flotilla of musicians, courtiers, maids of honour and servants. Some years ago two replicas of Tudor state barges were built just down-river, on **Trowlock Island**, for the film based on the life of **Sir Thomas More**, *A Man for All Seasons*.

You may not know that Hampton Court was the scene of **Alexander Pope**'s famous 'The Rape of the Lock':

> Close by those meads, forever crowned with flowers,
> Where Thames with pride surveys his rising towers,
> There stands a structure of majestic frame,
> Which from the neighbouring Hampton takes its name. . .

The view of the palace from the river is the best there is, a switchback rise-and-fall of roofs and gables, of chimneys twisted like barley sugar, rose-brick façades latticed with black, everything haze-mellowed by time. The south front, the part of the palace seen from the river, was created by Christopher Wren for **William III**. Wolsey's and Henry VIII's bit, exactly as King Harry left it, is the western portion.

Visiting boats tie up at the Barge Walk landing stage, just downstream of the clean-lined, red-bricked Hampton Court Bridge, and close to the dramatic **Jean Tijou** wrought-iron gates, exquisite as lace.

Hampton Court

'DOING' HAMPTON COURT AND BUSHY PARK

Only visitors with astonishing stamina can 'do' Hampton Court on a single visit, and they don't enjoy it. It's a place that needs to be lingered in. You should allow three hours at the very minimum, and it won't be anywhere near enough; four to five hours – all day, in fact – is better. You could, of course, just look at the palace from the outside and then walk or sail on by; that, however, would be foolish, for a visit to Hampton Court is a truly glorious experience. Its palace is a wonder, its gardens and parkland stunning, its history bewitching. What a disappoint-ment, then, that the powers-that-be have disinfected the place by ridding its interior of the spirits of period and time and left few clues to the great and famous who once lived and laughed and cried and loved within these walls. For all that, it is a place not to be missed.

Visitor information Opening times are always liable to change, but for the last few years the palace has admitted visitors Tue–Sun 09.30–18.00, Mon 10.15–18.00 (summer), and Tue–Sun 09.30–16.30, Mon 10.15–16.30 (winter). For physically handicapped visitors, there are accessible WCs. Access to some areas of the palace involves steps. Battery-powered cars are available free of charge for use in the gardens. Disabled parking is provided. Admission adult £11, child (aged 5–15) £7.25, concessions £8.25, family (five people) £33, child under 5 free. Be aware that prices, like times, are liable to change. For the latest information on admission charges, times of opening and facilities for disabled visitors, call 020 8781 9500 or visit www.hrp.org.uk.

DOS AND DON'TS

- Don't try to trail through all 31 of the palace's rooms – stick to ten at most (those described below should do)
- Take full advantage of the free audio guides in six languages, available throughout the palace
- If you are on a budget, don't use the Hampton Court refreshment places. Much better to pack a picnic or buy drinks and snacks outside the grounds.
- If you find the admission price to the palace too expensive (which it is – Queen Victoria ordered that there should be no charge when she opened the palace to the public in 1838), then bear in mind that it costs nothing to visit the 60 acres (24 hectares) of lovely, formal gardens and peer through the windows into the palace rooms. It's free to visit the **world's oldest grapevine** as well, and to wander the 1,800 acres of Hampton Court Park and the adjoining Bushy Deer Park on the other side of the Hampton Court Road. **General Eisenhower** located his 1944 D-Day headquarters at 16th-century **Bushy House**, which is now the National Physical Laboratory but is not open to visitors.

Bushy Park and Richard Dodderidge Blackmore

Bushy Park – as deep and fresh as green countryside – is the location for lots of gems, but of two in particular. The first is **Christopher Wren**'s magnificent **Chestnut Avenue**, which bisects the park from north to south, a double row of horse chestnut giants, seen at their best in the spring when their candle-blooms are a fizz of pink and white. The second is the **Great Diana Fountain** (referring to Diana the goddess, not Diana the princess), which played in the Hampton Court Privy Garden in **Charles I**'s day and was moved to Bushy by Christopher Wren. This is an elaborate affair created by **Francesco Fanelli** (a one-eyed Italian sculptor), with nymphs and sea monsters, boys holding dolphins and a graceful bronze Diana at the top.

Open from 09.00 to dusk, Bushy Park was originally fashioned from ploughed farmland into three separate parks by Cardinal Wolsey. Henry VIII turned them into his personal hunting ground. It is the second largest royal park in the British Isles, and contains a series of beautiful woodland glades and gardens, as well as streams and ponds fed by the 'Longford River', an artificial waterway, 13 miles in length, created by King Charles in 1639.

Richard Dodderidge Blackmore (1825–1900), famed for *Lorna Doone*, grew pears in Bushy Park. He was a true Thames man, born on the river's upper reaches (at Longworth, where his father was curate-in-charge). His mother died of typhus fever when Blackmore was only three months old, 'a crooked start to life', he recalled in later years. After taking a law degree at Oxford, then spending a spell as a barrister, Blackmore taught classics at Wellesley House School on Twickenham Common when he was 28. Life as a teacher depressed him:

> Considering. . .what occupation to follow, I decided to become a
> gardener and horticulturist. Having studied botany and agricultural
> chemistry. . . I felt I was well equipped for this calling.

He found, and purchased, 'suitable soil for pear cultivation for [sale to]
Covent Garden Market' at Bushy Park – 11 acres a dozen miles from London's
market. Well back from the road (there was no railway line in those days), he
built a plain but substantial house which he called 'Gomer'. The original
house, in what is now Doone Close in Teddington, was ripped down by a
moronic developer in 1938.

Blackmore lived in Bushy Park for the rest of his life, detached from the
world, writing and growing vines, peaches, nectarines, strawberries and pears.
Because his market garden never made much by way of profits, he wrote a lot
and often, hitting the jackpot with his third novel when *Lorna Doone* was
published in 1869. By all accounts, Blackmore was strong-willed, autocratic,
and self-centred – not an easy man to love. He died at Teddington on January
20 1900, the same day as John Ruskin.

Visitor information Free information leaflets on Bushy Park's attractions
and amenities are available from The Park Office, White Lodge, The
Stockyard, Bushy Park, Hampton Court Road, Hampton, Middlesex
TW12 2EJ; tel: 020 8979 1586; fax 020 8941 8196.

Hampton Court: a brief history

Cardinal Thomas Wolsey (c1475–1530) built Hampton Court in 1514 with
280 rooms and a staff of 500. Twelve years later, suspecting that the rug of
royal patronage was about to be pulled from beneath his feet, he gave it, stuffed
with goodies, to Henry VIII. This act, however, didn't save the devious prelate
from a doomed journey towards the Tower of London and death.

Henry VIII: fat and waddly

Henry VIII (1491–1547) liked
Hampton Court a lot. He junketed
in the Great Hall, jousted in the
Tilt Yard, hunted in the park, played
real tennis in the tennis court
(before he became fat and
waddly), and romped and
quarrelled here with his
lovers and queens.

Under the tower, on the
arched ceiling, is a pattern of
Tudor roses and the initials 'A'
for Anne and 'H' for Henry,

HAMPTON COURT'S GHOSTS

- Catherine Howard, distracted with misery, flies through the Haunted Gallery
- Jane Seymour, mother of Edward VI, shimmers white in the light of the taper she carries through the arch of Catherine of Aragon's Door
- The infant Edward's nurse, Dame Sibell Penn (whose effigy is at Hampton Church) still turns her spinning wheel in the southwest wing

twined in lovers' knots – a sad echo of a long-ago love affair. Anne Boleyn's glory lasted only three years before she was condemned to death, but not before giving birth to the daughter who was to become Elizabeth I (1558–1603).

On the day of her execution, the king ordered all traces of Anne be obliterated from the palace. But they weren't: the lovers' knots and the Boleyn family's crowned falcons are still there, one above the gateway named after her, some high on the carved ceiling of the Great Hall. Strangely, Anne's ghost doesn't walk the corridors of Hampton Court, although those of others do (see box above).

A pageant of 'royals'

All of Henry's wives, with the exception of Catherine of Aragon, lived here. So did other royals – and a single not-so-royal, Oliver Cromwell – until the accession of George III.

Mary Tudor (1526–58) – 'plain, pious and ill-dressed' – came here with her husband, **Philip of Spain**, and did what she could to sober the place.

Elizabeth (1533–1603), daughter of Henry and Anne Boleyn, was 26 when she came here as queen, coursed with greyhounds, hunted, flirted with courtiers, danced galliards, and enjoyed plays by Shakespeare and Ben Jonson in the Great Hall where Inigo Jones created colossal stage sets with baroque moving mountains. Elizabeth celebrated at least two Christmases at Hampton Court.

Charles I (1600–49) escaped from the palace across the river, and on towards Southampton and the Isle of Wight where, for a second time, he surrendered to the Parliamentarians.

Oliver Cromwell (1599–1658) lived here, as Lord Protector of the Commonwealth, in quiet domesticity.

After the Restoration, **Charles II** (1630–85) set up his spectacular and profligate court at the Palace of Hampton.

William (1650–1702) and **Mary** (1662–94) were the first monarchs to make dramatic changes to the palace, commissioning Christopher Wren to demolish the east wing and erect in its place a whole new series of state apartments. These were embellished with quoins and Portland ornaments, and pierced with sash windows. William died when his horse threw him while riding in Hampton Court Park.

Queen **Anne** (1665–1714) didn't much like the place, preferring Kensington, but she did come to hunt, even when she was fat and crippled by dropsy and could only follow hounds, 'furiously', in a horse and chaise.

George I (1660–1727) liked Hampton Court and sometimes lived here in Hanoverian plumptitude with his two German mistresses, one enormously tall and thin, the other fat. He often travelled on the Thames, always with a group of musicians. Handel's *Water Music* was written for Thames voyage, 'to drown out', say historians, the notorious 'water language' of Thames boatmen.

George II (1683–1760) was the last king to live in the palace, spending two months every summer here, mainly for the stag hunting.

George III (1738–1820) had his ears boxed in Hampton Court's gardens by his father, George II, and refused, ever after, to live there again. He much preferred Windsor Castle, and when was told there was a fire in the outbuildings of Hampton Court in 1770, he remarked, 'I should not have been sorry if it had burnt down'.

First step: exploring the parks and gardens

Before entering the palace, explore the gardens and parklands. In spring, the **Wilderness** is wild with daffodils and bluebells, the **Shrubberies** heavy with camellias. In early summer, the **Laburnum Walk** is a yellow tunnel of flowers. The combination of flowers, statues and fountains in the **Privy Garden** is considered formal gardening at its best, and the heady scent of the elaborate **Herb Garden** can be intoxicating. The **Rose Garden** is located in what was once Henry VIII's **Tilt Yard**. The **Knot Garden** re-creates the tortured complexity much loved by 16th-century gardeners. The famous 250-year-old **Great Vine** – oldest known vine in the world – still flourishes every year and bears 700lbs (318kg) of plump Black Hamburg grapes which are sold to visitors in August and September.

The maze: paying to get lost

It costs nothing to visit the Great Vine, but visitors have to pay to get lost in the maze the way Harris did in *Three Men in a Boat*:

> It's absurd to call it a maze. . . You keep on taking the first turning to
> the right. . . We'll just walk round for ten minutes and then go and
> get some lunch. . .

He was wrong. To get to the centre you must turn left on entering, then first
right and first right again – but don't let on I told you.

Second step: the palace itself
Lovely lavatories
In the palace itself, I particularly commend the lavatories; not the
'convenience' ones, but the regal ones which supported royal bottoms. **Celia
Fiennes**, in her 17th-century 'journeys' (*The Journeys of Celia Fiennes
1685–1712*), was as impressed as I am with the WC installed by William and
Mary:

> It is a closet that leads to a little place with a seate of easement of
> marble with sluices of water to wash all down.

Other 'must sees'
- The sun on the **astronomical clock** in the Clock Court, over Anne
  Boleyn's Gateway, revolves round the earth. It was made for Henry VIII
  in 1540 before people listened to what Galileo and Copernicus had to say
  about the earth spinning round the sun.
- An intricately modelled panel of **Wolsey's arms** – surmounted by the
  cardinal's hat – remains on the east side of the gateway, despite Henry's
  attempts to deface it.
- On the right of Clock Court, through a small door with the initials 'C W'
  above it, is the place where **Christopher Wren** lived when he was
  working here for William and Mary in between nipping down-river to
  work on St Paul's Cathedral.
- The vast **Tudor kitchens**, where an astonishing 1,000 meals a day were
  prepared.
- The **Great Hall**, where the same gigantic meals were eaten, and where it
  is possible, just, to picture Henry VIII, propped on sturdy calves beneath
  the towering hammer-beam roof, and surrounded by magnificent
  tapestries. A visiting Venetian ambassador described him,

> dressed entirely in green velvet, cap, doublet, hose, shoes and
> everything. . . [H]e covered his doublet with a handsome gown of
> green velvet and put on a collar of cut diamonds of immense value;
> and then dinner was served with incredible pomp.

- The **Tilt Yard** is where Henry VIII fought his tournaments:

> [A]fter [dinner] the King put on armour and jousted on a
> horse covered from head to foot in cloth of gold. . . [I]n this
> contest he was victorious, to tremendous applause, especially
> by the ladies.

- The **state apartments** of William III were restored after the fire of 1986 and still contain original paintings, tapestries and furniture. The **private apartments** of William and Mary reveal a more personal and intimate side of the palace, away from the pomp and ceremony of public life.
- The **queen's state apartments** took 30 years to complete and the result is breathtaking. Hung with rich tapestries and paintings, they offer views over the gardens and park.
- The **Georgian Rooms** provide some insight into the private life of George II, furnished as they were in 1737 at the final visit of the monarch to Hampton Court.

Getting there

By boat Riverboats ply their trade to Hampton Court from Greenwich, Westminster Pier, Richmond, Kingston and Windsor between the spring bank holiday and late September. Services operate at least every hour, and sometimes, in highest high summer, as often as every 20 minutes. The river journey from Westminster, including two locks, takes between two and four hours depending on tides. For general information, call (LTB) Rivercruise Information Service on 020 7373 9988.

By train Trains run to Hampton Court Station direct from London Waterloo.

By tube District Line to Richmond, then by bus (R68) to Hampton Court Palace.

By bus Nos 411, 111, 216, 451, 461, 513, 726, R68. Service No 267 runs on summer Sundays only.

By car From the M25, take either exit 10 on to the A307, or exit 12 on to the A308. Also accessible from the A3, after which you take the A309.

Hampton Court Bridge to Walton Bridge

Distances From Hampton Court Bridge: Molesey Lock 0.19 miles (0.31km), Garrick's Eyot 0.89 miles (1.43km), Sunbury Lock 3.17 miles (5.10 km), Walton Bridge 4.84 miles (7.63km)

A lot of the next section of the Thames Path is displeasing, although bits of it, especially the views across the river to the Middlesex bank, are delightful. The problem comes on the Surrey side, after the path changes banks over Hampton Court Bridge and travels tediously from the unlovable townships of East and West Molesey, past gloomy concrete reservoirs and on to the outskirts of Walton-on-Thames. One moment you are in deep country, the next in landscape so ugly that surely even the Middlesex trees cringe at the man-made unloveliness of it all. Boaters are much better off: they can't see above the Surrey bank.

HAMPTON COURT BRIDGE

Hampton Court Bridge, built of brick and stone by **Edwin Lutyens**, complements the palace nicely. People call it 'noble'. It replaced an ugly iron affair in 1930, which, in turn, had replaced a weird and operatic chinoiserie fantasy built in 1753. The latter was a seven-humped structure with turrets like Chinese pagodas at either end. I would like to have seen that.

Close by the bridge is the 300-year-old **Mitre Hotel** (tel: 020 8979 2264) covered in creeper. It was built by order of Charles II in 1665, on the site of a Tudor inn, to house courtiers who couldn't be crammed into the palace. Low ceilings, good furnishings, and some nice paintings by **Alfred Sisley** (the French impressionist who specialised in Thames Valley landscapes, 1839–99) give the Mitre style and charm. The food, the drink, and the ambience are goodish to good. There are three restaurants and seven bars, one of them in the old vaulted wine cellar. Doors from the Toll Bar open on to the riverside garden in the summer.

MOLESEY LOCK, ASH ISLAND, THE SWISS CHALET AND TAGG'S ISLAND

Turn your back on the unsavoury goings on at the Moleseys (see box, page 77), and concentrate instead upon the river. Within just a kilometre of

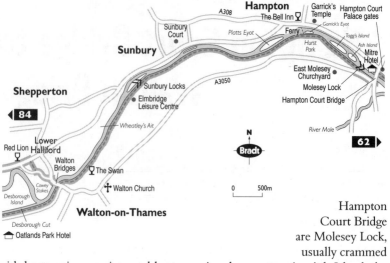

Hampton
Court Bridge
are Molesey Lock,
usually crammed
with boats going up-river and boats coming down, attractive Ash Island, the
astonishing Swiss fantasy chalet, and Tagg's island.

I like **Molesey Lock**. At 268ft and 4 inches (81.78 metres) in length, and
tree-lined, it is one of the longest, one of the prettiest, one of the busiest on
the river. It has always been a honey-pot for rubber-neckers, even during the
days of **Jerome K Jerome** in the 1880s:

> I have stood and watched it sometimes, when you could not see any
> water at all, but only a brilliant triangle of bright blazers, and gay caps,
> and saucy hats, and many-coloured parasols, and silken rugs, and
> cloaks, and streaming ribbons, and dainty whites . . . [B]oats are
> drawing near and passing away, so that the sunny river, from the
> Palace up to Hampton Church, is dotted and decked with yellow, and
> blue, and orange, and white, and red, and pink. All the inhabitants of
> Hampton and Moulsey dress themselves up in boating costume, and
> come and mooch round the lock with their dogs, and flirt, and
> smoke, and watch the boats, and altogether, what with the caps and
> jackets of the men, the pretty coloured dresses of the women, the
> excited dogs, the moving boats, the white sails, the pleasant landscape,
> and the sparkling water, it is one of the gayest sights I know of . . .

It is no longer anywhere near as colourful, but in high summer it still bustles
with people gathered on the lock side and the coming and going of boats. In this
sense it is very much the way it was when **A S Krausse** photographed Molesey
Lock for his *Pictorial History of the Thames* (published 1889), and declared it,

> [A] favourite lounging place for those who prefer to criticise the
> athletic abilities of others rather than exert themselves, and on
> Sundays during the summer is crowded with a large and not always
> too select concourse of people.

DARK DOINGS IN EAST MOLESEY

Dark doings used to take place in 19th-century East Molesey. So many corpses were stolen from the graveyard of **St Mary's Church** that the timbers of the demolished 'Chinese' bridge were used to make special thief-proof gates to the churchyard. However, they didn't stop thieves hauling newly buried corpses into waiting boats, then ferrying them downstream for dissection and dissertation at Guy's Hospital.

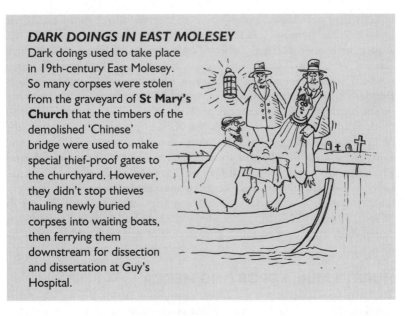

The American Anglophile, **Henry James** (1843–1916), observed something similar when he passed through the lock near the turn of the 20th century:

> I know of no other classic stream that is splashed about for the mere fun of it. There is something droll and almost touching in the way that on the smallest pretext of a holiday or fine weather, the mighty population takes to boats.

During the 'Great Frost' of February 1895, the river was frozen, hard and inches deep, from Molesey Lock to Sunbury. As recently as 1963 and 1967, the greater proportion of the Thames from Teddington to the source was frozen, but the ice was only thin and so nobody was able to roast sheep and oxen on the river the way they did in the 1800s.

Ash Island, by Molesey Weir, is pretty, but it can't be explored because it is private. Neither can the fretted confection on the Middlesex (left) bank – a genuine **Swiss chalet** imported bit by bit in 1900.

Next, comes **Tagg's Island**, joined by pontoons and catwalks to rafts of yachts and houseboats, and by a bridge to the Middlesex shore. There used to be lots more houseboat dwellers living here but they have been harassed away by developers and local fusspots.

Tom Tagg ran a thriving boat-letting trade on the island. In the late 1870s, he built a hotel here and it became the fashionable haunt of anyone who was anyone in London society. **Tubby Teddy**, Prince of Wales, who became Edward VII ('Tum-Tum' to his friends and 'Edward the Caresser' to the fondled), with luscious **Lillie Langtry** or **Alice Keppel** (**Camilla Parker-Bowles**'s great-grandma) on his arm, would frequent the place.

The hotel was in its heyday prior to World War I, when it was the property of Mr **Fred Karno**. He turned it into the 'Katsino' pleasure-dome – the home of 'Fred Karno's Circus', which included a dance hall, a casino, a theatre, and a menagerie. **Charlie Chaplin** learnt his trade here, as did **Stan Laurel**, **Bud Flanagan**, **George Robey**, **Will Hay** and **Max Miller**. Tagg's was England's once-upon-a-time university for knock-about comedy. Karno eventually went bust, ending up – by a twist of malevolent fate – running an off-licence in Lilliput, Dorset. His Katsino, one of the wackiest buildings in England, was demolished, but never rebuilt, by an American with ideas bigger than his money belt.

HURST PARK: A SPORTING MECCA

The nasty housing estate on the Thames Path, bank abeam of Tagg's Island, is Hurst Park. It used to be **Hurst Park Race Course**, and wasn't, apparently, any better-looking – 'a disgrace to the river and a blot on the landscape', declared 1950s Thames writer, **Eric de Mare** (*Time on the Thames*, Architectural Press, 1952). The race course closed in 1960. Civic planners had a chance to make good this blot; they didn't, replacing it with 'this drab new slum', as **Robert Nicholson** exquisitely described the Hurst Park housing estate in his 1969 *Guide to the Thames*. It doesn't seem to have weathered any better since.

It is hard to believe that this shambles of faceless conformity was once, in the 18th century, a sporting Mecca, not for bookies and jockeys and punters, but for duellers and prize fighters, and even aviators. An 18th-century letter reads:

> [W]ent . . . to see the great fight between Belcher and Cribb at Molesey Hurst near Hampton. The day was very fine and we had a charming drive out in our coach-and-four, and beat all the other coaches and chaises by the way. We had three hard runs with one post-chaise and . . . drove bogies, horsemen and all off the road into lanes and doors of houses.

Just imagine, here in the drabness that is now Hurst Park, sporting dandies and fops used to gather in the 18th and 19th centuries. The first game of cricket took place here in 1731, the first game of golf in England in 1758, one of the earliest balloon ascents in 1785, the first horse race in 1790.

THE BELL INN AND WENCHING

Garrick's Ait huddles close by the Thames Path on the bend of the river immediately upstream of Tagg's Island. Opposite is **Hampton Church** (built 1831) and the lofty **Bell Inn**, where Thames Street almost touches the river. The Great Cham of English Lit, **Dr Samuel Johnson** (1709–84), liked the

Bell, or Ye Olde Bell as it then
was: 'Aye, it hath old fashioned
appearance, neat without and
clean within.' It has a bit of
history, too. Servants and
courtiers from Hampton Court
Palace came to Ye Olde Bell,
slipping unseen, it is said, through a
network of tunnels linking the inn with the
palace. Cromwell's Roundheads used the inn, bean-feasting and wenching
and so forth.

Ye Olde Bell was destroyed by fire in 1892 and now has a modern interior
nothing like the one visited by **Oliver Twist** and **Bill Sykes** in Charles
Dickens's *Oliver Twist*:

> Here against the wall of a house, Oliver saw written up in pretty large
> letters, 'Hampton'. At length they came . . . into an old public-house
> with a defaced sign-board. The kitchen was an old, low-roofed room,
> with a great beam across the middle of the ceiling, and benches with
> high backs . . .

The Bell and the village of Hampton, on the opposite bank to the Thames
Path side, can be accessed via a **foot ferry** operating between West Molesey
Wharf, on the Hurst Park promontory, and Hampton's Thames Street, close
to the Bell Inn. The ferry runs during the months between March and
October only, weekends 11.00–18.00 and weekdays on demand. The notice-
board warns, however, that 'The council accepts no responsibility for
cancelled or delayed services'. It is best to call (tel: 020 8979 7471) to avoid
disappointment.

HAMPTON

Riverside Hampton is 16 miles as a racing pigeon flies from Charing Cross,
twice as far by the meandering river. The novelist **Anthony Trollope**
(1815–82) visited the river-hugging village in 1865:

GARRICK'S TEMPLE

Between the house and the river, visible from the Thames Path, is a
white octagonal temple, with Ionic portico, which Garrick built to
commemorate his successes. Erected in 1755/1756, it was recently
restored, with an exhibition to celebrate Garrick's life, and is now open
to the public between 14.00 and 17.00 on Sundays, from April to
September. Unhappily, it no longer contains the statue of Shakespeare
– 'the bust of the bard' – modelled by Garrick and sculpted by **Louis
Francois Roubillac** (1702–62); this was so good that the British
Museum swiped it for its own after Garrick's death.

> There are still some few nooks within reach of the metropolis which
> have not been be-villaed and be-terraced, and the little village of
> Hampton, with its old-fashioned country and inn and its bright,
> quiet, grassy river, is one of them . . .

The 18th-century actor, impresario and playwright, **David Garrick**
(1717–79), lived at Hampton House (now renamed Garrick's Villa) which he
bought in 1754 when he was king of the London stage. His friend Dr Johnson
loved 'Merry Hampton'. 'Ah, David,' he is reported to have said, 'it is the
leaving of such places that makes a death bed terrible.'

Horace Walpole was a frequent visitor:

> Today [in 1755] I dined at Garrick's. There was the Duke of Grafton
> and Lady Rochford, Lady Holderness, the Spanish minister . . . King
> Christian VII of Denmark, George Romney, the Duke of Devonshire,
> Hannah More, the Earl of Pembroke, Sir Joshua Reynolds, Queen
> Charlotte, Dean Stanley.

On August 19 1774, Mr and Mrs Garrick celebrated their silver wedding on
the lawns – now landscaped by the local authority into 'Terrace Gardens' – 'lit
by 6,000 lamps'. The lawn is open 07.30 until dusk daily, throughout the year.
Garrick's garden has been refashioned to echo its 18th-century layout,
complete with its original serpentine path.

Hampton Church is so ugly it barely seems worth a second look, but it
does contain interesting monuments, including one to **Mrs Sibel Penn**, who
was nurse to Edward VI, and whose ghost now wanders the Haunted Gallery
at Hampton Court Palace (see page 71). In the churchyard is the grave of
Huntingdon Shaw, who crafted the beautiful Jean Tijou-designed gates on
the riverfront at Hampton Court.

Jerome K Jerome wrote,

> Harris wanted to get out at Hampton Church, to go and see Mrs
> Thomas's tomb.
>
> 'Who is Mrs Thomas?' I asked.
>
> 'How should I know?' replied Harris. 'She's a lady that's got a funny
> tomb, and I want to see it.'

It's not a funny tomb at all, just a couple of marble pillars surmounted by a
coat of arms and the figure of Susannah Thomas, who 'departed this life on
the 4th of April 1731 in the 48th year of her age'.

GARRICK'S AIT TO WALTON-ON-THAMES

The 2.75-mile (4.5km) Garrick's Ait–Walton-on-Thames stretch of the Thames
Path is a claustrophobic one, strangled by the functional dreariness of Molesey's
huge reservoirs on the landward side, and by concrete anti-tank blocks erected
as World War II defences on the river bank. But it's not a dull walk, for all that,
especially on a Saturday afternoon or Sunday morning when the river buzzes

with sailing dinghies and rowing eights, and there's the tree-lined Middlesex bank to look at, a prettier and altogether happier one than the Surrey shore. The river is made particularly attractive by the chain of wooded islands through Sunbury Reach, ending at Sunbury Lock: **Platts Eyot**, **Purvis Eyot**, **Sunbury Court Island**, **Phoenix Island**, **Sunbury Lock Ait**, in that order.

Platts was once home of the famous Thornycroft boat works that built sleek gunboats for the Royal Navy. The island is linked to the Middlesex bank by a footbridge. Above the bridge are the moorings of launches used by the Metropolitan Police Thames Division, based at Shepperton, responsible for policing the river above Teddington.

Behind Sunbury Court Island, partly hidden behind the island's bungalows and difficult to see from the Thames Path, is **Sunbury Court**, the town's great mansion built in 1770 which is now the Salvation Army Youth Centre.

'Old' Sunbury: waterfront homes

Most of 'old' Sunbury is in narrow Thames Street, dominated by the strange tower and cupola of **St Mary the Virgin** parish church. Built in 1782, it was 'Victorianised' in 1856 to a 'quasi-Byzantine' style, and wonderfully described as 'peculiarly revolting' by the revered author of the monumental *Buildings of Britain* (50 vols, 1951–73), **Nicholas Pevsner** (1902–83).

In the churchyard is an old yew tree mentioned in *Oliver Twist* :

> As they passed Sunbury Church, the clock struck seven. There was a light in the ferry-house window opposite, which streamed across the road, and threw into sombre shadow a dark yew-tree with graves beneath it . . . and the leaves of the old tree stirred gently in the night wind. It seemed like quiet music for the repose of the dead.

There are handsome 18th-century homes overlooking Sunbury waterfront. In one of them – 'Wilmary', 'Orchard House', 'Darby House', nobody knows which – the **Reverend Gilbert White** (1720–93), author of *The Natural History of Selborne*, spent several summers. He wrote in 1867:

> I used to spend some weeks yearly at Sunbury, one of those pleasant villages lying in the Thames . . . In the autumn I could not help being much amused with those myriads of the swallow-kind, which assemble in those parts . . .

Admiral Edward Hawke (1705–81), who destroyed Napoleon's fleet in Quiberon Bay in 1759 and thus prevented the planned invasion of Britain, lived in the house called 'Hawke'.

Sunbury is well supplied with pubs; the **Flower Pot**, the **Magpie**, and the **Phoenix**, are all close to the water.

Jerome K Jerome found the river approach to Sunbury Lock Ait 'sweetly pretty . . . and the backwater charming.' There are two side-by-side locks, a larger, newer one on the Thames Path side of the river – opened in 1927 to handle barge traffic – and an older, original pound one (built 1811) which is still hand-operated and not used so often. Sunbury Lock Ait is joined by

THE DUKE OF WINDSOR AND A CIVILISED AFFAIR

David, who was Prince of Wales and chose to become **Edward VIII** when he was made king, before abdicating to become the Duke of Windsor, used to swim close by the weir above Wheatley's Ait in the 1920s when he was guest at the 18th-century house called Monksbridge (overlooking the river near Sunbury Lock).

The house was owned by Liberal MP, Dudley Ward, and the prince regularly bedded Ward's wife, Freda, there. It was all very civilised and provided the prince with the least rackety of his string of affairs with married women.

bridges to the next upstream island, Wheatley's Ait. This used to be the exclusive preserve of a commune of Victorian bachelors until they got bored and allowed women to join them – on the provision that they went home before midnight. Now Wheatley's is the second home for around a dozen families. A passenger ferry, available on request, operates from the 'Ferry House' boatyard of George Wilson and Sons between the island and the Middlesex shore. For details, tel: 01932 782067.

Much of the footpath walk alongside the arrow-straight **Walton Reach** from Wheatley's Ait to Walton Bridge is a bit of a slog – 2.7 miles (4.5km) – although made a trifle easier by four refreshment places positioned conveniently close to the path. First, there's the grandly Edwardian **Weir Hotel**, overlooking Sunbury Lock Weir. (For the benefit of walkers intending the join the Thames Path here, car parking is available close to the hotel.) Just ¼ mile (0.5km) on is the factory-block-style **Elmbridge Leisure Centre**, with typical leisure-centre-style public cafeteria, followed 1½ mile (2.5km) later – just beyond the small Wheatley's Ait weir, called, delightfully, 'Tumbling Bay' – by the notable **Angler's** and **Swan** public houses.

The Swan is where, in 1910, the up-and-coming American songwriter, **Jerome Kern** (1885–1945) – who was to write *Old Man River*, *Smoke Gets in Your Eyes*, and the Broadway hit, *Show Boat* – met his wife, Eva, who was the landlord's daughter. The Swan is one of a handful of pubs in southeast England where beer (the distinctive Young's) is sold cheaper in the 'Public' than it is in the other two bars.

Walton: a scold's bridle

Walton-on-Thames is a vast, straggling shopping centre without much going for it – a town to live in rather than to visit.

'We sculled up to Walton, a rather large place for a river side town,' wrote Jerome. He continued,

> There is an iron 'scold's bridle' in Walton Church. They used these things in ancient days for curbing women's tongues. They have given up the attempt now. I suppose iron was getting scarce and nothing else would be strong enough.

THE UGLIEST BRIDGE ON THE RIVER

There are two bridges crossing the Thames at Walton. The oldest is an add-on, prefabricated, lattice-steel structure erected by the Royal Engineers as a make-do affair in 1953. It's still there, the ugliest bridge on the river. The original Walton Bridge – a weird, but strangely attractive, geometrical contortion – was painted by **Giovanni Canaletto**. The second, opened in 1783, was painted by **J M W Turner**.

The 'scold's bridle' was stolen in 1964 but there is a copy in the vestry. The original was presented to the parish by a man called Chester in 1632. It bore the inscription, 'Chester presents Walton with a Bridle, To curb women's tongues that talk too idle.'

There are fine things in Walton's **St Mary's Church**, the finest being a monument pronounced 'worth a special journey' by the famous 19th-century German guidebook author, **Karl Baedeker** (1801–59). It's a statue by Frenchman **Louis François Roubiliac** (1702/5–62), commissioned in 1755, showing a daughter grieving over the death of her father who, remarkably cheerful, is leaning against a gun in the background. The monument is so big, so out of place in this nice Norman church, that the congregation complained – and rightly so – that it blocked out an entire window in the north aisle.

On the north wall is a curious 16th-century brass of **John Selwyn**, 'keeper of her Majesty's parke', showing off to Queen Elizabeth I by riding a stag towards her and cutting its throat at her feet.

Walton to Staines

Distances From Walton Bridge: Shepperton Lock (via Desborough Cut) 1.38 miles (2.22km), Chertsey Bridge 3.28 miles (5.28km), Penton Hook Lock 5.39 miles (8.67km), Staines Town Bridge 7.23 miles (11.64km)

The river divides above Walton, one branch heading northwest to meander, skittish as a kitten, past the villages of Lower Halliford and Shepperton, and the other running eastwards, canal-straight, before rejoining the main stream on the far side of Weybridge. Thames Path walkers have to make a choice of which route to follow.

The **'Desborough Cut'** is the direct, straight, and infinitely more boring of the two. It runs half a mile (0.8km) from Walton to a foot ferry operating downstream of Shepperton Lock where the Thames Path switches from the Surrey shore to the Middlesex bank. Grassy river banks sprout yellow sprays of golden rod along the edge of the path, towering poplars and hawthorn bushes are thick with splodges of cream blossom in late spring on the other.

The alternative is to cross over the river and take the longer, **waymarked footpath** (1 mile/1.6km), via the M-shaped river-wriggle, through the outskirts of Lower Halliford and Shepperton villages, to rejoin the Thames Path at Shepperton Lock ferry. Sections of this route are pretty, bordered by willows and, in summer, willow-herb, teasel and purple loosestrife; other parts peer voyeuristically into the gardens of modest riverside homes. It is this latter route which we shall explore first.

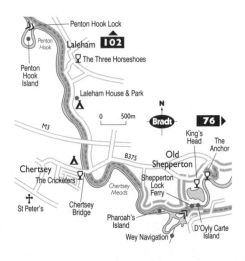

84

VIA HALLIFORD AND SHEPPERTON

After crossing over the river, there is a stretch of parkland called **Thames Meadow** on Ordnance Survey maps and **Cowey** (or Causeway) **Stakes** by the locals. It's a famous courting area, where passions are sometimes dampened by the river in flood.

Julius Caesar crossed the river at this very spot, so they say, following his battle with the British chieftain, Cassivellaunus. He built a bridge on stakes across what was then a swamp – hence the name 'Cowey Stakes'. One of the stakes used to be held by the British Museum, inscribed 'this was on the 16 October 1977 drawn out of the bottom of the river, in which at least five-sixths of its length were embedded'. I believe it has been lost, or was pinched, or has crumbled to dust.

The *Compleat Angler*'s **Isaac Walton** fished the river banks at Lower Halliford and Shepperton, where there are fishy stretches so shallow that boats constantly run aground. Onlookers find it ever so funny, and the red-faced skippers may later be found hiding in one of the bank-side pubs: the wisteria-veiled, oak-panelled and old-beamed Red Lion, Ship Hotel, Anchor, Warren Lodge, and King's Head, in that order.

Shepperton

The 16th-century **Anchor Inn** on the edge of Shepperton's delightful village square is one of the most popular; it has an old brick inglenook fireplace, worn flagstone floors, panelled walls, and furniture from the Beaconsfield home of Prime Minister **Benjamin Disraeli** (1804–81). An ancient pistol was once found in the pub's beams, perhaps wedged there by one of the **highwaymen** who frequented the bar. Famous people have patronised the Anchor, including **Lord Nelson** and **Lady Hamilton**. Nelson came to mix nooky with fishing. Others came to drink. **Elizabeth Taylor** and **Richard Burton** used to be regulars. The pub was frequented by other movie stars too, including **David Niven** and **Gregory Peck**, and starlets from Shepperton Studios (a couple of miles from Shepperton village), where scenes from such top box office hits as *Cleopatra*, *The Dam Busters*, and *The Guns of Navarone* were shot. Taylor and Burton, it is said, once fought each other – and anybody who got in the way – with sausage rolls in the bar of the Anchor.

Close to the inn is the site of the most famous **prize-fighting ring** in the whole of England, and an oil painting of such a fight hangs in the bar. Boats would lie close to the bank of the river, waiting to whisk pugilists and their patrons to the Surrey shore in the event of the fight being interrupted by 19th-century law keepers.

The **village square**, almost touching the water, is the heart and soul of old Shepperton – a startling survival of 300 years and more. A row of genteel 18th-century houses huddle close to **The King's Head**; the king was **Charles II** who, according to local history, shared several brandy and oranges here with his mistress, 'pretty, witty' **Nell Gwyn**.

The **church** was rebuilt in 1614 on piles driven through the river mud. It has a fine, square, brick tower, added in 1710. There are two outside staircases, one leading to the public gallery, the other to the private pew belonging to the nearby **Manor House**. The huge, white 19th-century Manor House has lawns – 'Mrs Lindsay's lawns' they are called, although I can't tell you why. They sweep down to the river's edge, the way all good riverside lawns should.

The novelist **George Eliot** (1819–80) wrote episodes from her *Scenes from Clerical Life* – a series of stories seen through the eyes of a clergyman, and her first major work – while staying at the manor with her married lover, **George Henry Lewes** (1817–78). To the north of the church is a handsome rectory where a curate, **J M Neale**, wrote the carol 'Good King Wenceslas' during the reign of Henry VII.

Lower Halliford: a gem

Lower Halliford, next door to Shepperton, has been described as 'one of the gems of the river'. The village has a lot of pretty cottages, snug and squat, some with larkspurs and lupins and hollyhocks in the gardens. The 19th-century novelist **Thomas Love Peacock** lived in Peacock House near the corner of the green from 1826 until his death in 1866. He is buried in Shepperton churchyard. So is his daughter, Margaret (1823–26), who died aged three. Peacock so lamented her death that he wrote his most moving poem in her memory; it is inscribed on her tomb, and made me cry:

> Long night succeeds thy little day
> Oh blighted blossom, can it be
> That this grey stone and grassy clay
> Have closed our anxious care of thee . . .

Peacock was, I think, an especially nice eccentric who would only drink or eat in a pub after discovering whether its mustard pots were clean. He was one of the local landmarks during his time. One evening, two men were rowing past the house at Lower Halliford. 'Is this old Peacock's?', asked one. Back came the thunderous response from over the garden wall: 'Yes, this is old Peacock's and this is old Peacock himself!'

His son-in-law, another famous novelist, **George Meredith**, lived in Vine Cottage on the other side of the green. He had a disastrous marriage to Peacock's widowed daughter.

VIA DESBOROUGH CUT

Now we shall take the shorter, Thames Path route to Shepperton Lock, via Desborough Cut (dug in 1935 to provide a short cut for river users), which is named after **Lord Desborough**. He was a philanthropist, an avuncular politician, and an outstanding athlete who swam the Niagara rapids twice, climbed the Matterhorn three times, was 'Amateur Punting Champion of the Upper Thames', and rowed across the English Channel; he subsequently described the latter achievement as 'a typical British feat – quite useless, exceedingly dangerous and thoroughly worthwhile'. In his day, he was a 'worthy man', serving on 115 committees at the same time as he was the longest-ever-serving chairman (1904–37) of the Thames

Conservancy. He planned and oversaw the building of the Desborough Cut. While he was still plain Mr William Henry Grenfell, and a newly elected Member of Parliament, a gossip writer in the *Evening News* swooned over him:

> [H]is broad, level brow beneath curling light hair, his straight, but
> not classic nose, his clear, far-seeing eyes, are typically English. His
> strong neck rises from a pair of broad, supple shoulders, and his arms
> are as massive as those of some hero of the classic sculptures.

Weybridge

Weybridge lies tucked beyond the trees running parallel to the Thames Path on the Surrey-side of the Desborough Cut. It's a stockbroker-Tudor commuter town, balanced precariously on the 'twixt and between of London urban and suburban – goodness only knows where the city begins and ends these days, or where it is going to.

Wealthy business tycoons and pop stars with pots of money live in the luxurious parts of Weybridge like St George's Hill. In other parts there are industrial estates such as the one near the old Brooklands motor-racing circuit (now an airfield, mainly helicopters). This is where early-20th-century drivers, dressed like Mr Toads in flapping leather helmets and oil-smeared goggles, nursed high-wheeled racing machines around the concrete banking still visible from the London–Portsmouth railway.

In the 19th century, the Shakespearian actress **Fanny Kemble** (1809–93) lived in Weybridge. She was famous for her debut sensation as Juliet at Covent Garden when she was 20, after which she went to the United States to marry, and eventually divorce, a southern planter called Pierce Butler. She wrote affectionately about the village it then was:

> [It is] rural and rather deserted-looking and most picturesque . . .
> with the desolate domain of Portmore [now Burwood] Park, its
> mansion falling into ruin, on one side of it, on the other the empty
> house and fine park of Oatlands.

Oatlands Park House, its rooftops visible above the trees on the left bank above the Thames Path, 'overlooks the Temms,' **Edward Lear** told a friend. The house, originally a palace belonging to **Henry VIII**, is now a posh hotel, so posh that it has its own helicopter pad.

Henry built the palace, a stupendous pile spreading over 14 acres, for his third wife, **Anne of Cleeves**, who didn't like it. His fourth wife, **Catherine Howard**, did, and Henry, always the romantic, married her in the chapel here. **Edward VI**, **Elizabeth I**, **James I** (who bred silk worms at Oatlands for his 'King's Silk Works') and **Charles I** all lived here at different times. A fine cedar tree beside the hotel drive is said to have been planted by Charles I to commemorate the birth of his son Henry at Oatlands.

The palace was destroyed by Parliament during the English Civil War. It was rebuilt, pulled down, and rebuilt again – the last time, in 1794, as a rococo Gothic fantasy in the style of Walpole's Strawberry Hill – by the last 'royal' to call it 'home', the Duke of York, second son of George III. The composer **Haydn** and the dandy **Beau Brummel** (who went anywhere for a free meal where there were toffs) were regular guests of the Yorks. Mrs York, the duchess, was dotty about animals, and the headstones from her dogs' cemetery are still near the present hotel's lounge-bar patio. She must have been a popular lady for, after her death in 1820, the townsfolk of Weybridge paid for a tall Doric column to be erected in her memory at the bottom of **Monument Hill**, outside the town's 17th-century **Ship Inn** – and a proper eyesore it is too!

Oatlands Hotel has entertained some famous guests in its time: **Émile Zola**, **Anthony Trollope**, **Edward Lear**, to name just three. Lear described the hotel in a letter to his friend, Fortesque, whom he addressed as '40sque':

> [It is] large and sumptuously commodious . . . with nice broad terrace walks and wonderful views over the river and the surrounding landscape . . .

Lear had come to change his image from funny man, with a genius for nonsense rhymes, to that of serious artist, choosing the hotel's magnificent cedar trees as subjects for his paintings. However, he couldn't resist knocking out a bit of nonsense as well, inscribing a cartoon he drew while staying here, 'Lear feeding "unfortunate birds" at Oatlands Park Hotel, Weybridge'. Copies of the cedar tree painting and the cartoon are in the hotel.

The Desborough Cut passes through two bridges, the first just under a mile (1.5km) from Walton, the second about half a mile (750m) down-river from Shepperton Lock ferry. Both provide Thames Pathers with access to and from a dog-walk trail round Desborough Island.

D'Oyly Carte Island

D'Oyly Carte Island is immediately downstream of Shepperton Lock ferry, which is downstream of the confluence of the Thames and Wey Navigation, which is downstream of Shepperton Lock.

The river below and about Shepperton Lock is like a wide lake, studded with islands, motor boats buzzing like gnats, canoeists flailing through the white water at the fall of the weirs.

D'Oyly Carte Island is at the tail of the lake. It is named after the impresario, Richard d'Oyly Carte (1844–1901), who owned it. He built **Eyot House**

SULLIVAN – A DEDICATED THAMESIDER

Both Gilbert and Sullivan were dedicated Thamesiders, but Sullivan was particularly so. He lived for 12 years at 'River House' in Walton (1884–98), and stayed for long periods of time either in 'Grove House' (now 'Bridge House') in Weybridge (where he wrote the music for *The Gondoliers*), or on the Shepperton side of the river at 'Ladye Place' in Ferry Lane near the Middlesex-bank ferry landing stage (where those who walk the Desborough Cut route will land after being carried across the river by the Shepperton ferry).

During Sullivan's final visit to Ladye Place in July 1890, he finished *Te Deum* for the Peace Celebration Service at St Paul's Cathedral. The weeping-willow trees on Shepperton's river bank are said to have inspired the *Mikado* and the song *Tit-Willow*.

there, intending it as a summer annex to London's Savoy Hotel in which he had interests, but the authorities refused to grant a drinks licence so he abandoned the idea and set up house there instead. He is best known for producing a string of Gilbert and Sullivan operettas from 1875. **Sir William Schwenck Gilbert** (1836–1911), who wrote the librettos, and **Sir Arthur Seymour Sullivan** (1842–1900), who composed the music, were frequent guests at ugly Eyot House. Some people maintain that the pair's famous partnership, begun in 1871, was actually formed here on D'Oyly Carte Island, where they roughed out the outlines for what was to be their first huge success, *Trial by Jury*, produced under D'Oyly Carte's management.

The entire D'Oyly Carte opera company, the 'Savoyards', were richly entertained on the island every summer. This was depicted in the film *The Story of Gilbert and Sullivan*, which showed the Savoyards aboard a Salter Company's steamer, decorated with Chinese lanterns, howling choruses from Gilbert and Sullivan operas. Today, the house is divided into flats and the island is linked to the Weybridge bank by a picturesque footbridge.

SHEPPERTON LOCK FERRY – CROSSING A CONFUSION OF WATERS

Sullivan, and almost certainly Gilbert, regularly rode the Shepperton Lock ferry. We are about to take it from the landing stage close to D'Oyly Carte Island, across the confusion of waters where the Wey Navigation runs into the Thames, to rejoin the Thames Path at Ferry Lane on the Middlesex shore.

Summon the ferry by ringing the bell. It operates quarter-hourly weekdays – 08.30–17.30 (May–Aug 08.30–18.30), Sat 09.00–17.30, Sun 10.00–17.30 (May–Aug 10.00–18.30) – but it might be advisable to confirm ferry times beforehand by ringing the office at Ferry Lane, Shepperton; tel: 01932 254844. If the ferry isn't running, you will need to cross the bridge at Walton and take the alternative, waymarked route through Lower Halliford and Shepperton villages.

THE 'WATER POET': GRIM VERSIFIER

The most famous Thames ferryman was a waterman, John Taylor, born in 1580, who called himself the 'Water Poet'. He wasn't only a ferryman but a tax collector as well, responsible for collecting dues payable on wine being transported up-river. He was also a showman, at  one time making and sailing a brown paper boat for 36 hours on the Thames, kept afloat by eight pigs' bladders and propelled by sticks tipped with dried fish. Deeds such as this, rather than his rhymes, made him famous. As the 18th- and 19th-century writer, Robert Southey (1774–1843), chronicled,

> Kings and Queens condescended to notice him, nobles and archbishops admitted him to their table, and mayors and corporations received him with civic honours.

Taylor was commissioned to devise and organise royal river pageants on the Thames. No doubt the royals had to listen to the 'Water Poet's' rhymings. Taylor himself admitted that

> [S]ome through ignorance, and some through spite,
> Have said that I can neither read nor write.

In 1630 he published a collection of his verses, since reissued by the Spencer Society of Manchester in eight thick volumes. Some of it is funny, much historically important, most all of it grim versing. A single stanza serves as ample demonstration:

> We went into a house of one John Pinner
> And there eight several sorts of ale we had
> All able to make one stark drunk, or mad.

The Wey is not a river, but a 'navigation' – a canal opened in 1760 to link the Thames and the actual River Wey at Guildford and Godalming. It is still navigable as far as Guildford, but the four-mile section from there to Godalming is largely disused, although canoes are able to make the voyage which requires a lot of lug and tug (or so I am told).

There has been a ferry at Shepperton Lock for over 500 years, with the exception of a 26-year period between 1960 and 1986. In the 15th century –

during Henry VI's reign – the ride was free. In the 1700s it cost a shilling to ferry a 'drove' [herd] of cattle. During the first half of the 20th century, passengers paid a penny (1d) and cyclists two pence (2d). Today there's a charge of £1 a head.

Our Mutual Friend's **Plashwater Weir Mill**

Shepperton Lock is Plashwater Weir Mill in Charles Dickens's *Our Mutual Friend*, where Lizzie Hexham – 'a dark girl of nineteen or twenty' – rescues the almost murdered Eugene Wrayburn whom she eventually marries. There's a small shop at the lock where the lock-keeper's wife serves light refreshments. There are also toilets and a water point.

The river weaves some weird turns over the next 1.8 miles (3.1km), heading sometimes east, sometimes north and sometimes south, until it straightens itself out, after an S-bend at Chertsey Mead, beneath the M3 motorway bridge at Chertsey. For nearly a mile (1.3km) – past Pharaoh's Island and Chertsey Mead meadows on the far bank – this section of the Thames Path is on a riverside road with grass strips by the water's edge. Upstream of Shepperton Lock, bungalows line the bank, green and red toys from a Monopoly set, veiled by trees, while moored houseboats – floating houses, really – curtsy in the river on passing washes.

PHARAOH'S ISLAND – A GIFT TO NELSON

Pharoah's Island commemorates the **Battle of the Nile** and was presented by a grateful nation to **Nelson**, who said 'thank you very much', and gave it back again. A lot of the present properties on the island have Egyptian names such as 'Rameses', 'Sphinx' and 'Thebes'. The actor **Ian Hendry** used to live here.

Once past Dockett Point, and through a kissing gate, there's open country and space to breathe nearly all the way to Chertsey Bridge.

CHERTSEY MEAD ABBEY AND 'HANDFULLS OF BONE'

The meadowland of Chertsey Mead on the Surrey side is the site of a once great **Benedictine abbey**; only a few foundation stones and traces of monks' fishponds remain. It was ravaged, first by **Vikings** who destroyed the buildings and slew the abbot along with about 90 of his monks, then, after rebuilding, by **Henry VIII** 200 years later. The antiquary **William Stukeley** (1687–1765) – who was to blot his reputation by mistakenly linking Stonehenge and Avebury with druid ceremonies – expressed himself stunned at the demolition job committed by Henry's forces:

> So total a dissolution I scarcely saw . . . [N]othing remains. Human
> bones of abbots, monks . . . were spread thick all over the garden, so
> that one might pick up handfulls of bits of bone . . . everywhere
> among the garden stuff.

I was told a story – a true one, I was promised – at **Chertsey Museum**. (Chertsey Museum – Windsor Street, Chertsey – used to be the Italianate town hall and is open Tue–Fri 12.30–16.00, Sat 11.00–16.00; closed Sun and Mon. Admission free.) The story concerns the curfew bell of St Peter's Church, which still tolls every evening from Michaelmas (29 September) to Lady Day (25 March). It was introduced, long ago, as a precaution against fire in the days when houses were built of wood and conflagrations were frequent. The curfew (or '*couvre-feu*') was a metal case placed over the ashes in the hearth to extinguish them; the curfew bell tolled at sunrise and sunset to remind people to extinguish or rekindle the ashes. And now to the story:

Blanche Heriot, a beautiful Chertsey girl, and a lad called Neville were lovers in the time of the stormy Wars of the Roses. Neville, who had fought long and fearlessly, was captured by the Yorkists and condemned to die at Chertsey Mead on the first chime of next morning's curfew. But there was still hope; a messenger had been sent to the king begging a pardon for Neville. Although it was granted, the messenger had only reached Laleham ferry, some two or three miles away, by the time the first toll of the bell should have rung and poor Neville put to death. No bell was heard.

Suddenly the messenger galloped on to the mead, his horse steaming with sweat and flecked with foam. Neville was saved. And why had the bell not chimed? Because Blanche Heriot, distraught with grief, had climbed to the curfew tower and thrown herself on to the clapper of the great bell, thus preventing it from being rung.'

The bell tolls for Henry VI

The very same bell tolled for the funeral of Henry VI when, after his brutal murder in the Tower of London, he was carried to Chertsey by water, and buried 'without priest, clerk, torch or taper, singing or saying' within the grounds of the abbey. Twenty-two years later his tomb had become such a place of pilgrimage that his body was removed and taken, again by river, to Windsor.

Chertsey Bridge gets a mixed press. One travel guide calls it 'handsome', another 'dignified', and a third 'uneasy'. It was built, seven arches wide, of Purbeck stone in the 1780s.

CHERTSEY: 'THE SILLIEST OF TOWNS'?

Most of Chertsey – 'the silliest of towns', according to poet **Matthew Arnold** (1822–88) – is a mile to the south (about 15 minutes' walk from the Thames Path), so the river hereabouts has rural charm. There are some attractive bits and pieces to be found in the town, which is where Oliver Twist was wounded when Bill Sikes forced him to commit burglary at Mrs Maylie's house (the location of which I have never identified, and I doubt if anybody else has either).

One-time home of Charles Fox

Chertsey

Chertsey parish church, rebuilt in 1808, isn't attractive. But it is interesting. The interior is large and airy, painted in simple, earth-coloured tones. There's a memorial tablet to the famous Whig statesman, Charles James Fox (1749–1806). In old age he lived in a large house on the southern slope of Chertsey's **St Anne's Hill**, where he entertained great people, **Charles Dickens** and **Matthew Arnold** among them. Fox revelled in rural life, which St Anne's provided in those days. One visitor observed 'Fox . . . at home, sitting on a haycock, reading novels and watching jays steal his cherries.'

Another, the poet **Samuel Rogers** (1763–1855), recalled:

> I remember his calling out to the Chertsey hills, when a thick mist, which had for some time concealed them, rolled away: 'Good morning to you! I am glad to see you again'. There was a walk in his grounds through which the farmers used to pass, and he would stop them and talk to them about the price of turnips . . . I was one day with him in the Louvre when he suddenly turned from the pictures and, looking out of the window, exclaimed, 'This hot sun will burn my turnips at St Anne's Hill'.

St Anne's Hill (near where the M3 and M25 cross, almost three-quarters of a mile/1.2km from the centre of Chertsey) is worth visiting on a clear day, when there are good views of the town.

There are three main streets in Chertsey: London, Guildford, and Windsor. The latter retains some of the grace of the 18th century and is probably the

---

PUB RENAMED THANKS TO LOVABLE PAINTER

The **Cricketers Hotel**, on the Surrey side of the bridge, used to be the Holly Bush Inn until that loveable drunkard painter, **George Morland** (1763–1804), couldn't afford his lodgings and so settled the account with a painting of Chertsey cricketers playing against a Hambleden XII. The landlord changed the name of his pub accordingly. A big collection of ties used to be displayed in the bar – perhaps they still are – each bearing the name of its one-time owner and regiment, school or club. One dates back to the Zulu Wars.

most interesting because it contains **Curfew House**, which was originally a school, built in 1725 in a style called 'Vanbrughish' after the baroque architect **Sir John Vanbrugh** (1664–1726). He was best remembered, by those who remember such things, for designing Woodstock's **Blenheim Palace**, which so appalled the Duchess of Marlborough that she refused to pay for his work.

Andrew Cowley: scholar and poet

For the last two years of his life, the now little-quoted (even less read) royalist poet Andrew Cowley (1618–67) lived in a Jacobean timber-framed house in Guildford Street called **Cowley House**. Cowley led a busy life, studying, writing and promoting the royalist cause. He had long looked forward to owning 'a small house and a large garden, with very moderate conveniences joined to them' and to cultivating fruit and flowers and studying nature. He asked, in his poem, 'The Garden',

> Who that has reason, and his smell
> Would not among roses and jasmine dwell
> Rather than all his spirits choke
> White exhalations of dirt and smoke
> And all the uncleanness which does drown
> In pestilential clouds a populous town?

His retirement did not last long. He caught cold one summer evening while helping to bring home the last loads of hay, and died on July 28 1667. His body was carried by State barge down river to Westminster and buried in the abbey; famous scholars, especially dead ones, were treated royally in those days.

Campsites: Chertsey and Laleham

Chertsey Lock is against the Middlesex bank, between Chertsey and the M3 bridges, facing the mouth of the Abbey Stream, on the banks of which there is a campsite. **Chertsey Camping Club** (Bridge Road, Chertsey, Surrey KT16 8JX; tel: 01932 562405) is open all year, and accessed from the Surrey side of Chertsey Bridge. It's a policy of the site never to turn a backpacker away, I was told – 'We couldn't, even if all our pitches were full, because otherwise it would be a long walk if they had to move on to the next site,' said the lady in reception. There are 225 pitches, and the facilities include toilets, showers, wash-basins, laundry/ironing points, a recreation room, a children's play area and a shop. Cost per backpacker varies between £3.95 for members of the Caravan and Camping Club and £5 for non-members (Jun–Sep), and £3.60 for members and £4.65 for non-members outside these months. Close by, on the downstream side of Chertsey Bridge, are a telephone and a good-sized service station with a shop.

For half a mile (0.87km), from Chertsey Lock to the riverside houses, bungalows and houseboats at **Laleham**, the Thames Path is almost rural. **Laleham House**, on the right, cannot be seen from the towpath, but since it is of no great architectural beauty – square and plain, red brick with a large Doric portico – it doesn't much matter. The house was for centuries the seat

LUCAN – THE MAN WHO SACRIFICED THE LIGHT BRIGADE

The third earl, who took the Light Brigade into the Crimea's 'Valley of Death', lived in Laleham House, as did **Donna Maria**, Queen of Portugal, as a child. The personal feelings of animosity between the Earl of Lucan and another aristocratic general, Lucan's brother-in-law, James Thomas Brudenell, 7th Earl of Cardigan (whom we shall meet again, in Hambleden – page 156), are said to have led the light cavalry brigade to its destruction with a fatal charge against enemy guns at Balaclava in 1854. The glorious charge is described in **Lord Alfred Tennyson**'s famous poem:

'Forward, the Light Brigade!'
Was there a man dismay'd? Not tho' the soldier knew
Some one had blunder'd:
Theirs not to make reply,
Theirs not to reason why,
Theirs but to do and die:
Into the valley of Death
Rode the six hundred.

We shall meet the dislikeable Laleham Lucans again, in church (see page 96). Not, however, the obnoxious ninth Lord Lucan, who did a bunk, accused of murdering his children's nanny, and who is now probably lording it over peons in Paraguay. Or perhaps he's dead?

of the strutting, pompous earls of Lucan, until it became a convent that has now been turned into flats. About half the surrounding estate is a public park where **Laleham Camping Club** (Thameside, Laleham, Middlesex TW18 1SH; tel: 01932 564149) is located, accessible by following a signed footpath from the Thames Path. The campsite is open from early April until the last week in September, and costs £4 per head per night. 'Goodness knows how many pitches we've got,' said the lady in reception when I asked her. 'It's a blooming big site, that's all I know, and I shall be glad when the end of the season comes! I'm blown right out, I am.'

LALEHAM AND 'QUEER SUGGESTIONS OF OLD HOUSES'

There was a **ferry** in Laleham until the 1950s, its one-time presence marked on the Surrey shore by a Georgian ferry cottage, now sagging beneath the weight of time and lichened tiles. Strange, the reasons why some places and things have a claim to fame; Laleham ferry's is that Bing Crosby and Bob Hope apparently used the ferry to get to the golf club on the opposite side of the Thames.

It is easy to miss the village of Laleham, barely visible from the river bank; the artist-craftsman-designer-writer **William Morris** (1834–96) observed that all you can see of the place is 'enormous willow trees and queer suggestions of old houses'. Many of the willows, giant and ancient-limbed, were lost in the storm of the late 1980s and now saplings, grown taller with time, once again begin to shelter Laleham in shy retreat beyond their boughs.

A short stroll up Blacksmith's Lane leads directly into Laleham, more a hamlet than a village, a delightfully rustic scattering of houses, a few cottages, three pubs and a brick church.

All Saints Church
All Saints Church was crudely restored in 1932, but it is queerly picturesque nevertheless, with a broad ivy-mantled tower and little dormer windows. It looks Victorian, but the tower, brick with a parapet, is 18th-century.

The resting place of Matthew Arnold
The scholar-poet Matthew Arnold (1822–88) is buried in the churchyard, near the south porch, almost within sound of the river his 'Scholar-Gipsy' wandered by. His father, the famous **Thomas Arnold** (1795–1842) of Rugby School fame, portrayed in Thomas Hughes's (1822–96) *Tom Brown's Schooldays*, tutored in Laleham.

Matthew Arnold was born in Laleham, at a house (now gone) where his father, several years before becoming headmaster of Rugby in 1828, kept a small private school. Lessons began at 07.00 and continued until 15.00, with just a half-hour for breakfast. At 19.00 lessons were resumed until 21.30. Dr Arnold taught for some 54 hours a week, and in his spare time either wrote or begat lots of children, all of whom he nicknamed. Matthew was known as 'Crab'. The boy's first report was written when he was six months old. His father recorded that he was 'backward and rather bad-tempered'. The site of Matthew's birthplace is marked by a cedar tree, which was part of the Arnolds' garden. During the last 15 years of his life Matthew lived close to Laleham, in Pain's Cottage at Cobham.

It was Dr Arnold's unfulfilled wish to return to Laleham in old age. According to **Dean Arthur Penrhyn Stanley** (1815–81), his biographer and a family friend,

> [He would] often revisit Laleham and show his children his former haunts, his favourite views on the great plain of Middlesex, and the lonely walks along the quiet banks of the Thames.

Bumptious Lucan – an aristocratic prat
Inside Laleham church is Lucan Chapel, actually owned by the earls of Lucan. The most bumptious of the Lucans, George Bingham (1800–88), made an aristocratic prat of himself concerning the chapel.

Soon after he became third Lord Lucan in 1839, he picked a row with the rector of Laleham over the family sittings in Laleham church. In Lucan's opinion, these were inadequate and the family chapel was badly sited. As a consequence, he brought an architect down from London to rebuild the church according to his convenience. The earl declared in a letter,

> [S]ince the building is so old, having a Norman character . . ., a clean sweep can be made and the view of the church will not be obstructed by Norman pillars.

The rector, however, thought otherwise, whereupon Lucan flew into a passion, consulting and insulting ecclesiastical authorities who were told that he was entitled to do whatever he pleased:

> I consider I have exclusive and entire control over the Manorial Chancel, may exclude even the minister from passing through and may occupy it in any way I prefer . . . I claim exclusive power and control.

Swans: still fouling and preening

Year after year, Lucan harried the rector about the manorial chancel. Nor was this his only grievance at Laleham. There were trespassers on the family seat as well – swans. Lucan declared they were, 'truculent, destructive, untidy, abusive, and foul'. On December 8 1853, he wrote to the Lord Chamberlain:

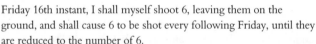

> Sir, I have within the last hour seen more than, if not quite, 70 swans in my fields. I can and will submit no longer to so intolerable a nuisance. I therefore and hereby give you notice that unless the swans are removed on or before Friday 16th instant, I shall myself shoot 6, leaving them on the ground, and shall cause 6 to be shot every following Friday, until they are reduced to the number of 6.

He didn't. The swans won in the end. Today, and on nearly every day of the year, there are more swans in Laleham Reach and on the surrounding water-meadows – ripping up the grass, preening, sleeping it off, fouling – than most people ever see in one place in their lives. Bless 'em!

The Three Horseshoes – once reserved for a chosen few

As far as I know, the third earl never called at Laleham's picturesque pub, The Three Horseshoes. Strange, because a lot of other toffs did, at one time or another. There was an inn here as early as 1624. Its most famous landlord was **William Clifton**, mine host from 1884 to 1925. He reserved the bar parlour (now the King's Room) exclusively for a chosen few, among them **King Edward VII** (who invariably paused here on his visits to Laleham House) and **Sir Arthur Sullivan** of Gilbert and Sullivan fame.

PENTON LOCK AND CHARMING PENTON HOOK ISLAND

Above old Laleham Ferry, the river is hemmed by houses on the right and bungalows and villas on the left, almost all the way into and out of Staines which is unlovely for the most, although a tiny bit of it, beside the river, is surprisingly good. First, though, the Thames Path – partly road, partly gravel track – crosses the intake to Thames Water's enormous **Queen Mary Reservoir** then accompanies Penton Lock through the thin neck of the pear-shaped Penton Hook Island.

The lock – 81.28m in length – shortcuts the river's wild U-bend by about half a mile. It's a charming spot. Penton Hook was a famous place long before the green and wooded island was created with spoil from the lock diggings in 1812. Back in the 17th century, when folk talked of ''im [or 'er] lying out at Penton 'ook', it was a mass grave, a burial place during the **Great Plague of 1664**. If you have time, cross over one of the lock gates, then over the weir, and explore the path around the island. There's good fishing from its banks, but anglers must obtain a weir permit from the lock-keeper.

A notice at the lock announces, '78 miles to Oxford, 34 miles to London'. The **lock cottage** (1814) is attractive; it was the highest of the locks controlled by the City of London, which is why the City's arms are on the cottage wall. '**John the Lock**' was the name of the lock-keeper when I came this way. His assistant, another John, was 'Norwich John'. On a busy day they were getting something like 130 boats passing through. 'John the Lock' said it used to be more than 300 a day, sometimes 600 on a weekend; he blamed the fall on a downturn in the hiring of boats and a demise in use of the river by private owners. You can buy books, magazines and postcards at the lock-side office.

STAINES

With Staines railway bridge ahead, just under a mile (1.5km) from Penton Hook, the Thames Path passes by **St Peter's Church**, opened in 1894. The church is interesting not for its beauty, but because its considerable construction costs were borne by one man, **Sir Edward Clarke**, KC, a lawyer who was to lead the defence at the trial of Oscar Wilde. He lived, with his wife, in a villa not far downstream and craved a church on the banks of the Thames like one the couple had visited beside the River Dart in Devon. So they bought the land and built themselves a church. Oh, the things wealthy Victorians could undertake on a whim!

Staines railway bridge is painted with yellow stripes to stop swans from flying into it. Apparently they work. Just upstream of the bridge, the old barge tow-path (but not today's Thames Path, which continues on the Middlesex bank all the way to Staines Bridge) used to switch banks at a stone slipway called 'Shooting Off Point', next to cottages called 'Hook On' and 'Shoot Off'. In the 19th century, a local by-law forbade horses to tow barges through Staines along the Middlesex tow-path. Instead, they were 'hooked on' or 'shot off' here, according to whether their loads were heading upstream or down, and the horses led barge-less through town, over Staines

TRUSS'S ISLAND WAS, THEN WASN'T, NOW IS AGAIN

Reclaimed Truss's Island, in the bight of the first right-hand bend after Penton Hook, was an island, then it wasn't, now it is again. It's not very big – just 200 yards (182.8m) long and seven yards (6.4m) wide – but it has an interesting history. It is named after a barge-owner and City of London clerk of works, **Charles Truss**. Truss spent 36 years, from 1774 to 1810 (when he was 82), restoring the entire heavily obstructed river and its eroded banks between London and Staines. The City appreciated his efforts so much that when he retired, a corporation mark-stone was set up on the island, engraved with the City's arms and inscribed, 'TRUSS'S ISLAND 1774'.

Their duty done, the City then forgot about it, so much so that by 1865 Truss's successor complained, 'this so-called island practically joins the right bank now.' It continued to be neglected, and had almost completely disappeared until Runnymede Borough Council restored it to island status in 1992. Truss's stone is still there, not far from the Thames Path.

Bridge, and back to the barge which had been poled and man-handled to the other side of the river.

Most of modern Staines is ugly. I read somewhere, although I can't recall where, 'No-one would go to Staines for a holiday.' You might go there for the shops, though, which are good, and there is a twice-weekly market on Wednesdays and Saturdays, held in the pretty **Market Square**. The square is situated beside the clock-towered **Town Hall**, which replaced the Old Market Hall where **Sir Walter Ralegh** was committed for trial in 1603.

The river reach and the town promenade, where thoughtful development has been instigated, are pleasant, despite some distressing architectural blemishes. Views from the bridge, upstream and downstream, are good. The monumental, granite **Staines Bridge** (1829–32) was built by **John Rennie**. It's a practical, rather than handsome, structure. Like many major Thames bridges, there is a pub at each end of it – in this case the **Swan** one end and the **Bridge Hotel** the other.

Corners of old Staines, close by the river, aren't bad, especially the 'villagey' area around the Gothic-revival parish church of **St Mary's**. To find the church, walk up **Clarence Street** (some of which has an old-fashioned-market-town air about it) on the Middlesex side of Staines Bridge. St Mary's was rebuilt by Victorian 'restorers' in 1828; fortunately, they didn't get around to spoiling the three-stage, red-brick tower built in 1631 by **Inigo Jones**, who lived in Staines for a time:

> [W]hen a lofty pile is raised,
> We never hear the workmen praised,
> Who bring the lime or place the stones;
> But all admire Inigo Jones.

PEPYS AGAIN

Between 1659 and 1662, Samuel Pepys visited the Swan Tavern several times and noted the visits in his famous diary. After a glass or two, and a meal, he travelled back to Westminster by rowing boat, a distance of 40 miles, which must have taken some considerable time. A century or two ago the inn used to issue 'Swan tokens' to bargees as change instead of coins, thereby ensuring their return; the tokens are now collectors' items.

Near St Mary's is **Ashby Recreation Ground**, running to the edge of the Thames where the **London Stone** was erected on a pedestal in 1781 (almost hidden from the Thames Path side of the river by trees). A replica now replaces the much-vandalised original stone. It is inscribed 'God preserve ye City of London', and used to denote the upstream limits of the jurisdiction of the City of London, which lasted from 1285 to 1857 when the Thames Conservators took over. Today the stone marks the boundary between the old county of Middlesex and Buckinghamshire. Three-quarters of a mile upstream from Staines Bridge, a similar function is served by the islands of Hollyhock and Holm, which mark the boundary crossing into the Royal Borough of Windsor. The future **Edward VIII** and **Mrs Simpson** used a house called 'The Nest' on the half-obscured Holm as a hideaway during the 1930s.

Runnymede to Windsor

Distances From Staines Bridge: Bell Weir Lock 1 mile (1.6km), Old Windsor Lock 3.92 miles (6.30km), Romney Lock 7.92 miles (11.13 km), Windsor Bridge 8.35 miles (11.92km)

The Thames Path crosses Staines Bridge from Middlesex to Surrey and soon the river begins to shed more of its urban shackles. Bungalows and houses become fewer, tubs and flowerbeds increase in number and colour, trees and parks and meadows and wooded hills begin to predominate; living is more spacious and the river preens, with good reason, for we are reaching towards a place of supreme importance in English history.

RUNNYMEDE

The approach to Runnymede, just under a mile (1.5km) from Staines Bridge, is marked by the Runnymede Hotel and, next to it, Bell Weir Lock, on the upstream side of the thunderous M25 double-bridges.

Dating from 1817, **Bell Weir Lock** (which has toilets) is named after its first weir keeper and ferryman, Charlie Bell, who opened The Angler's Rest Hotel here in the 18th century. Its successor, **The Runnymede Hotel**, has a Charlie Bell's café-bar. The weir is recommended for fly-fishing.

The Thames Path runs through the entire 1.25 miles (2.9km) of Runnymede riverside meadows, grassland and broadleaf woodland, backed by lovely, tree-covered **Cooper's Hill**. Everyone should climb Cooper's Hill for the views are enormous and wonderful, made famous by a poem, 'Cooper's Hill', completed in 1655 by **Sir John Denham** (1615–69), poet, gambler, royalist, High Sheriff of Surrey and sometime governor of Farnham Castle. He once persuaded **Charles I** to spare the life of a fellow poet, Roundhead **George Wither**, arguing that while Wither lived, 'I shall not be the worst poet in England'. Denham's poem contains the following lines:

> My eye, descending from the hill, surveys
> Where Thames among the wanton valley strays;
> Thames, the most loved of all the Ocean's sons
> By his old sire, to his embrace runs
> Hasting to pay his tribute to the sea
> Like mortal life to meet eternity.

On the hill's summit is an open common called **Englefield Green**, along with the **Commonwealth Air Forces Memorial**, a quadrangular structure designed by **Sir Edward Maufe** in 1953. The memorial bears 'the names of 20,456 airmen who have no known grave'. Below the hill is the **Magna Carta Memorial**, also designed by Maufe, presented by the American Bar Association in 1957 as a tribute to 'freedom under law'. A short distance away is the **Kennedy Memorial**, on an acre of land given to the American people in 1965 'in memory of John F Kennedy, born 19 May 1917, President of the United States, 1961–63, died by an assassin's hand 24 November 1963'.

Runnymede, administered by the National Trust (tel: 01784 432891; fax 01784 479007; email: runnymede@ntrust.org.uk; web: www.nationaltrust.org.uk/historicproperties/runnymede), should be visited because it is there, a milestone in the history of democracy. Ideally, you should visit before the great crowds start arriving not long after sunrise, or at twilight time, after they have left:

> It is a fine summer morning – sunny, soft and still . . . Gay-cloaked companies of knights and squires have ridden in, all travel-stained and dusty . . . And now lo! down upon the road that winds along the river bank from Staines there comes towards us, laughing and talking together in deep guttural bass, a half a score of stalwart halbert-men – Barons' men, these . . . And so, from hour to hour, march up along the road ever fresh groups and bands of armed men, their casques and breastplates flashing back along the long low lines of morning sunlight . . . And all the river down to Staines is dotted with small craft and boats and tiny coracles . . . It is noon . . . front and rear, and either flank, there ride the yeomen of the Barons, and in the midst King John . . .

> From *Three Men in a Boat* by Jerome K Jerome

As every English schoolchild knows, Runnymede was where wicked **King John** signed **Magna Carta** (or, rather, he sealed it, because he couldn't write). The charter limited his powers, made the barons more powerful and wealthier, supposedly paved the way for all men to become equal before the law; in reality, though, it did not do much at all for ordinary people.

Given by our hand in the meadow that is called Runnymede, between
Windsor and Staines, on the 15th day of June in the seventeenth year
of our reign [1215].

Did the opposing forces – the barons, who forced the king to wax his seal to
Magna Carta, and the king's men who didn't agree with the Carta's clauses –
occupy opposite banks of the river? Did they meet on the island now called
Magna Carta Island and was Magna Carta sealed there? Did King John
really rest the document on a flat stone, now in the 1834 Gothic villa on the
island, or use a proper table as surely seems more probable? And was the
famous charter the progressive document preceding democracy, as some say it
is, or did it merely prolong the power of the rich for generations as the authors
of *1066 and All That* maintain? We may judge for ourselves, for a copy of the
document is posted at the memorial site; it contains the following key words:

No man shall be taken, imprisoned, outlawed, banished or in any way
destroyed, nor will we proceed against or prosecute him, except by
lawful judgement of his equals and by the law of the land.

Rudyard Kipling (1868-1932) was intrigued by Runnymede – its mystic, its
place in English history. In his *Puck of Pook's Hill*, the sprite Puck tells of 'the
Law that was signed at Runnymede' and of 'Magna Carta signed on the island
in the Thames that carries its name'. In the last verse of *The Reeds of Runnymede*,
Kipling develops these ideas:

And still when Mob or Monarch lays
Too rude a hand on English ways
And whisper wakes, the shudder plays,
Across the reeds at Runnymede.
And Thames, that knows the moods of kings,
And crowds and priests and suchlike things
Rolls deep and dreadful as he brings
Their warnings down from Runnymede!

Visitor information Runnymede is open all year for walkers and cyclists,
day and night. For visitors arriving by car there is a riverside grass car
park open daily Apr 1–Sep 30 (10.00–19.00). For the remainder of the
year cars must use the hard-standing at the Magna Carta Tea Room,
which is open daily Apr 1–Sep 30 (08.30–17.30) and Oct–Mar
(09.20–16.30), except Christmas Day. There is a small shop at the
tearoom where hand-held audio 'wands' and braille guidebooks can be
hired for self-guided tours. In addition, there is an extensive programme
of guided walks throughout the year (for details, tel: 01784 477110).

The nearest railway stations are Egham (½ mile from Runnymede) and
Wraysbury (1 mile from Ankerwycke). While cycling is permitted on the
Thames Path, it is not in Coopers Hill Woods or on the meadow slopes.

On the opposite bank of the Thames, about midway along the Runnymede meadow, is **Ankerwycke Park**, acquired by the National Trust in 1998 and containing remains of the 11th-century Ankerwycke House, once the site of St Mary's Priory where **Henry VIII** sometimes met **Anne Boleyn**. Some of the Ankerwycke trees – in particular a huge yew, with a 33ft girth, near the priory ruins – are said to be over 2,000 years old. Jerome and his companions anchored for the night at Ankerwycke's 'Picnic Point', better known to boating people as 'The Picnic', a charming little wooden house with a thatched roof.

FROM RUNNYMEDE TO OLD WINDSOR

The Thames Path passes two of **Edwin Lutyens** gatehouses as it leaves Runnymede; the one across the road houses the Magna Carta Tea Room (see *Visitor information*, page 103). From here to Old Windsor, the Thames sweeps from Surrey into Berkshire on a ripple of green silk. It passes through woods

THE BELLS OF OUZELEY

A famous inn called **The Bells of Ouzeley**, which used to be picturesque but isn't now, stands next to the Thames Path. You will pass by it, a quarter-mile or so from the western end of Runnymede. It used to be tiny and snug, with a tea garden on the water's edge and tables wrapped round the trunks of apple trees. The present Bells of Ouzeley pub dates from 1936, when Jerome's 'picturesque inn' was pulled down and rebuilt. It is now a dreary mock-Tudor substitute, with a vast tarmacked car park, run by the Harvester Inns group.

Tradition has it that there was a hostelry here in the 12th century. The name stems from the 1530s dissolution of the monasteries, when, it is said, the bells from Oxford's **Osney Abbey** were spirited down river by monks trying to save them from Henry VIII's vandals. When the barges went aground the bells were hidden in the oozing mud. They have never been found. Only five glass bells on top of a cupboard in the bar serve as a reminder of the story that gave The Bells its name.

and meadows, marred only a little by rashes of north-bank bungaloidism, stretching two miles from Wraysbury to the weir stream at Ham Island above Old Windsor Lock. It's hard to believe the Thames has barely left Greater London.

Approximately three-quarters of a mile up-river from The Bells of Ouzeley (see box, page 104), between the Thames Path and the A308, is a general store and a post office.

The grave in Old Windsor churchyard

Attractive corners of Old Windsor remain, but by and large it is now bleak surburbia with little going for it. What it does have, though, beneath a fir-tree in the little churchyard of St Peter and St Andrew, is whatever is left of the once-beautiful **Mary Robinson** (1758–1800). Robinson was an actress and author, who in 1779 became one of the several mistresses of the future **George IV** when he was 17 and still 'prinny' and Beau Brummel's 'fat fwend'.

Mary was lovely, according to 18th-century tastes for chins, ivory plumpness and breasts like air-beds. In her later years she was '**Sappho**', the poet who turned out daily poems for the *Morning Post*. While her poetry is not great, it did find mention in Southey's *Annual Anthology* and a small place in the archives of the Romantic Movement. Before turning poet and, in later years, novelist, she was '**Perdita**', royal mistress and actress. **David Garrick** acted with her and coached her to play Cordelia at his Hampton villa. After a disastrous marriage, the Prince of Wales wooed her by letter (calling the 21-year-old Mary 'Perdita' – her acclaimed role in Shakespeare's *A Winter's Tale* – and himself 'Forizel'). In the end – after Mary caught her husband bonking a maid – George bribed her into bed, used her until he found someone raunchier, and then sent her on her way with a present of £20,000. This she exchanged for an annuity of £500 a year – not bad earnings for two years' off-and-on employment as a rpya; bed-mate. She 'retired' to an elegant riverside villa and was painted by **Joshua Reynolds**, **Thomas Gainsborough** and **George Romney**. She died before her time from a rheumatic complaint.

Her grave is a sad one, showered these days not with roses left by lovers but dead pine cones and needles. At one time, the grave was visited by gentry, by verse-makers, and by 'Perdita's' romancers. The poets **William Wordsworth** and **Samuel Coleridge** came, Coleridge, in particular, because he was in love with her verses and her memory.

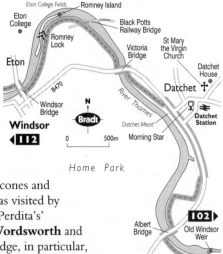

I discovered, by chance, the writings of a forgotten Victorian who describes meeting an ancient labourer in Old Windsor churchyard. He told the writer:

> There's not much in the churchyard to please you; only, maybe, like the rest of the gentry, you want to see what we used to call 'The tomb of the Fair Shepherdess'. She was a play-actor once. They say a king's love fell upon her like mildew, and, for all her beauty, withered her up; and then she died, poor thing. I can tell over the inscription to you – 'Mrs Mary Robinson, author of poems, and other literary works; died on the 26th of December, 1800, aged 43 years.' Why, you'll hardly believe it, now, when the gentry come and ask which is 'Pedita's' tomb? And I tell 'em, maybe they'll hardly damp their shoes to look at it, and ask each other what poems 'twas she wrote, and no one knows – not one can tell! But some fifty years ago, I've seen some, and from the Castle, too, who would tell them all over plain enough.

'Perdita' wrote the following bitter lines for her own memorial:

> On Thou! Whose cold and senseless heart
> Ne'er knew affection's struggling sign,
> Pass on, nor vaunt the Stoic's art,
> Nor mock this grave with tearless eye.
> No wealth had she, no power to sway;
> Yet rich in worth, and learning's store;
> She wept her summer hours away,
> She heard the wintry storm no more.

Memorials of interest inside the church include the recumbent effigy of **Sir Charles Augustus Murray**, a Victorian diplomat who gave London Zoo its first hippopotamus. A famous early artist, **Thomas Sandby** (1725–1809), who has been called 'the father of England's watercolour school' is also commemorated. In the churchyard is the box tomb of **Mrs Brinsley Sheridan**, wife of the 18th-century playwright.

Old Windsor Lock, Friday Island and Dr Grant

The Thames Path doesn't enter Old Windsor, but follows the riverbank, touching **Windsor Home Park** (open to the public for cricket matches, the Royal Windsor Horse Show and other genteel jollies) on the left-hand side. A mile ahead (1.6km) is **Old Windsor Lock**, which marks the start of a half-mile-long '**New Cut**', picturesque as an ancient canal, built in 1822. The original river course travels a mile-long hook round the back of **Ham Island** where there are sewage works. A short way downstream of the lock, on the far bank, is the thatched **Honeypot Cottage**, home of actress **Beryl Reid** from 1952 until 1996. A bank-side fisherman with whom I passed the time of day recalled her being 'as deliciously dotty as the parts she played' and 'giving a home to any stray cats found wandering around the place.'

Friday Island (footprint-shaped, hence its name) stems the weir stream (which runs furiously in flood) on the far side of Old Windsor Lock. The inventor of Marmite (which he didn't like!) and edible papers for secret agents, **Dr Julius Grant**, lived in the island's tiny two-bedroom cottage, served by its own well. He stayed there for 25 years, from the late 1960s until he died, aged 89, in 1991. Old Windsor lock-keeper, Roy Dunstan, was Dr Grant's neighbour and friend for eight years. He recalled,

> When [Dr Grant] went on to the island, he said it felt it was like going a million miles away . . . [I]t was like owning half of Australia, it was so secluded.

Dr Grant was a leading criminologist in his day, known as 'the man all forgers feared'. His most celebrated case was that in which he denounced the 'Hitler Diaries' – the very same diaries that had hoodwinked German and British experts. Dr Grant, however, detected that the paper they were written upon was 11 years too young to have belonged to the genuine Hitler.

DATCHET

Leaving Windsor Home Park on the left, the Thames Path crosses into Datchet over **Albert Bridge**, with the grey mound of **Windsor Castle** glimpsed through trees rigid as guardsmen, an appropriate simile for hereabouts.

Even now, although swollen into a large dormitory suburb of Windsor, Datchet manages to retain the 'villagey' traces of a long and sleepy past. This is where Shakespeare's **Falstaff** suffered at the hands of the servants of the *Merry Wives of Windsor* – in **Datchet Mead**, near the end of Datchet Lane. This 'gross watery pumpkin . . . carried in a basket, like a barrow of butcher's offal' was 'thrown in the Thames . . . the muddy ditch close by the Thames-side' to be 'cooled, glowing hot, in that surge, like a horse-shoe; think of that – hissing hot – think of that'.

Falstaff would have drowned had the river's edge not been 'shelvy and shallow', which it still is. He was never really slung into the Thames, or course. Or was he? A master at Eton College, **Samuel Evans**, hauled an ancient bronze fibula – a brooch for pinning clothing in place – out of the Datchet Thames in about 1874. It was in exceptionally good condition, about

DATCHET AND THE HERSCHELS

It's strange the people and things you come across when you don't expect them. I had known about Falstaff's ducking at Datchet, but I knew little about the famous astronomer **William Herschel** (1738–1822), or anything at all about his equally remarkable sister, **Caroline** (1750–1848), nor their connections with Datchet.

A man I met in the Morning Star public house, at the corner of the green near Datchet church, put me right. The pub is a fine one with wooden floors, simple furniture and an old stone fireplace; in the main bar are artefacts relating to Sir William Herschel. As best I can recall, this is what my acquaintance told me:

> Sir William Herschel lived here, in the village, along with his sister, Caroline Herschel, who was also an astronomer. They were German, like the family at the big house on the mound [the royal family at Windsor Castle], and they both had a scientific sort of friendship with the king, George III. They often went to soirées at Windsor Castle to tell the royal family about celestial things.
>
> William was so well-thought-of by the king that he was given a royal pension with which he bought a house in Datchet in 1772, mostly so that he could be close to his royal master. Caroline moved in with him. They watched the heavens through their telescopes together, and it was at Datchet [and at a later home, 'Observatory House', in Slough] where William observed and made notes about the Milky Way, which he called 'the island universe'.

The couple lived in Satis House, next door to Cedar House, which has now been replaced by a block of flats. It was here that Caroline Herschel carved her own considerable astronomical reputation by discovering eight comets between 1786 and 1797 and three nebulae in 1783. After her brother's death in 1822 this remarkable lady married and returned to Germany where she stayed until she died aged 97.

four inches long, with seven amber and two blue glass beads. It is now in the Myers Museum at Eton College. Could it have belonged to Falstaff? I wonder.

Old Datchet remains a 'seemly' little place – a row of red-bricked, river-folks' homes called 'The Beach', a ravel of Georgian-elegant streets, several detached early-Victorian yellow-brick villas, and a pleasant village green. Near the river are **Datchet Lodge** and bow-fronted **Old Bridge House**. The 17th-century **Cedar House**, with a fine cedar tree in the front, has a small powder room where gentry powdered their wigs. **Datchet Manor House**, with a plaster cat chasing a mouse over the roof, now houses an antiques business. **Ditton Park**, once Ditton Manor Estate, was used as the Admiralty Compass Observatory (1917–79) for researching space and other spooky things. It now belongs to the Calor Gas Company.

The considerable **St Mary the Virgin** village church, in London Road, was rebuilt in the 1850s, but contains some good 18th-century monuments and a brass of 1593. A tablet records the death of **Robert Baker**, who printed the Authorised Version of the Bible in 1611. The tower is octagonal and excessively ornamented. Above the inner doorway is an impressive royal coat of arms, made for the church in 1683 and restored not long ago; it was once compulsory to show a royal coat of arms in all churches 'by order of King Charles II'. The chancel has two interesting brasses: one to the memory of **Lady Katheryn Barkeley** and the other erected in 1593 to the memory of **Richard Hambery**.

Datchet House, next to the church, is an 18th-century building where a film star, **Laura La Plant**, lived in the 1930s. She had the whole roof lowered seven inches and her bedroom walls painted with tropical scenes.

There's a 'cats' cemetery' in Datchet, or what remains of one. When **Lady Mabel Cholmondeley** died at Leigh House in the early 1920s, her will ordered that the 30 cats buried in the garden's shrubbery, together with coffins and tombstones, should not be disturbed. Ever. When the house was pulled down in the 1930s to make way for **Leigh Park Estate**, the island of shrubs was left in the middle of the road. It's still there, I am assured, but all trace of the tombstones has gone.

After Datchet, the Thames Path returns to the Windsor side of the Thames via **Victoria Bridge**. It then dips under the ugly **Black Potts railway bridge** (which carries the South Western line from Staines into the Windsor and Eton Riverside station) on the bend before the granite steps and trim garden of **Romney Lock** (water tap and toilets). On the right, beyond **Romney Island**, are the **Eton College** playing fields. Ahead, at the end of the cut beyond the lock, is the squat grey mound of **Windsor Castle's Round Tower** which, incidentally, is not as round as it looks.

Isaac Walton – the father of angling books, who believed 'angling is somewhat like poetry, men are born to be so' – used to fish from Romney Island in the company of **Charles Cotton** (1630–87). The latter wrote a much-revered treatise on fly-fishing for the fifth edition of Walton's *Compleat Angler*. Sometimes the sublime **John Donne** (1572?–1631), poet and Dean of St Paul's, accompanied them. Another fisherman, **Charles II**, used to fish the Thames from a punt in the Black Potts reach, with **Antonio Verrio** (1640–1707), an Italian painter commissioned by the king to decorate Windsor Castle. **Alexander Pope** wrote:

> Methinks I see our mighty monarch stand,
> The pliant rod now trembling in his hand;
> And see he now doth up from Datchet come...

Windsor and Eton

WINDSOR

Books have been written, and will continue to be written, about 'Royal' Windsor. Snippets of its history, things, and people, are the best I can offer.

Windsor Castle

At least three-quarters of the people who visit Windsor, and probably more than that, only come to see the castle. Its Disneyland towers and turrets are everyone's idea of what a fairytale castle should look like. And, of course, the Queen and her Court live there, in Regency hard-but-regal comfort. **William the Conqueror** built the first Windsor Castle, judging its location

> . . . a place appearing proper and convenient for a royal retirement on account of the river and its nearness to the forest for hunting, and many other royal conveniences.

Henry II rebuilt it. Other monarchs, especially **Edward VI**, **Henry VII** and **Henry VIII**, did their bits as well, but none of them had much to do with the way the castle looks today. That's down to the Georgians and then the Victorians, and one in particular: **Sir Jeffrey Wyattville** (1766–1840). His demolition, restoration and embellishments spanned three reigns: those of George IV, William IV and Victoria. He tore down the buildings overlooking the river and replaced them with towers and whatnot. His work, say knowing architectural critics, is 'clumsy', 'unromantic', 'uninspired', and the end result cleverly described as 'an enlarged toy fort'.

Ummm, well, other people admire it and there is no denying that the whole, viewed from the river above the bridge, is picturesque and impressive.

Wyattville may not have been a great architect, but he was a great snob. His name was really Wyatt, but he changed it, partly to avoid being mistaken for his uncle (a much

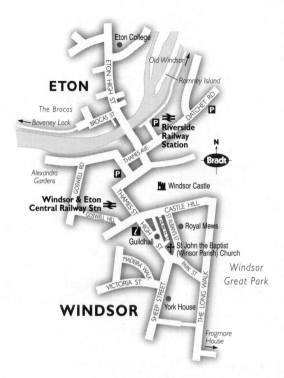

better architect) but mostly because he decided 'Wyattville' had a more orotund echo about it, sounding much more 'the thing' when he was promised a knighthood. The story goes that he asked if it was all right for him to add 'ville' to his name. The king replied: 'Veal or mutton – call yourself what you will.' So he did.

What you do, what you see, depends on how much time you've got. Given the greater part of a day, then you can cover quite a bit of ground. Given less, then it's best you take the bus tour (information at the TIC; see page 114), taking in Windsor, Eton and its college, Datchet, the Long Walk, and the Home Park.

You are certain to visit the castle. Mr and Mrs **Samuel Pepys** did. They were enchanted:

> [T]he most romantic castle that is in the world. But, Lord! the
> prospect that is in the balcone in the Queene's lodgings, and the
> terrace and walk, are strange. . . being the best in the world, sure.
> Infinitely satisfied I and my wife with all this, she being in all points
> mightily pleased too, which added to my pleasure.

The main castle entrance is by **Henry VIII's Gateway**, not far from **No 2 Castle Hill**. Here there is a plaque to a forgotten author and publisher, **Charles Knight** (1791–1873). He was proprietor of the *Windsor and Eton Express* from 1811 to 1821, and the first publisher of 'penny populars' such as

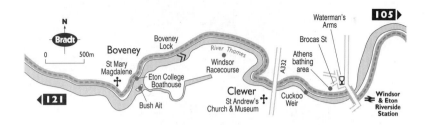

the *Penny Cyclopaedia* (1833–44) and the *Popular History of England* (1862). But these are not the reasons why he is remembered, if he is remembered at all. His father, a Mayor of Windsor, kept a bookshop and one of his customers was **George III**. The latter was once observed, outside the shop, eagerly reading Tom Paine's newly published and revolutionary *Rights of Man* (1791–2) – regarded as unsuitable reading for a monarch.

Visitor information Changing of the Guard takes place Mon–Sat at 11.00 (April to end of June), or on odd calendar days of the months for the remainder of the year (except Sun).

The castle precincts and State Apartments

The castle precincts, leading to the State Apartments, provide some spectacular views over the Thames and surrounding countryside. In August and September the formal gardens at the end of King Henry VIII's north terrace are open to visitors.

Visitor information The castle precincts are open daily 10.00–17.00 (sometimes closing earlier). It used to be free to walk through the castle precincts but it's not any more. In fact it costs a whopping £11.50 for adults, £9.50 for senior citizens, £6 for children – but the price of admission does include each and every one of the castle's attractions, including the State Apartments and St George's Chapel. There are shops and toilets. For general enquires, tel: 01753 868186 ; for 24-hour recorded information, tel: 01753 831118.

The State Apartments are the heart of the working palace, used for ceremonial and official occasions. They are magnificent – most of the 16 rooms are open, despite the devastating fire of November 20 1992. Miraculously, only one painting was destroyed by this fire – and it was one that **George III** had wanted to burn some 200 years earlier! On view is an amazing collection of bric-a-brac: tapestries, armour (including a suit belonging to **Henry VIII**), furniture, paintings by Rembrandt, Van Dyck, Rubens, Holbein and others, and, of course,

the remarkable 'Queen's Dolls' House'. Designed by **Sir Edwin Lutyens**, and originally shown at the Wembley Exhibition in 1924–5, it is over eight feet long and five feet wide, contains miniature books and paintings by contemporary artists, and has working plumbing and electric lighting. Next door is an exhibition of drawings from the Queen's priceless collection; the display, changed from time to time, usually contains works by Holbein, Leonardo da Vinci and Michelangelo.

Visitor information The State Apartments are generally open whenever the castle precincts are open (daily 10.00–17.00). These hours can vary, however, so it is best to check before visiting (tel: 01753 868286). The State Apartments are also closed three times a year, when the queen is officially in residence at Easter, during June, and in December.

St George's Chapel

St George's Chapel is breathtaking, a spectacular example of perpendicular-style architecture. Its wedding cake pinnacles, flying buttresses and delicately fretworked parapets are all in dramatic contrast to the sturdy surrounding castle buildings. Begun by **Edward IV**, completed by **Henry VIII**, the chapel took 51 years to build, and hasn't been changed much since the heraldic badges in the roof were finished in 1518. The banners of Garter Knights splash the choir with colour; behind are knights' coats of arms in burnished metal; and high above is a stupendous web of fan vaulting. Ten monarchs are buried here, the **Black Prince** married the '**Maid of Kent**' here, and **Henry VIII** lies beneath the choir floor with his favourite wife, **Jane Seymour**.

Visitor information Open Mon–Sat 10.00–16.00, Sun 14.00–16.00. Free entry to services Mon–Sat 07.30, 08.00, and 17.15 (sung evensong, excluding Wed), Sun 08.30, 10.45, 11.45 and 17.15 (sung evensong). Note that St George's Chapel closes to prepare for special occasions. For information, tel: 01753 865538; for 24-hour recorded information, tel: 01753 831118.

The town

Personally speaking, I've 'done' the castle so many times that these days I prefer to amble through the medieval cobbled lanes of bustling Windsor town, or wander into the ravishingly beautiful 4,800-acre **Windsor Great Park**.

Visitor information Follow the finger-post signs to the tourist information office in Thames Street to pick up a town map, guide and leaflets. Tourist information centre open Apr–Oct Mon–Sat 09.30–18.00, Sun 10.30am–17.30; Nov–Mar Mon–Sat 09.30–17.00, Sun 11.00–16.00.

You could try telephoning the TIC on 01753 852010, but I wouldn't if I were you. I knew a man who once actually talked by telephone to someone at Windsor's TIC. We used to pat him on the back and buy him drinks because we were so proud of his achievement. Most other callers hang up because the number is always engaged or, if they do make a miraculous breakthrough, find themselves listening to one of those disconnected voices that offer options on this or that, but never the options you want. If I were you I would call in person at the TIC, and only then if you don't mind standing in seemingly endless queues.

Opposite Henry VIII's Gate on Castle Hill is the cobbled **Church Street**, Windsor's old market area. This is where **Eleanor 'Nell' Gwyn** lived (see box opposite). The **Old King's Head** pub, oldest of Windsor's many inns, is also in Church Street. It was here, in 1648, that leading Parliamentarians met to declare that **King Charles I** 'should be prosecuted for his life as a criminal person'. A reproduction of the signed death warrant is on the wall of the building.

At the ruined red-bricked building, framing a tiny garden, in Church Street, turn right to the monumental **Guildhall**, built by **Sir Christopher Wren** in 1713. It contains an exhibition of royal portraits and a display of Windsor's silver plate. The Guildhall's six sturdy columns down the centre of the hall were added by Wren after the burgesses complained the building was going to fall down. Wren gave them their pillars, but ended them an inch short of the ceiling to prove they were unnecessary.

Visitor information The Guildhall is open Mondays only, 10.00–14.00. Free admission. There are toilets immediately opposite, in High Street.

Next to the Guildhall is the quaint, leaning, **Market Cross House**. It is now a tearoom, and seemingly in danger (though not) of toppling over. Almost

NELL GWYN'S HOUSE

Eleanor 'Nell' Gwyn (1650–87), the actress and royal mistress, lived in Church Street. She inhabited the uncharacteristically straight and narrow house marked with a tablet, 'Nell Gwyn's House', one of two homes she occupied in Windsor; the other is in what is now the Royal Mews in St Alban's Street. Nell is the best-remembered of **King Charles II**'s 17 acknowledged mistresses. Small, with long, shapely legs, generous breasts, a heart-shaped face, hazel eyes and chestnut hair, she had graduated from her mother's brothel to become an orange seller, actress and king's mistress while still a teenager. Before climbing into the king's bed for the first time in 1667, soon after Charles had tired of Lady Castlemaine, Nell had pleasured a good many others, including the poet **John Dryden**. She was the rage of London. **Pepys** called her, first, 'pretty and witty Nell' after seeing her as Florimel in Dryden's *Maiden Queen*; later he revised his description, referring to her as 'that jade' and 'a bold merry slut' after 'the King did send several times for Nell'. She bedded King Charles after liaisons with an actor and an aristocrat, each called Charles; as a consequence, she dubbed the king 'my Charles the third'. A doggerel verse about her was soon making the rounds of Windsor:

> She hath got a trick to handle his prick
> But never lay hands upon his sceptre.

Nell maintained a permanent place in the king's ménage (even though she was temporarily eclipsed by Moll Davis), providing him with an irresistible and arousing mix of relaxation and entertainment. Charles judged this mix to be worth every penny of an annual £5,000 pension for services rendered, and begged, upon his deathbed, 'Let not poor Nelly starve'.

opposite is a plaque recalling **H G Wells**'s apprenticeship to a firm of Windsor drapers here, portrayed in his novel *The History of Mr Polly*:

> Mr Polly was not naturally interested in hosiery and gentlemen's outfitting. . . He was apprenticed in one of those large, rather low-class establishments which sell everything from pianos and furniture to books and millinery, a department store . . . There he remained six years. He spent most of the time inattentive to business, in a sort of uncomfortable happiness, increasing his indigestion.

We shall meet Mr Wells, a bit of a Thamesider, and Mr Polly again, a little further up-river.

Turn left into **High Street** and visit the 1872 **Windsor parish church**, which contains a royal pew with **Grinling Gibbons** carvings, and a painting, *The Last Supper*, by **Franz de Cley**, James I's painter. This was presented to the church by **George III**, who delighted in giving away paintings he didn't like.

Windsor Home Park, Frogmore House, the Long Walk and Windsor Great Park

You are going to get fed up with crowds in Windsor; the place is too small to cope. It is possible to shake them off – well, some of them – by visiting parts of Windsor which the castle-crammers don't get to in quite so many numbers: Windsor Home Park and Frogmore House, The Long Walk and Windsor Great Park.

We passed the eastern end of **Home Park** on the way into Windsor. The north part of the park is always open to the public, but the eastern end, containing the delightful 18th-century royal mansion, **Frogmore House**, and its gardens, is the queen's retreat and only open to you and me a few days every year (see opposite for details).

Frogmore has been used by royals as a hideaway ever since **George III** and his **Queen Caroline** bought it in 1792. They played 'mothers and fathers' here, this quite likeable monarch and his faithful wife, who were portrayed almost kindly in Alan Bennett's play (which was made into a film), *The Madness of King George*. Until then, poor George had not been treated well. One eminent Victorian, **William Edward Hartpole Lecky** (1838–1903), called him 'ignorant, arbitrary, narrow-minded'. Yet during his reign no monarch had been more popular, and he was regarded with widespread sympathy for the illness (since diagnosed as porphyria, genetic disease) which imprisoned this sad man, sometimes in Frogmore but mostly in Windsor Castle. He was faithful to his wife, a faithfulness which sired 15 children, some conceived, it is said, in the gardens of Frogmore which 'Mister King' and 'Missus Queen' loved with a passion. I believe it was here, in one of his insane times, that the king wandered through the garden wondering how it was that apples managed to get inside an apple dumpling.

Equally fond of Frogmore were **Queen Victoria** and **Prince Albert**. She loved the place so well that she wrote of it,

> All is peace and quiet and you only hear the hum of the bees, the singing of the birds.

Victoria broke with royal tradition and had herself and her husband buried in a lavish mausoleum in the 30 acres of landscaped and picturesque gardens. The poet John Betjeman wrote, in his contribution to *Murray's Berkshire Guide*:

> The Queen's grief still sobs through its [the mausoleum's] interior as though she had left her sorrow on earth to haunt this rich, forbidding temple to her loneliness.

The Long Walk and **Windsor Great Park** are found at the top of elegant **Park Street**, off High Street, through lantern-topped, stone-pillared park gates. To the left are stunning views of the State Apartments, and the pedestrian-way to Frogmore House and gardens; to the right is The Long Walk, straight as a die (three miles long, to the perimeter of Ascot race course), laid out by **Charles II** and **Queen Anne**. The royal family passes this way during Ascot week, first in cars, then changing into open horse-drawn carriages just past the '**Copper Horse**' (an equestrian statue of George II, riding in Roman toga without stirrups) at the end of The Long Walk.

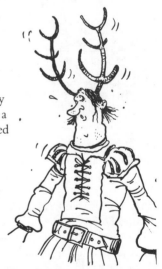

Windsor Great Park sprawls 4,800 acres, a mere remnant of a much vaster royal hunting forest which once covered most of southern Berkshire south of Windsor Castle. Dusk is the best time of all to visit the park for then you may hear the hunting horn of **Hearne the Hunter**, a favourite huntsman of **Richard II**. When mauled by a deer, Hearne exchanged his hunting skills with a wizard in return for saving his life. The wizard secured a set of antlers to Hearne's head and so he became the hunted instead of the hunter. Grief-stricken, he hung himself from a tree in Windsor forest, almost plumb in the middle of Windsor Home Park, still known as '**Hearne's Oak**' and said to be impossible to find.

Shopping

It's easy to find tourist-style souvenir shops in Windsor, but not so easy to track down good old, run-of-the-mill stores selling ordinary, everyday provisions. Find **Goswell Road** and **Goswell Hill**, and you've as good as cracked it. Immediately on the right up Goswell Hill, there's a flight of steps leading to a new shopping precinct, King Edward Court, where you will find a supermarket, shoe shops, department stores, Boots and Dixons, and more of that sort of thing. The court connects with **Peascod Street** where a Marks & Spencer, a Woolworth, and a post office are located. At the top end of Peascod Street is High Street, where there are four major clearing banks with hole-in-the-wall cash-dispensing facilities.

ETON AND ITS COLLEGE

The Thames Path crosses from garter to gown, from Windsor to Eton, via **Windsor Bridge**, an early example (1824) of cast ironwork, and therefore interesting rather than lovely. It is closed to motor traffic.

'The river throws its arm about Eton with an ample swing,' wrote the critic and biographer, **Percy Lubbock** (1879–1965). 'The Thames is a very lordly water, in these middle reaches.'

Eton is essentially a single narrow high street, well filled with antique shops and genteel cafés for the stuffing of young Etonians by visiting mothers and fathers. **Eton College** is at the end of the street. It was founded by **Henry VI** in 1440 to serve 'ten sad priests, four lay clerks, six choristers, twenty-five grammar-scholars, and twenty-five poor men to pray for the king.' Noblemen and gentlemen have since taken possession, though never to the entire exclusion of 'poor scholars'. Some 1,280 boys, aged 13 to 18, are nowadays taught by no less than 143 masters (a ratio of about nine pupils to every teacher) and ruled by ancient customs and taboos. 'Eton,' declared **Daniel Defoe**, 'is the finest school that is in Britain, perhaps in Europe.'

The boys confetti the high street, hatless, in coat-tails, diving in and out of book shops, bun shops and the sort of gentlemen's outfitters found nowhere else in the world outside London, Oxford, and Cambridge. Most visitors come to goggle at the boys in long-tailed fancy dress, some to wander in and wonder at the college's ramble of old buildings, and a few because famous men, when they were boys, once ambled across the cobbled School Yard. The school has bequeathed England a historic pedigree, not to mention its jacket and collar, its 'crop' and the awful 'Eton Boating Song'.

The most famous Etonian of all is, perhaps, the **Duke of Wellington**, victor at Waterloo and later prime minister. He didn't much care for the school, left when he was only 13 and never played ball games here, so it seems unlikely he ever declared, as people believe, that 'The battle of Waterloo was won on the playing fields of Eton'.

OLD ETONIAN WRITERS

There are 98 names included on the college lists of Old Etonian 'Writers, Poets, Wits, Scholars, Schoolmasters'. Below is a flavour of some the school has produced.

The poet **Thomas Gray** (1716–71), best remembered for 'Elegy Written in a Country Churchyard', loved his Eton days, even though he forever referred to himself and his fellow pupils as 'little victims'. He was himself a 'little victim', despised by his peers as a 'fop' for reading instead of hunting and walking instead of riding. 'Walking' for Gray meant strolls in nearby Burnham Beeches, where he discovered 'mountains and precipices'. His best friend at Eton was **Horace Walpole**, with whom he frequently stayed in later years at Strawberry Hill. He recalled his schooldays at Eton – of which he declared, 'where ignorance is bliss, 'tis folly to be wise' – in his first published poem, 'Ode on a Distant Prospect of Eton':

> Of Windsor's heights the expanse below
> Of grove, of lawn, of mead survey,
> Whose turf, whose shade, whose flowers among
> Wanders the hoary Thames along
> His silver-winding way.

Shortly before Gray arrived at the college, the novelist **Henry Fielding** (1707–54) was here, girding his loins for a life of amorous adventures not unlike those retold in his rumbustious *The History of Tom Jones*. Fielding had barely left Eton, at 17, when he set about abducting a comely young heiress from her home in Lyme Regis, Dorset, failed, was bound over to keep the peace, and sent abroad.

The Thamesider poet **Percy Bysshe Shelley** (1792–1822), whom we shall meet again further up-river, was another Etonian eccentric. His explosive schoolboy experiments with chemicals and his outspoken opinions earned him the nicknames 'Mad Shelley' and 'Atheist Shelley'. **Algernon Swinburne** (1837–1909), another eccentric, was at Eton. So were **Eric Blair** (better known as **George Orwell**; 1903–50), who said he d dn't learn much, and **Ian Fleming** (1907–71), who said he did, and smoked cigarettes in a long holder, even then.

A good many other prime ministers came out of Eton, 19 in all, stretching from **Robert Walpole** (1676–1745; prime minister 1721–42) to **Harold Macmillan** (1894–1986; prime minister 1957–63) and **Alec Douglas-Home** (1903–95; prime minister 1963–4). The names of former Etonians carved on a desk panel at Upper School include those of Walpole and **Pitt the Elder**. (For details of some Old Etonian writers, see box, page 119.)

Aldous Huxley (1894–1963) briefly taught at Eton in 1917; so, too, did **David Cornwell** (also known as **John le Carré**; born 1931). Longest serving, and arguably the most remarkable master in Eton's history, was **Dr Keate** (1809–34). He was also the college's greatest flogging head and once flogged 80 boys, one after the other. He was caricatured by the historian **Alexander Kinglake** (1809–91):

> He was little more (if more at all) than five feet in height, and was not very great in girth, but within this space was concentrated the pluck of ten battalions. You could not put him out of humour, that is out of the ill-humour which he thought to be fitting for a Head Master. His red, shaggy eyebrows were so prominent that he habitually used them as arms and hands for the purpose of pointing out any object towards which he wished to direct attention. He wore a fancy dress, partly resembling the costume of Napoleon, partly that of a widow woman.

A fine orator, Keate taught boys to use voice and gesture. Two of his pupils became prime ministers: **Derby** and **Gladstone**. Keate founded the Eton Society in 1811; initially a debating society, it met in Mrs Hatton's lollipop shop on the site of what is now School Hall, and became known as 'Pop' (derived, perhaps, from lollipop, or from the Latin *'popina'* meaning 'eating house'). 'Pop' is now responsible for maintaining school discipline.

Visitor information Windsor Tourist Office's (see box, page 114) guided afternoon tours (May–Oct) around Eton College are recommended. The chapel (a replica of the chapel of King's College, Cambridge; the most striking of buildings, containing exquisite 15th-century paintings), the cobbled School Yard (the first quadrangle, entered through a building called Upper School), and the Cloisters, are open daily 14.00–17.00, and 10.30–12.30 during school holidays. For information on Eton College, tel: 01753 863593.

Eton College's annual festival is held on the nearest Saturday to June 4, birthday of **George III**. George regularly used to stroll down from his castle home on the hill to the college for a chat, and remains Eton's favourite royal patron. The festival is marked by a procession of boats on the backwater behind **Romney Island**, the wearing of weird naval uniforms, much guzzling of strawberries, a tailback of Rolls Royces, and recitations from literature by senior boys wearing tailcoats, knee-breeches, and black silk stockings.

Windsor Bridge to Maidenhead

11

Distances From Windsor Bridge: Boveney Lock 1.9 miles (3.06km), Bray Lock 5.07 miles (7.16km), Maidenhead Town Bridge 6.53 miles (10.51 km)

The names of Thameside towns and villages above Windsor and Eton read like a Betjeman litany: Boveney and Bray, Cliveden and Cookham, Marlow and Hurley, Bisham and Henley, Pangbourne, Streatley, Goring . . .

Upstream of Windsor Bridge, the ever-narrowing middle reaches of the Thames are fine. Beyond Maidenhead they are finer still, some say as good as they get: great beechwoods roll down to the water's edge, limbs as sheen as silk-stockinged legs; little grebes – gleaming chestnut in summer plumage – dive like conjuring tricks; coots tail-waggle from sight; and comely stone cottages, ochreous and time-worn, squat content beside the greening river.

Motor launches, steamers, punts and skiffs slip past at a snail's pace.

Here are willow-fringed Edwardian villas with velvet lawns, inns gay with umbrellas, terrace gardens shadowed by giant willows, weirs, ancient locks, historic houses and abbey ruins. This is a still-rural England where cows graze hock-deep in buttercup meadows and old men with walnut-crinkled faces keep guardian eyes on clouds, the weather, their cattle – and passing strangers.

It is right and proper that after Eton (left down Brocas Street and beyond the Waterman's Arms and Eton College Boathouse) the Thames Path passes through a meadow, Brocas

Meadow. Here the river appears to be greener than it was down-river of the bridge. Behind, majestic Windsor Castle towers over the town. Opposite, a man with a dog, and a boy and girl, linked by hands and each other, wander the promenade of Alexandra Gardens. Ahead is a railway bridge, and the Elizabeth road bridge carrying the A355 link; then, on this bank, is a featureless platform with a bench and a tablet explaining this is 'Athens', traditional bathing place for Eton College boys. School law requires that 'boys who are undressed must either get at once into the water or get behind screens when boats containing ladies come in sight.' On the opposite bank is enclosed Cuckoo Weir, where junior Eton boys bathe, Clewer village beyond, and Windsor Racecourse behind the trees upstream of that.

CLEWER VILLAGE

There are some intriguing pieces of history's jetsam in Clewer, where there is a youth hostel close to **St Andrew's Church** and a local history museum (for opening times, contact Windsor TIC on 0753 852010).

The upright Victorian prime minister, **William Gladstone** (1809–98), used to send prostitutes to Clewer when he had finished doing whatever he did with them. He would pick them up at night, 'comfort them', 'save them', and give them their train fare to Clewer where they were 'rehabilitated' in a convent in Hatch Lane.

In the churchyard is the grave of **Sir Daniel Gooch** who was the Great Western Railway's first locomotive engineer and created the great railway centre at Swindon in Wiltshire. He designed superb broad-gauge locomotives, attaining speeds and reliability not previously considered feasible nor exceeded since. He later helped inaugurate telegraphic communications between England and America, sending the first cable message across the Atlantic in 1866; for this he was made a baronet. Also buried in Clewer churchyard are some of the victims of the Titanic disaster, and 'Nanny Mary (Mary Ann Hull)' who looked after Queen Victoria's children (or so it claims on her tombstone).

BOVENEY LOCK

Abreast of Windsor Racecourse, two miles (3km) upstream of Windsor Bridge, is Boveney Lock. It is lovely, especially in lilac time. A simple wooden footbridge spans the lock. To the right, a stone's throw from the river, wrapped cosy in a nest of tall, thick trees, are the large, timber-framed Tudor buildings of Boveney, scattered around a green – 'so heavily restored as to give doubts as to their authenticity', according to one authority.

OAKLEY COURT – COUNT DRACULA'S CASTLE

Three miles (4.7km) up-river of Boveney Lock, on the opposite, Berkshire, bank is gothic-weird Oakley Court (Windsor Road, Water Oakley; tel: 01753 609988), a 92-bedroomed bric-a-brackery of spooky towers and fanciful stone animals crouching on the roof. It is so rich in Victorian flummery that you wonder why a generation so wealthy in literature was so poor in architecture. Add a puff or two of dry ice over the lawns, which stretch nearly three quarters of a mile along the river, and the house could serve – indeed, probably has served – as Count Dracula's castle. You will have seen the property before, lots of times, if you watch ageing horror movies. The house and grounds used to be the property of **Hammer Films** in the 1950s and 1960s, when they starred in a good many of their very worst films as well as some quite good ones: *St Trinian's*, *Half a Sixpence* and *The Rocky Horror Picture Show*. The French general, and later first president of the fifth republic, **Charles de Gaulle** (1890–1970), lived at Oakley Court during World War II. He used to stalk the lawns reflecting on the perfidy of the British and the nobility of the French. The house is now a hotel.

It's a pity the building is on the wrong side of the river for Thames Pathers because you can get a good full cream tea on the lawns here.

Boveney's strange little chapel of **St Mary Magdalene** stands alone on the riverbank. Services are no longer held there, but a key may be borrowed from **Boveney Place** (see notice-board outside the chapel for directions).

DOWN PLACE

Behind Oakley Court (see box above) is another big house; neat, well-bred, and devoid of fiddly ornamentation, Down Place is not a bit like Oakley Court. Only just visible from the Thames Path, it was the one-time home of **Jacob Tonson** (1656–1736), a bookseller who purchased the copyright of *Paradise Lost* from **John Milton**, shrewd fellow. He was also founder/secretary of the **Kit-Kat Club**, which flourished from 1700 to 1730 and whose members – including statesman **Robert Walpole** (1676–1745), dramatist and poet **William Congreve** (1670–1729), and essayists and politicians **Joseph Addison** (1672–1719) and **Richard Steele** (1672–1729) – met in the Great Hall. Addison, in particular, looked forward to his visits to Down Place. In a letter to a friend he described its rural attractions:

> I want to invite you to a concert of music which I have found in a
> neighbouring wood. It consists of a blackbird, a thrush, a robin
> redbreast and a bull finch. There is a lark by the way of an overture,
> the whole is concluded by a nightingale . . .

In theory the club was a literary one, but in practice it plotted to replace the Stuarts with the House of Hanover. At full strength there were 48 members, whose portraits, now in London's National Portrait Gallery, were painted by German-born **Sir Godfrey Kneller** (1646–1723). The club's name, by the way, honoured a Thames baker called Kit Catt who supplied the membership with mutton pies – or so the story goes.

DORNEY COURT

Just over half a mile further upstream on the Thames Path bank – almost abeam of Queen's Ait and Bray Marina in **Dorney Reach** – is another big house, the enchanting 16th-century manor of Dorney Court. It is huddled close to the small stone-and-flint church of **St James**; a footpath, the 'Barge Path', leads from the riverside to the house. This is quintessential England, a nest of timelessness, unchanged over the last 600 years. Yet no more than half a mile away the M4 growls its unceasing growl and, in the fields behind the house, JCB diggers prowl fields which are soon to become Eton College's new boating lake.

Astonishingly, here stands a perfect Tudor manor, its roof dipped by time, its gables fitted with barge boards. It grows from the earth, guarded by fat, sculpted yew hedges and backed by a delectable church. The house has been in the possession of the Palmer family since the 1500s. A Palmer – Peregrine – sometimes conducts visitors through the house today.

Charles II's mistress, **Barbara Villiers**, was a Mrs Palmer. In 1669 she married Roger Palmer, who was created Earl of Castlemaine – which, apparently, he considered adequate compensation for her being bonked by the king. Charles used to strut his stuff with Barbara at Dorney. She was lovely; at a recent National Portrait Gallery exhibition of 'Restoration Ladies', an entire room seemed to be positively intoxicated by her charms. **Samuel Pepys** even dreamed about her, describing 'the best [dream] I ever dreamed. [I was] having my Lady Castlemaine in my arms, and was admitted to use all the daliance I desired of her.' Pepys even chronicled his monarch's bedroom doings with the lady: 'The king and she did send for a pair of scales and they did weigh one another'. (Everyone to their own!)

The long-term affair, looked upon as a bit of a romp by Joe and Josephine Public, was no secret. Charles even offered a reward of £1,000 to whoever unmasked the rogue who had penned the rhyme:

> The reason why she is not duck'd
> Because by Caesar she is . . .

In the king's honour, the Dorney gardener **Charles Rose** produced the first 'king-pine' (pineapple) to be grown in England. He presented it to Charles in 1668, an event recorded in a copy of a painting by **Hendrik Danckerts** (1625–79) – the original is believed to be in America – which shows the merry monarch looking extremely chary of the thing. There is also a pineapple carved from wood in one of Dorney's rooms.

The church next door, unpretentious and un-Victorianised, is delightful. There are some 16th-century seats, a 12th-century font, a 17th-century musicians' gallery and a splendid tomb of the **Gerrard family**. The Gerrards were grocers who owned the court and gave their name to Gerrards Cross; the Palmers married into the family in the 16th century.

Visitor information The house, appearing as 'Syon' in the film *Lady Jane*, is open July–August (Mon–Thu 13.00–16.30), and bank holidays (and the preceding Sun) in May. Admission £5.50.

Just upstream of the footpath leading to Dorney is a new footbridge over the Thames, opened in 1996 primarily to carry a conveyor belt hauling gravel from the Eton College rowing-lake excavation behind Dorney Court. When completed the 1.5-mile rowing trench will be known as Dorney Lake Park and Nature Reserve.

MONKEY ISLAND

After Summerleaze footbridge, the Thames Path passes **Monkey Island**. This is in fact no longer an island but leashed to the Berkshire shore, on the opposite side of the river, by a footbridge. Linking this once-solitary island to the mainland is a strange thing to have done; until 1956 it was still a proper island, could only be reached by boat, and all the more romantic for it.

The Monkey Island building is a hotel serving visitors with lunches and teas and allowing them to lodge there providing the management approves of the cuts of their jibs. On their release from prison the '**Birmingham Six**' stayed here, so they must have passed muster.

Inside hangs an Edwardian photograph of a regal luncheon party held on the Monkey Island lawn. The bearded face of King Edward VII dominates the gathering and beside him, solemn in a sailor suit, sits his young grandson who was to become, briefly, Edward VIII and then the Duke of Windsor. Two other sovereigns are in the photograph, the future George V and George VI.

The island is very redolent of the raj, with resident peacock, fishing lodge and pavilion set in more than four acres. It gets its name from a series of ceiling pictures of monkeys doing human things, which the third Duke of Marlborough commissioned for the main building in 1738. It became a hotel in 1840 and the paintings are still there, in the banqueting hall. No-one knows who painted them. Mr and Mrs Hall in their *Book of the Thames* (1859) described the ceiling:

> The most ludicrous scene occupies the centre . . . and is a burlesque
> on the triumph of Gallatin. Even the cupid attending her is
> represented as a winged monkey with fluttering drapery, strewing
> flowers on the nymph, who, with her attendant Tritons and sea-
> nymphs, are also represented as monkeys.

The composer **Edward Elgar** (1857–1934) was a regular visitor while he was living in a house on the riverbank overlooking the hotel; he composed his violin concerto there, when the house was still called 'The Hut'. It was later to become the home of racing driver **Sterling Moss**.

Lovers and novelists **H G Wells** and **Rebecca West** used regularly to visit Monkey Island. He used to travel up-river from his uncle's pub, the Royal Oak in Datchet Road, on the edge of Windsor. She lodged there and used the island as the idyll for lovers Chris and Margaret in her novel *The Return of the Soldier*. Her descriptions of the island, where the young man and girl meet, reflect her own passionate meetings with Wells on the lawns of Monkey Island. She writes of

> the liquefaction of colours which happens on a summer's evening, when the green grass seemed like a precious fluid poured on the earth and dripping over the river, and the chestnut candles were no longer proud flowers . . . but just wet lights in the humid mass of trees.

> . . . In front were the dark green glassy waters of an unvisited backwater; and beyond . . . a bright lawn set with many walnut trees and a few great chestnuts, well lit with their candles, and . . . a low white house with a green dome rising in its middle and a veranda whose roof of hammered iron had gone verdigris colour with age and the Thames weather.

West word-paints a portrait of Wells towards the end of the novel, almost certainly as a private joke:

> [A] little man with winking blue eyes, a flushed and crumpled forehead, a little grey moustache that gave him the profile of an amiable cat, and a lively taste in spotted ties.

Visitor information Amerden Caravan and Camping Site (Old Marsh Lane, Dorney Reach, Maidenhead: tel: 01628 627461) is on the riverside, close by the M4. There are 30 pitches, WCs, showers, wash basins, a telephone and a shop. Open Apr 1–Oct 31. Pitches cost £6–10 per night (depending on size of tent).

About half a mile downstream of the M4 New Thames Bridge, the Thames Path leaves open country to pass along the bottoms of large gardens and doesn't regain it again, green and pleasant, until Bray Lock, approximately a quarter-mile on the other side of the bridge.

BRAY

Bray Lock is among the most pleasing of all the pleasing locks on the Thames; some say it is the best and the prettiest which, perhaps, it is. You must judge for yourself. It has a lovely garden, and has done ever since **Mr Baldwin** was lock-keeper back in the 1950s and often won the 'big' cup for the best lock garden on the river. The trophy used to be presented every year by the avuncular Thames Conservancy, which cared, deeply, not just for the river but for its locks and its lock-keepers. Once a year the board would travel up-river by official launch, a stately craft, in order to judge the best-kept garden and present the trophy to the winner. Regrettably the Environment Agency – successor to the Thames Conservancy – doesn't continue this tradition; in fact, when I asked an agency spokesman about the once-treasured gardening trophy he had to admit that as far as he knew it had been lost.

Bray, on the Berkshire bank (there is access over the lock from the Thames Path), has retained its 'villagey' charm, despite the coming of arty-crafty, cosmopolitan, well-heeled city folk, and its fake half-timbered cottages – urban stage-set imitations of genuine rural up-river originals.

Yes, this was the village of the famous **Vicar of Bray**, the turncoat parson celebrated in verse for turning his coat according to the religious conviction of the ruling monarch of the time. The famous song, composed around 1720, celebrates how the 16th-century reverend, Simon Alleyn, survived half a dozen reigns in 48 years, umpteen changes of religion, and a stack of political hithers and thithers without losing his head or being burned at the stake:

> Until my dying day, Sir,
> That whosoever King shall reign.
> I'll be the Vicar of Bray, Sir.

He began as a High-Church parson when Charles I was on the throne, decided on a spot of lower-Churching under Charles II, became a Catholic when James II was crowned, turned Protestant on the succession of William and Mary, an Anglican and Tory for Queen Anne, and a Whig for George I:

> The illustrious House of Hanover,
> And Protestant succession,
> To these I lustily will swear,
> Whilst they can keep possession . . .
> George my lawful King shall be,
> Except the Times should alter.

Simon's well-preserved, largely 13th-century church is approached via a fine brick gatehouse of 1460. The snooker champion **Steve Davis** was married in the church, something of which the villagers are ever so proud. They love their celebrities, among whom they count **Rolf Harris**, who lives here because it reminds him of his riverside home in Perth, and **Michael Parkinson**, who is also rich enough to afford the place. **Gerald Ratner**, the jewellery retailer who goofed by admitting his stores sold trash, used to live at the riverside house called Somerville (the one just upstream of Bray with an

American-style wrap-around balcony) but sold up for £1.7 million when all the adverse publicity got too much for him.

The **Jesus Hospital almshouses** in Holyport Road are worth viewing, although you can't go inside them. They were the favourite subjects of excellent Victorian painter **Fred Walker**, ARA, (1840–75), and are depicted in his *Harbour of Refuge*, one of the best-loved pictures of the Victorian age and now in London's Tate Britain. It is one of two Walker paintings (the other is *Marlow Ferry*) that epitomise the tranquil loveliness of the Thames before Queen Victoria's 'golden age' of progress and development troubled its peaceful waters. Should you be interested, there is a word-portrait of Fred Walker contained in **George de Maurier**'s novel *Trilby*, where he appears as Little Billee,

> small and slender . . . , a straight white forehead veined with blue, large
> dark blue eyes, delicate, regular features, and coal-black hair. He was
> also very graceful and well built, with very small hands and feet . . .

There are some good eating places in Bray, although not everybody can afford them. The journalist **John MacCarthy**, who was a captive in Lebanon with Terry Waite, came to eat at the Michelin three-starred **Waterside Inn** (which has a notice outside warning 'Restaurant only', in case anybody thinks the inn is an inn, which it isn't) but took one look at the prices and went somewhere else. Diners here, apparently, have included 'Fergie', the Duchess of York, and 'escort'.

Just as the Waterside Inn isn't an inn, the **Hind's Head Hotel** in Bray High Street isn't a hotel, although the old sign outside maintains it is. The hotel (?), inn (?), pub (?), restaurant (?) is old, probably built in the middle of the 16th century, with wood panelling, old beams and high-backed settles. **Queen Elizabeth II** and **Prince Philip** dined here once on saddle of lamb, treacle tart (made to a 15th-century recipe still on the menu) and Stilton. There's a room called the 'Vicar's Room' which is said to be the sleeping place of Simon Alleyn, the Vicar of Bray (see page 127), although for the life of me I can't think why it would have been.

MAIDENHEAD

The distance from Bray to Maidenhead is about a mile. On the left are large Edwardian mansions with sumptuous gardens lining the bank. In one of them, although I have never discovered which, the beautiful, red-haired **Lillie Langtry**, Edward VII's mistress, held court.

Ahead is the Great Western Railway's **Maidenhead Railway Bridge**, by far the best of all the middle-Thames railway bridges. It was built in the late 1830s by **Sir Isambard Brunel** (1806–59), who responded to the challenge to span both towpath and river in one by creating what are still the widest, fattest brick arches in the country, measuring 128ft (38.8m) wide with headroom in the centre of only 24ft (7.3m). The artist **J W Turner** (1775–1851) painted the bridge, with a GWR broad-gauge express thundering over it, in his famous study 'Rain, Steam and Speed'. As you pass under the bridge on the Thames Path it is the done thing to shout loudly and wonder at the strength of the returning echo.

A quarter-mile further on is another bridge, Maidenhead's elegant road crossing, and immediately upstream of that, on the Thames Path side of the river, is **Skindles Hotel**, once the 1920s hub of Maidenhead pleasure seeking. It was the 'in' place, the 19th-century 'jewel of the Thames', where playboys and débutantes came to wine, dine and fornicate. 'Are you married or do you live in Maidenhead?' was a famous little quip of the time. When the site of the one-time Maidenhead Brigade of Guards Club was excavated, gold wedding rings galore were discovered in the rubble, apparently abandoned by young ladies preparing to return home after a wild weekend on the town.

British novelist **Michael Arlen** (1895–1956) – originally born Dikran Kouyoumdjian in Bulgaria of Armenian parents – called the Skindles Hotel 'the hymen of London', implying that it was where maidens lost their virginity. Through the early years of the 20th century the town enjoyed a notorious reputation in the divorce courts, thanks to the fondness of the upper classes for bedding each other's husbands and wives in Skindles. It was much patronised by Prince 'Tum-Tum' (the future **Edward VII**, when Prince of Wales), who brought Lillie Langtry, and goodness knows who else, to share his favourite lunch of mutton chop, dry champagne, a little brandy with soda, a cigar . . . and bed. It was the hotel's *louche* reputation that *Three Men in a Boat*'s Jerome leered over when he declared Maidenhead,

> too snobby to be pleasant . . . the haunt of the river swell and his
> overdressed female companion . . . the town of showy hotels,
> patronised chiefly by dudes and ballet girls. The *London Journal* duke
> always has his 'little place' at Maidenhead and the heroine of the
> three-volume novel always dines there when she goes out on the
> spree with somebody else's husband.

There used to be over 90 coaches going helter-skelter through Maidenhead streets in the heyday of coaching. Great coaching inns sprouted here, the first stop on the great road to the west. One such inn was the Greyhound in the high street, burned down in 1735, where **Charles I** was brought prisoner from Caversham to be reunited with his children – 'to his infinite content and joy', according to the chronicler **Edward Hyde Clarendon** (1609–74).

The Thames Path crosses over Maidenhead Bridge, from Buckingham into Berkshire and, officially speaking, from Taplow into Maidenhead proper. The 'three men in a boat' went 'through Maidenhead quickly', a good example to follow as it is a dull, dormitory town, ugly, shapeless and noisy. It deserves only to be glanced at from the river. In any case, better and lovelier things lie ahead: Boulter's Lock, Cliveden Reach and Cookham.

Maidenhead to Cookham

The Thames Path continues along a 'promenade' road through Maidenhead, reached over the bridge and through a public garden where there is a refreshment hut, normally open daily through the year, and WCs in the garden. For a little over half a mile, to just past Boulter's Lock, the riverside houses of **Taplow** are on the opposite, Buckinghamshire, bank, followed by Taplow Court Estate, sheltered by trees. **Taplow Mansion**, Victorian-Tudor brick, romantic with towers and gables, was the home of **Lord Desborough** who built the Desborough Cut at Walton (see pages 84 and 86–8).

BOULTER'S LOCK

Boulter's Lock is famous the world over, largely because of **Edward John Gregory**'s painting, 'Boulter's Lock – Sunday Afternoon 1895' (now at the Lady Lever Gallery, Port Sunlight; tel: 0151 4784136). The painting shows a bustle of colour, of parasols and blazers, of punts and canoes and skiffs and steam launches crowded into this best known of Thames locks at the height of summer. The original painting, on which Gregory worked for six years, was sold in 1905 for just under 8,000 guineas, not such a measly sum in those days. He was a resident at various times of Maidenhead, Cookham Dean and Marlow, a retiring man, happiest cycling alone in the Thames Valley countryside, or paddling his boat into shady backwaters. He died in 1909 and his grave can be visited in Marlow churchyard, within a few yards of the red-bricked wall at the edge of the Thames; a palette and brushes are carved on his tomb.

The Sunday following Royal Ascot used to be the big day for

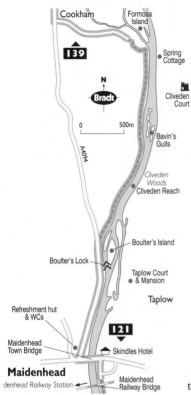

Cookham
Formosa Island
139
Spring Cottage
N
Bradt
Cliveden Court
0   500m
Bavin's Gulls
A4094
Cliveden Woods
Cliveden Reach
Boulter's Island
Boulter's Lock
Taplow Court & Mansion
Taplow
Refreshment hut & WCs
121
Maidenhead Town Bridge
Skindles Hotel
Maidenhead
denhead Railway Station
Maidenhead Railway Bridge

visiting Boulter's by 'Arries and Arriets' – **Jerome K Jerome**'s hoity-toity nicknames for the less-than-middle classes who dropped their aitches. They crowded around the lock at Boulter's, striving to outdo each other, and the river-borne wealthy and famous, in sartorial elegance. Great was the excitement when the **Prince of Wales** passed through in the steam launch *Duchess* to stay with the **Astors** at Cliveden in 1886. And great, again, in 1904, when his wife, **Queen Alexandra**, came with Lord Desborough from Taplow Court to board an electric launch at Boulter's. **Oscar Wilde** passed through the lock one weekend with **Melba** (Dame Nellie), the Australian-born prima soprano, and caused a great fluster among excited bystanders.

Today, Boulter's is no longer the place where people come to watch the well bred, the rich and the famous. Strangely, though, there remains an air of Edwardian naughtiness about the place, this river Piccadilly where people-watchers now arrive just for the fun of watching boats jostling for space and people falling in – which a lock-keeper told me they do at least once a week.

As you will realise, when you come, Boulter's is a sort of village gathered around the lock: an inn, a restaurant, and, not so long ago, a mill as well. The lock's name is derived from the word 'bolter' meaning 'miller' which the first lock-keeper, Richard Ray (appointed 1773), doubled as.

For over 20 years (1880–1904), the entire complex was presided over by one of the most famous lock-keepers ever to work on the Thames: **W H Turner**. Described by a local newspaper as 'well built and muscular, with bronzed face and hands, and a sturdy look which fears no man', Turner had earlier served before the mast on three-decked

men-o'-war as a gunner and cutlass instructor. He ruled Boulter's, justly, benevolently, courteously, and bravely, rescuing no less than seven people from drowning. Such was his skill as a locks-man that the local newspaper reported he packed in boats and launches 'like barrelled herrings'.

Everybody who passed through Boulter's in those days remembered Turner – and his prize-winning garden, heavy with the scent of roses, described by the *Maidenhead Advertiser* as 'the prettiest on the Upper Thames . . . in spring, full of tulips and other spring flowers, later a wealth of choice begonias, roses, pinks, honeysuckle and carnations'. Turner retired in 1905. His health failed in 1914 and, one evening in June, he was taken ill with heart failure and died within a few minutes. I have been unable to discover his grave.

CLIVEDEN

Beyond Boulter's Lock is Cliveden, 'perhaps the sweetest stretch of all the river' (*Three Men in a Boat*). It is breathtaking. High above the river, in woods of beech stretching from Maidenhead to Hedsor, is **Cliveden** (pronounced 'Cleeveden') **Court**, the backdrop to many political intrigues and scandals, culminating in the 1960s '**Profumo Affair**' which brought down a government (see page 135).

First you get just a glimpse of the house through a gap in the trees, then a bit further on the gap widens so that the fragment of a house becomes a vast mansion, perfectly sited on a plateau terrace overlooking one of the most graceful curves on the Thames. It is all very beautiful. The gad-about diarist **John Evelyn** (1620–1706) thought so too. He came in July 1679, and observed that 'it is a romantic object, and the place answers the most poetical description that can be made'. Jerome K Jerome considered all of Cliveden – its woods, the house, the river reach – an 'unbroken loveliness'.

Of the original Cliveden Court, built in the 1660s, nothing remains but the terrace. The present, 1850s' building is not beautiful, but gigantic and imperious, ornamental and graceless. It was fashioned by a Victorian architect much in love with Italianate flummery, **Charles Barry** (1795–1860). **Queen Victoria**, who visited often, thought it 'a perfection of a place, first of all the view is so beautiful, and then the house is a bijou of taste'.

Like Victoria, a number of highly respected critics still regard Cliveden Court as one of Barry's 'masterpieces'. Others, equally respected, don't; soon after the house was completed, one commentator declared it 'easily imitated by three or four packing cases', another, 'an example of the wild vicissitudes of taste'.

A lot of visitors, I am told, experience vague déja vu when they visit the court. I did. It is perhaps because the Beatles' film *Help* was in part shot here when the house doubled as Buckingham Palace. The place has always been popular with 'luvvies'; actors **Kenneth Branagh** and **Emma Thompson** were married in the grounds in 1989.

Lots of nobs have lived here. The first great house was built for the second Duke of Buckingham (1628–87), who fought a duel on the terrace for the love

of a 'piece of trash' (I shall tell you more shortly). It was enlarged by the Earl of Orkney, of whom I know nothing, and rented by the Prince of Wales, father to King George III, who heard the first performance of 'Rule, Britannia' here. The music for the latter was composed by **Thomas Arne** (1710–78), the words by the Scottish poet **James Thomson** (1700–48), who received a pension from the prince for his trouble.

The original house was burned down in 1795, and rebuilt, before being burned down again, the last time by a housemaid reading by candlelight in bed. The present court was erected in 1850; there were then subsequent additions by the American Astor family.

Cliveden has an intriguing and dubious past. First, there was the Duke of Buckingham scandal, then an Astor-family scandal, and then, juiciest of all, the 'Profumo Affair', involving a government minister and a prostitute.

The duel between Buckingham and Shrewsbury

On January 16 1667, an infamous duel was fought – between not two antagonists, but six. On one side were **George Villiers**, second Duke of Buckingham, and his friends **Sir Robert Holmes** and **Captain William Jenkins**; on the other **Francis Talbot**, the eleventh Earl of Shrewsbury, **Sir John Talbot** and **Bernard Howard**, grandson of the Earl of Arundel. Each man was wounded, and two – Shrewsbury was one of them – were killed. Samuel Pepys wrote in his diary the following day:

> [T]hey met yesterday . . . and my Lord Shrewsbury is run through the body, from the right breast through the shoulder; and Sir John Talbot all along up one of his armes; and Jenkins killed upon the place, and the rest all, in a little measure wounded.

The duel was fought because Shrewsbury had discovered the 'rake' Buckingham in bed or in the bushes (history is unsure) with his wife, or, more probably, her in bed with him. Pepys noted:

> The woman herself was a typical piece of trash; she chose to watch the duel, disguised as her lover's page.

The 'piece of trash' was **Anna Maria**, Countess of Shrewsbury, perhaps the most notorious, the must buxom, of Restoration beauties. She was the daughter of Robert, Lord Brudenall, afterwards second Earl of Cardigan, and ancestor of the seventh Earl of Cardigan. The latter had helped Lucan send the Light Brigade into the valley of death in the Crimea (see page 95), and gave English ladies and gents their 'cardies', named after the knitted wool jacket he wore against the cold of a Crimean winter.

Anna Maria's passionate affair with Villiers cost her husband his life. He died on January 17 1668 of a wound received in the duel with Buckingham. Anna Maria, apparently, held the bridle of Buckingham's horse while he ran her husband through, and afterwards they made love, frenzied and saturated in the blood of her husband. Her portrait is in the National Portrait Gallery: insolent, contemptuous, cruel . . . and superb.

The Astor scandal

Cliveden was the home of **Nancy Astor**, Viscountess Astor (first woman ever to take her seat in 1919 as a member of parliament), from the time of her marriage to Waldorf Astor in 1906 – 'I married beneath me, all women do' – until her death in 1966. The daughter of a southern American 'gentleman', she was gifted with beauty, wit and intelligence. There is a portrait of her in the Great Hall; it was painted by the American artist **John Singer Sargent** (1856–1925), whose home we visited in Chelsea (see page 34).

Nancy made Cliveden the centre for political weekend parties. The playwright and pamphleteer **George Bernard Shaw** (1856–1950) was a regular guest, as were political leaders of the day. A journalist, **Claud Cockburn**, writing in his 1930s scandal sheet *The Week*, began rumours of an Astor plot to give Germany's Adolf Hitler a free hand in Europe so long as he left Great Britain alone to be ruled by rich and powerful landowners. History now regards it as an unlikely piece of journalistic mischief-making.

Britain's World War II leader and prime minister, **Winston Churchill**, was a frequent visitor to Cliveden, but never a friend of the Astors. After one of the

Visitor information There is no direct access to Cliveden from the Thames Path, but you might like to try what I did and hitch a ride on one of the boats passing through Boulter's Lock. Ask the skipper to land wherever he can – there are lots of grassy landing and mooring places on the Buckinghamshire bank. A walk of about half a mile will take you to Cliveden Court on the A4094, two miles north of Taplow Road.

Cliveden's woodland is open all year, 11.00–17.30 daily in the summer, 11.00–16.00 Nov–Mar (closed Christmas Day and New Year's Day). Cliveden Court is now let by the National Trust as a hotel, but three ground-floor rooms are open to the public twice a week between April and October (Thu and Sun 15.00–18.00). Admission adult £1, child and concessions £0.50. The gardens are open daily between March 12 and December 31 (11.00–18.00 until Nov 1, 11.00–16.00 afterwards). Admission adult £6, child and concessions £3.

There is a shop, and refreshments are available in the conservatory restaurant. Dogs are allowed in specified woodland areas only. Various open-air festivals are held throughout the year – check beforehand for dates. For more information, call the estate administrator on 01628 605069.

DANGEROUS FOREIGNERS

Not all foreign imports are as harmless as the mandarin ducks (see page 136). The man I met from the Environment Agency was also keeping an eye open for signs of the American mink, which was brought to this country for its fur, then absconded into our waterways to bring a reign of terror to the otter and the harmless water vole. Mink are born to kill and, I was told, they have decimated the water voles – 'Ratties', from **Kenneth Grahame's** *Wind in the Willows* country. A horrifying 90% of Thames water voles have been wiped out in just a couple of decades. But not around here, I was told. The saviours of the water voles, would you believe, are Cookham's dogs? In the drainage ditches off Cliveden's main stream the waterfront burrows of water voles still bustle with life because the creatures have found unexpected allies in the form of domestic dogs. Walked daily alongside the river, these dogs have kept the dreaded mink at bay. Isn't it wonderful that here – in the very heart of *Wind in the Willows* country – 'Ratty' is alive and well?

crowded dinner parties, he snarled, 'Thirty dishes and no damn room to eat them'. Other regulars included **Henry James**, **Hilaire Belloc**, **Charlie Chaplin**, **Bernard Shaw**, **Lawrence of Arabia**, **Oswald Mosley**, and goodness only knows how many political leaders. One of them, **Harold Macmillan**, when told the mansion was to become a hotel, quipped, 'My dear boy, it always has been.' **Franklin D Roosevelt**, 32nd President of the United States, came, liked it, and returned again.

Cliveden's tenure by the wealthy Astors began in 1893 and lasted until 1966, when the house and estate were handed over to the National Trust, who still owns it, although the family continued to live there in considerable style until the 1970s.

The Profumo Affair

At the foot of Cliveden's wooded cliffs, close by the Thames and not far from the site of the old My Lady Ferry (no longer operating), is fairy-tale-gabled Spring Cottage, scene of the infamous 'Profumo Affair', as far-reaching in its time as Nixon's Watergate scandal and Bill Clinton's 'Zippergate' affair.

Back in the early 1960s, the cottage was rented out by Lord Astor to a London osteopath and socialite, **Stephen Ward**, who organised assignations at Spring Cottage for the rich and the famous. The 'Profumo Affair' involved a married Conservative MP, and minister of defence, **John Profumo**. He had sex at Spring Cottage – and probably in the bedrooms of Cliveden Court – with one of Ward's luscious, leggy call-girls called **Christine Keeler**. It was 'a screw of convenience', Miss Keeler later told reporters, but one which turned out to be exceedingly inconvenient for Mr Profumo when newspaper reporters discovered that Miss Keeler was also bedding a Soviet naval attaché,

Yevgeny Ivanov. As the newspapers spelt out, in the coy language of the '60s, Miss Keeler was in danger of passing on all manner of defence secrets picked up in pillow talk with Britain's minister of defence. The scandal forced Profumo to resign from office and resulted in the downfall of the Harold Macmillan government.

Visitor information The riverside Spring Cottage, named after a nearby mineral spring that was a favourite picnic place for Frederick, Prince of Wales, in the 18th century and Queen Victoria in the 19th, is now rented out as a holiday-let by the National Trust.

Cliveden Reach

The artist **Stanley Spencer** (1891–1959), who lived close by, once said, 'You can't walk by the river at **Cliveden Reach** and not believe in God'. It is so enchanting that it would be difficult to leave, were it not that from here on, round nearly every turn of the Thames, there are things so pleasing it is tempting to canter on in order to peer round the next bend to see what's in store. You never know whom you are going to meet. I got into conversation with an Environment Agency ecologist when I was ambling by the banks of Cliveden Reach. He was looking for ducks, 'tree-nesting foreign escapees' he called them – exotic mandarin ducks and drakes with swept-back, 'Adams family', cockscomb crests. Apparently a whole raft of mandarin ducks have escaped from private collections into the wild, and are now thriving just as well on the River Thames as they do in their native China. The leafy waterways at Cliveden suit them perfectly. The duck raises her family in the branches of a tree and, when they are fledged, the youngsters fling themselves with whirling wing stubs into the river and scoot about like crazy tops.

COOKHAM

From the site of the old My Lady Ferry, the Thames Path turns inland, through woods, to Cookham village. A warbler was singing here when I walked this path, and once, at twilight, from the deck of a boat in Cliveden Reach, I listened to nightingales singing their hearts out somewhere on the Cliveden hills.

The Thames Path bypasses **Cookham Lock**, which is a pity for it is another of the pretty ones. It is certainly the most magically sited, tucked beneath woods in front and behind, up-river and down, so that in April the air is rich with birdsong, and in October the lock is a reflected flame of colour. To reach it, Thames Pathers must make a half-mile diversion, there and back, soon after leaving the My Lady Ferry riverside, following the road on to **Formosa Island** where the lock is located. Two Thames channels enclose the island, which has an area of about 50 acres and is the largest on the river.

Like Boulter's, famous lock-keepers were once in charge of Cookham Lock. One was '**Mister Hill**' – nobody, as far as I can make out, ever used his Christian name. He retired in 1914 and was so famous that the national *Daily Express* mourned his leaving:

> He was a master of both tact and sarcasm . . . equally adept at holding
> up a launch of noisy trippers, ridiculing a 'mug' punter with irony,
> and sympathetically helping ladies inexperienced in the skills of
> boating.

His wife was famous for her cream teas, sold at one shilling a time in 1901, and

> served with a plentiful supply of bread and butter (nicely cut) and
> cake and two kinds of jam, in tip-top style. There is not stint, and into
> the bargain, one has the pleasure of being waited upon by a nice-
> looking, courteous and business-like waitress.

Stanley Spencer

Cookham Village is attractive, meticulously and conscientiously preserved. There's a ford, a village green, cottages of red brick glistering with white paint . . . and, of course, there's Stanley Spencer. Or at least there was, until 1959 when he died at the age of 68.

Spencer was born in Cookham, lived and painted here, in this 'village from heaven', for most of his life, at the house he was born in near the chapel where there is a permanent exhibition of his work. He was so much part of the village, so devoted to it, that his fellow art students at London's Slade Art College nicknamed him 'Cookham' because he was forever talking about the place, nor was at rest when he was away from it. He was born in a semi-detached Victorian villa, 'Fernlea', in the High Street on the day a crow fell down the chimney of the living room; it was considered a good omen.

Spencer grew up to become an eccentric English oddity. Once dubbed 'the divine fool of British art', he divorced one wife to wed a lesbian who refused to consummate their marriage before eagerly taking him for everything he owned when she got around to throwing him out.

To this day, Cookham residents remember him pushing a child's pram full of paints through the village, and fondly recall how he wore pyjamas under his clothes when the weather was cold. One resident remembers him as a 'bony man with glasses and wild hair who put up his easel in the village with a notice reading, "Mr Spencer would be grateful if visitors would kindly avoid distracting his attention from his work"' (now in the Stanley Spencer Gallery – see box below).

His biblical-theme paintings, located in Cookham, were not initially well received by critics who failed to share his view of the Thameside village as 'the new Jerusalem'. They regarded him as dotty, quaint, and his subjects as clever caricatures of local yokels. Regard one time was so low that his only painting at London's Millbank Tate was hung just outside the lavatory. Things have changed since, and from time to time the Tate now gives pride of place to several Spencer paintings. But it's not the best place to see them, as an article in the *Guardian* pointed out:

> Today it's at Cookham you'll find the Stanley Spencer Gallery in the chapel where he attended Sunday School, with some of his best works. They belong here . . . more happily than they do in the Tate; their shock value lies in the strange meeting between the powerful yet poignant subject of his paintings and the gentle settings that house them.

Visitor information The Stanley Spencer Gallery is in 'The King Hall', Cookham High Street, not far from Stanley's 'Fernlea' home. There's a permanent collection of his work, letters, documents, memorabilia, and the battered old pram. Open daily from Easter to October (10.30–17.30) and Saturday, Sunday and bank holidays from November to Easter (11.00–17.00). Admission adult £1, concessions £0.50, child up to 16 free. There is a shop with facsimile reproductions, etc; good disabled access. For further information, tel: 01628 471885.

The path back to the river runs left of the church where the actress **Susan George** was married in 1984. The churchyard features in Spencer's *The Resurrection* – the artist's grave is to the left of the path. His *Christ Preaching at Cookham Regatta*, is set at the back of the **Ferry Inn**, just downstream of Cookham Bridge (built in 1867) , and 'Swan Upping' (see box, pages 140–1) at the bridge itself, close by where the Thames Path rejoins the river.

Cookham to Marlow

Distances From Cookham Lock: Cookham Bridge 0.49 miles
(0.78km), Bourne End Railway Bridge 1.54 miles (2.46km), Marlow
Lock 4.38 miles (7km)

WIND IN THE WILLOWS COUNTRY
Cookham Dean

From here, practically all the way up-river to the source, we are travelling
in *Wind in the Willows* country. Living for a while around the next great
bend, at **Cookham Dean**, and for a good deal longer nearly 30 miles
further up-river in **Pangbourne**, author **Kenneth Grahame** knew these
reaches intimately.

He was born in Scotland in 1859. When he was five his mother died and he
went to live with his maternal grandmother at 'The Mount' in Cookham
Dean. The house was beautiful and rambling, with a 300-year-old oak in the
grounds, which bounded the river. Close by is **Quarry Wood**, the dreaded
Wild Wood in *Wind in the Willows*. Grahame roamed freely through the house
and grounds, wandering through the meadows to the edge of the River

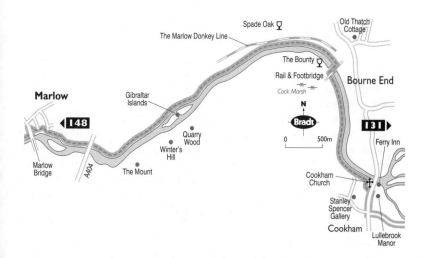

SWAN UPPING

The annual ceremony of 'swan upping' is at least seven centuries old, and probably a good deal more than that – a celebration of an exotic and eccentric tradition, when a fleet of swan uppers' skiffs passes beneath Cookham Bridge on a long-distance swan-gathering, a five-day upriver round-up. It's as colourful as a bag of hundreds-and-thousands, dating back to a time when a swan was a prize worth eating and protecting. As a result, it was established that there were only three legal swan owners on the Thames: the monarch and two London livery companies, the Vintners and the Dyers.

Joshing and laughing, most of them 'likely-lads' in their 50s and 60s, the muscular rowers swoop beneath the bridge in a flotilla of gleaming varnished skiffs with giant pennants flying from the stems, and senior swan uppers, great panjandrums, sitting magisterially in the stern. The three seniors are paid honorariums for their work. The queen's man is Swan Marker and wears a scarlet blazer with brass buttons, white trousers, and a peaked cap. The Vintners' Marker wears a bottle-green blazer with rings on the cuffs and swan badges on the lapels; he sports a long swan feather in his cap. The Dyers' man wears a blue blazer and cap.

Whenever a pod of swans is sighted a long howl is passed from boat to boat: 'A-a-a-a-l U-u-u-up!' It's as daft as morris dancing, as silly as the maypole, a wonderful fragment of English pageantry. Its pointless purpose: to round up and mark ownership of the Thames's young cygnets before they can fly.

Thames. He remembered this part of his life so vividly that when he brought his own family to live beside the Thames, in 1906, he wrote:

> I feel I should never be surprised to meet myself as I was when a little chap of five, suddenly coming round a corner . . . I can remember everything I felt then.

When Grahame was nine he was sent to school in Oxford. He left school in 1876 and quickly rose from the lowly position of bank clerk to become Secretary to the Bank of England in 1898. The following year he married Elspeth Thomson, and they had a son, Alastair, in 1900.

From babyhood, Alastair Grahame was nicknamed 'Mouse'. He was blind in his right eye and squinted with his left, was awkward and shy. In 1906, aged 47, Grahame decided the river air would do Alastair the world of good. He moved the family back to his childhood haunts when he bought a house called 'The Hillyers' not far from 'The Mount' in Cookham Dean. Later they moved to the larger, thatched 'Mayfield', described by Grahame as 'an idyll of elms and buttercups and old red brick'. We shall constantly be bumping into Kenneth Grahame and his riverbank creatures between here and Pangbourne where the author spent the last years of his life.

The boats form a fence round the birds to prevent their escape. Parent cobs (males) and pens, in moult and therefore unable to fly, are scooped from the water with their two- or three-month-old offspring. Their legs are gently tied with twine, their wings pinioned by a stout arm, and then they are marked – a single nick in the beak for birds claimed by the blue-vested Dyers, two nicks for the white-shirted Vintners, none for the birds of the Queen's Men who wear red.

These days, swan uppers are river-men, boat-builders, boat operators and ferrymen with a lifetime spent on the Thames. They take five days over the voyage, leaving Sunbury on a Monday morning every July and finishing at Abingdon on Friday afternoon, stopping on the way at riverside pubs for sumptuous lunches and pints of good bitter. As they go through Windsor they salute the sovereign by standing to attention in their skiffs and presenting arms with their sculls. At the end of each day a coach picks them up and takes them to a hotel. Every year they 'up' an average of 179 cygnets and 99 parent birds.

Some people say that **Lullebrook Manor** in Cookham's Ferry Lane was his inspiration for **Toad Hall**, but that's not entirely true because Toad's mansion was a Kenneth Grahame amalgam of several stately riverside homes, each of which I shall point out as we travel up-river. Yet there are, as it happens, two links between Toad and Lullebrook. First, the owner of the manor in Grahame's day was the first person in the area to own a motor car; and second, the house is not far from **Bourne End** (next township upriver, 1.05 miles/1.69km from Cookham Bridge), where Toad went to steal a motor car after escaping from Toad Hall:

> [H]e strode along, his head in the air, till he reached a little town,
> where the sign of 'The Red Lion' reminded him that he had not
> breakfasted today.

Cookham to Bourne End

Between Cookham and Bourne End the river is wide and open from the west, providing fair winds for sailing craft; all very 'yellow wellies', 'oilies' and 'bobstays'. There's the **Upper Thames Sailing Club**, the **Bourne End Cruiser and Yacht Club**, the **Bourne End Marina** – each spewing out so many boats that the river seems to have difficulty coping. On the Bourne End bank, seen from the Thames Path, the Edwardian riverside villas are 'refeened' left-overs from the 19th-century 'model' estates, tweely marketed as 'cosy make-believe' and 'subtopian fairy world', and which the architectural historian **Pevsner** declared 'picturesque'. Oddly, they are.

The Thames Path crosses the river via a 1993 footbridge attached to the Bourne End Railway Bridge, which carries the Maidenhead–Marlow 'Donkey Line' rail bus.

The old **Red Lion**, where Toad pinched a motor-car without so much as a 'poop-poop!', is still at Bourne End. So is the rambling, 16th-century '**Old Thatch Cottage**' where the popular children's author **Enid Blyton** lived from 1929 to 1937.

> It is perfect, both inside and out . . . just like a Fairy Tale house and
> three minutes from the river. . . [T]he whole place has a lovely feel to
> it – friendly, happy, welcoming.

She used the house and its setting many times in her stories.

About half a mile after Bourne End Railway Bridge, past the **Spade Oak** pub and a level crossing over the 'Marlow Donkey' branch line, the river sweeps into lovely Bourne End Reach. Here the Thames Path comes level with Wootten's Boatyard and **Quarry Wood** on the far bank, just downstream of the Gibraltar Islands. 'Dear old Quarry Wood! with your narrow, climbing paths, and little winding grades' wrote Jerome K Jerome.

Quarry Wood

Quarry Wood is the 'Wild Wood' of Kenneth Grahame's *Wind in the Willows*.

'We don't go there very much, we river-bankers,' Ratty told Mole. There are 'little evil wedged-shaped' faces staring through the trees in the Wild Wood, 'the pat-pat-pat of little feet' and 'whistling . . . very faint and shrill it was, and far behind . . .' All very frightening.

In truth, Quarry Wood is not like that at all. It is actually as chummy as any wood gets, venerable and beautiful, its dome-headed beech trees rising thick from the river. This entire reach would vie with Cliveden's were it not for the rash of bungalows on the northern Thames Path bank. The poet **Percy Bysshe Shelley** (1792–1822), who lived in Marlow and spent hours boating on the river, describes the woods, the islands, in one of his epics, *The Revolt of Islam*:

> . . . where the woods frame a bower,
> Whose interlaced branches mix and meet,
> Or where with sound like many voices sweet,
> Waterfalls leap among wild islands green,
> Which frame for my lone boat a lone retreat
> Of moss-grown trees and woods.

Very old folk who live in these parts, those with memories stretching back to the last years of the 19th century and the early ones of the 20th, recall a time when they heard the soprano voice of prima donna **Nellie Melba** (1861–1931) singing in Quarry Wood. She used to live in a cottage among the trees.

If you are ever roaming the opposite bank of the river, and have the opportunity, then climb **Winter Hill** on the far side of Quarry Wood. Its top is only 225 feet high, but the view is spectacular, much as it was when writer-cum-historian-cum-politician **Lord Thomas Babington Macaulay** (1800–59) looked down on 'that beautiful valley, through which the Thames rolls round the gentle hills of Berkshire'.

MARLOW

Marlow is a 'wow' of a town, just as it is described in *Three Men in a Boat*:

> [O]ne of the pleasantest river centres I know of . . . a bustling, lively little town; not very picturesque, on the whole, it is true, but there are many quaint nooks and corners to be found in it . . . There is lovely country round about it, too.

Just downstream of Marlow's famous suspension bridge are the weir and lock, famous beauty spots. The view from the bridge is justly famous, an accidental grouping no artist could improve: the pinnacled church spire, the remarkable 1836 suspension bridge, and the lawn of the **Compleat Angler Hotel**. The best of Marlow lies along the river and in West and High streets. In the latter you will find the Marlow TIC (31 High Street; tel 01628 483597). If you are lucky, you may get a response to a telephone call, but in my experience this is one of those rarely-answer-the-telephone information centres.

It's a quiet town, as towns go, except during the annual regatta. At most other times it is easy-going and relaxed, if a bit 'county', as though every day is a Sunday. There is no escaping the overworked word 'picturesque', which the best of Marlow's Thameside certainly is, and even the most modern riverside bits have been built to look just like a white, weatherboarded mill.

Despite being vandalised by Victorian do-gooders (who in fact did-bad), the **church** has somehow or other retained its ancient dignity. Inside is a wall monument to **Sir Miles Hobart** who, when Speaker of the House of Commons in 1628, locked the door of the House and kept the key in his pocket so that MPs were unable to escape an interminable debate on 'the illegal imposition of Tonnage and Poundage'. For this he was imprisoned in the Tower of London and soon after his release was killed by a runaway coach on London's Holborn Hill.

In the vestry is a portrait of the 'Spotted Boy', a young Caribbean negro whom a showman, **John Richardson**, famous in his day, bought as a slave for £2,000 and put on exhibition for Victorian rubber-neckers to gawk at. Richardson was buried in the churchyard at his own request next to his 'Spotted Boy' who died in 1812, a pathetic little fellow only eight years old. Another grave in the churchyard belongs to **Edward John Gregory** who painted the famous *Boulter's Lock – Sunday Afternoon 1895*. He lived at No 100

in the High Street and we met him when we stopped at Boulter's Lock (see page 130).

Marlow's most remarkable structure is the small **suspension bridge** (built 1829–32) over the river, designed by **William Tierney Clark** who was also responsible for the Hammersmith Suspension Bridge and the famous bridge which linked Hungary's Buda with Pest until it was destroyed in World War II. With its two heavy stone pylons, and white-painted ironwork, the Marlow Bridge is a little beauty.

The town baker told me a story concerning the bridge which bears repeating:

A long time ago the Marlow baker got fed up being told by visiting bargees that he wasn't putting enough meat in his pies. So he got hold of some drowned puppies, cooked 'em and crammed 'em into a gigantic pie. The bargees loved it, and after

that everyone in Marlow used to jeer 'Who ate the puppies under
Marlow Bridge?' whenever a visiting bargee got lippy.

The best, most attractive buildings in Marlow include some **Georgian
houses**. Those in Marlow Place, Station Road, are said to have been built in
1720 for George II when he was Prince of Wales. There are two in West
Street, one called 'Remnantz', with fine brick gate-piers and a cupola over
the stables, and the other next door, 'West House', with a handsome shell
hood of moulded plasterwork over the doorway. There's a nice house at No
72 in the High Street as well, and a 14th-century 'Old Parsonage' in St
Peter's Street, long and rambling with many gables, probably the oldest
house in town.

At one time or another, most rivermen find themselves in one of Marlow's
three riverside hostelries. The 18th-century **George and Dragon** and the
Two Brewers (visited by Jerome K Jerome) are both downstream of the
bridge on the Buckinghamshire bank, and **The Compleat Angler** is beside
the bridge, on the Berkshire side.

Lots of famous writers have visited and written about The Compleat
Angler. In his delightful *A Pictorial History of the River Thames*, published in
1889, A S Krausse described it as

> the most delightful riverside resort on the Thames . . ., old-fashioned,
> rambling, one-storied [sic] . . . with a gabled roof and quaint chimney
> stacks.

It has changed a bit, metamorphosed into a large and modern hotel, with the
sort of exterior you wonder why planners allowed, waiters and waitresses
instead of Krausse's buxom, apple-cheeked barmaids, and his simple plates of
bread and cheese exchanged for expense-account menus.

The poet Shelley and the creator of *Frankenstein* who doubled as his second
wife, **Mary Wollstonecraft Shelley** (1797–1851), lived briefly in 1817 and
1818 at **Albion House** in West Street (now called **Shelley House** and
marked by a plaque; not open to the public). A close friend and one of their
West Street neighbours was fellow author **Thomas Love Peacock**, who lived
in 47 West Street (now buried beneath a car park) while he was writing
Nightmare Abbey. Shelley kept a skiff on the river called *The Vaga* in which the
three used to voyage, once as far up-river as Lechlade, just a few miles from
the source (see page 217).

The wandering World War I poet **Edward Thomas**, who came to Marlow
in search of Shelley's roots, observed that 'from the time he went to school to
his last residence in England, Shelley was never long away from some part of
the River Thames'.

At the Gothic Albion House on the edge of Marlow, Shelley worked on *The
Revolt of Islam* while Mary, pregnant, worked quietly away at Frankenstein's
monster. When they weren't on the river, Shelley and Peacock ranged the
surrounding countryside to within a radius, they meticulously recorded, of 16
miles. They only halted for a pub meal once Peacock had asked the landlord,

without explanation, for a mustard pot; they based their decision on whether to stay or leave upon the condition of the pot.

There remains one other famous poet to mention before we leave the town – **T S Eliot**, who lived at 31 West Street (house not open to the public) a century after Shelley's time there.

Visitor information The Shelley Theatre at the Thameside Court Garden – on the Buckinghamshire bank just upstream of Marlow Bridge – commemorates Shelley and his associations with the town. Court Garden is a beautiful 18th-century house forming part of the Court Garden Leisure Centre, with café, bar, squash courts, tennis courts, swimming pool and other facilities. Open daily 09.00–22.00. Admission is free.

Marlow to Henley

14

Distances From Marlow Suspension Bridge: Temple Lock 1.51 miles (2.4km), Hurley Lock 2.15 miles (3.44km), Medmenham Abbey 3.73 miles (5.96km), the Ferry Pot Inn 3.73 miles (5.96km), Hambleden Lock 5.81 miles (9.3km), Temple Island 6.65 (10.6km), Henley Bridge 8.09 miles (12.9km)

If you've been thinking the trip up-river has been good, you ain't seen nothing yet. Upstream of Marlow Lock and Weir, the river curves among trees girdled by hills, and on the hills are more trees, the beech woods of Buckinghamshire. They are lovely in the spring, an unending blue mist of bluebells, serene and silent as a cathedral in high summer, the colour of a bonfire embers in the autumn. Wide-girthed, gnarled and stunted, lopped and re-grown by foresters in ancient times . . . these are the patriarchs of 'Beechy Bucks'.

Just outside Marlow, not yet far beyond the town's clutter and still not into untamed Thames, the Thames Path passes the park and mansion of **Higginson**, built in the 1760s as the home of **Dr William Battie**, a mental-illness specialist who provided posterity with the word 'batty'. The opposite side of the river is littered with a rash of expensive houses and maisonettes lacking the grace to retire quietly into the background. One day, the developers who create such eyesores, and the planners who permit them, will be put to law the way other polluters of our lovely land are, or should be, flayed into submission.

BISHAM

Among the trees on the other side of the Thames is the riverside **Bisham Church**, where floodwater once engulfed the pulpit. A quarter of a mile further, also on the far bank, is **Bisham Abbey House**, at whose handsome bay window **Queen Elizabeth I** sat when she was a princess and held prisoner there.

Bisham Abbey

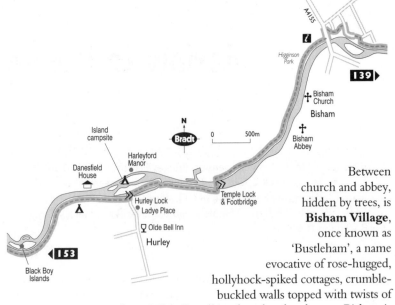

Between church and abbey, hidden by trees, is **Bisham Village**, once known as 'Bustleham', a name evocative of rose-hugged, hollyhock-spiked cottages, crumble-buckled walls topped with twists of moss-mellowed tiles. For all its chocolate-box beauty, Bisham is an unhappy reflection of English villages. Since I first came, 20, 30 . . . goodness knows how many . . . years ago, the little shop and the village hall have gone. So has the resident parson, the Mother's Union, the Women's Institute, the social club and the annual children's Christmas party in the **Abbey Hall** (when the kids wore Christmas-cracker hats and the conjuror drowned his watch in a jug of milk, then smashed it with a mallet, but, magically, never broke it). Most of the old villagers, too, have been elbowed out by commuting in-comers who think the village is quaint but couldn't really give much of a toss for its yesterdays. One ancient resident, clinging on, grieved that 'with the Big House and the vicarage gone, there's nobody to look after us any more.'

The poet **Percy Bysshe Shelley** loved this reach. He used to laze here, drifting on the stream, slumped in the bottom boards of his skiff. He told his buddy Peacock:

> [Bisham] runs with the blood and bones of a thousand heroes and
> villains, and no doubt the water is sour with tainting; but the scene is
> most satisfactory, you must agree.

I do, I do! It is difficult to imagine that any other English village, even one four times the size, has so many famous men with memorials either in the church or the abbey. There is **Richard Neville**, Earl of Salisbury, king-maker and king-destroyer, who was killed by one of the first cannonballs to be fired in battle; **Edward Plantagenet**, Earl of Warwick, imprisoned by Henry VII for 14 years and beheaded in 1499 for trying to escape from the Tower of London when he was still only 24; and **Thomas de Montacute**, 'the mirror of all martial men', who died, 'valiantly', at the siege of Orleans in 1428. What waste, what wonder, to die 'valiantly'.

Apart from its 12th-century square tower and its 16th-century chapel, the church was restored by wretched do-gooding Victorians. They at least left the nave and tower as they found them, but not the remainder. The chapel contains some fine monuments. It is called the **Hoby Chapel**, pronounced 'hobby', after the name of the local lords from the time of the dissolution right up to the 18th century.

Most stunning of the monuments is a free-standing stone pyramid edged by four swans, wings outstretched; it is called the **Swan Monument** and was erected by **Sir Edward Hoby**, son of the chapel's creator, in memory of his wife, **Lady Elizabeth Hoby**, aunt of the philosopher **Francis Bacon** (1561–1625) who came here often as a boy. The monument depicts her kneeling at a prayer desk beneath a canopy, her face refined, intelligent . . . but cruel, which she was, if legend is to be believed, for she beat her son to death for blotting his copybook and still haunts the neighbouring Abbey House, wringing her guilty hands.

I was ready to doubt than any woman could kill her own son for such a tiny misdeed until I discovered that workmen had unearthed parchment-dry and badly blotted 16th-century copybooks while renovating the one-time abbey home of the Hoby family in 1840. It does make you think, doesn't it? Whatever the truth, Lady Hoby was not a loving mother. She called another son a 'spindle-shanked ape', and he is said to have been the model for Sir Andrew Aguecheek in Shakespeare's *Twelfth Night*.

What remains of the ancient Abbey House is mainly Tudor. **Henry VIII** seized it after the Dissolution and gave it to **Anne of Cleves** (the 'Flanders Mare') as a sort of compensation for divorcing her and, no doubt, as a way of getting rid of her for he never liked her too close to hand. She lived here for a piece, mooching along the river banks, but never enjoyed the place. She soon exchanged it for a Kentish manor belonging to **Sir Philip Hoby**, who moved to Bisham where he was appointed gaoler to the future **Elizabeth I**, who was imprisoned for three years at Bisham during her sister Mary's reign.

The abbey is now the National Sports Centre, not open to casual visitors. However, if you are as desperate to see the Abbey Hall as I was, you might try telephoning 01628 476911 and moaning as loudly as I did about not being able to visit one of our national treasures. I didn't get in either!

HURLEY

At Thames-trim **Temple Lock**, elegant with topiary and majestic with giant chestnut trees, the Thames Path changes sides again, from Bucks to Berks. It crosses the longest hardwood footbridge (150ft/54.6m span) in the country, then travels half a mile along one of the shortest and sweetest reaches on the river – through an avenue of trees and lawns, fringed by banks of meadowsweet and foxgloves, wild-sown forget-me-nots and agrimony – to enter **Hurley Lock** through a weave of islands and backwaters, of which Jerome K Jerome observed

> [I] often thought that I could stay a month without having sufficient
> time to drink in all the beauty of the scene . . . The village of Hurley,
> five minutes walk from the lock, is as old a little spot as there is on
> the river.

There is a best-in-the-business Environment Agency campsite with ten pitches on one of the islands, between the lock and the weir, run by the lock-keeper who allows passers-by, as well as campers, to take advantage of the lock-side rubbish disposal facilities, WCs and freshwater supplies. The lock has a wonderful relic of the not-so-long-gone past – a timber weir winch. This was used in the 18th century to pull boats up through the old flash lock against a froth of flood water which surged upon them when the weir boards were removed prior to the pound lock being constructed in 1790. There is another ancient capstan, fully restored, a pace or two up-river beside **Henley Weir** at Medmenham. Yesterdays are never so very far away from Hurley Lock. **Freebody's Boatyard**, for instance, just downstream of the lock, is one of the few remaining boatyards still building wooden boats.

Visitor information Hurley Lock Campsite (Mill Lane, Maidenhead, Berkshire S6 1SA; tel: 01628 824334) has WCs, showers, washbasins, shaver points, fishing, and canoe-landing point. It is open Apr 1–Sep 30, and costs £5.50 for a two-man tent. The nearby Hurley Village has a shop, post office and pubs. There is excellent fishing for those with weir permits, obtainable from the Evironmental Agency (tel: 0118 953 5000).

Some parts of Hurley, best reached by a footpath at the top end of the lock, have been hurt past mending by the intrusion of new and unseemly housing estates. But the best bits, only yards from the river, remain as good as ever they were: the church, next door's Edwardian mansion of **Ladye Place**, a few half-timbered cottages, a green, and the **Olde Bell** inn (claimed to be the oldest in England). That's about it – but it's enough.

The long and narrow nave of Hurley's **St Mary the Virgin** is all that remains of a priory founded here in 1087 for Benedictine monks. Inside is a famous monument to Hurley's **Lovelace family**, a coloured memorial, with

LADYE PLACE AND JOHN LOVELACE

The original Ladye Place (demolished during the early 19th century and replaced by the present Edwardian building) contained an underground vault in which, **Macaulay** recorded, 'some zealous and daring opponents of the government held many midnight conferences'. In plainer terms, a 17th-century Lovelace descendant, John, third Baron Lovelace of Hurley (1638–93), used his cellar as the headquarters for plotting against **King James II**, who had resolved to impose Roman Catholicism on a nation which would have none of it. Lovelace staked everything he possessed on overthrowing the king. One night he and 70 of his supporters crossed the river at Hurley, and galloped through the darkness into Gloucestershire where they intended to raise a rebellion. But the militia confronted them, and ordered them to put up or fight. They fought, were overpowered, and taken as prisoners to Gloucester Castle. Lovelace survived to see James deposed and Protestant **Mary** and **William of Orange** imported from Holland. He died in 1693, probably from drinking too often and too well, especially his regular morning tipple comprising a quart of brandy . . . at least. William of Orange, and later successive Hanoverian kings, came in homage to Ladye Place.

kneeling Elizabethan figures. They lived next door, in Ladye Place (see box above), built by a Tudor sea-dog ancestor, **Sir Richard Lovelace**, who paid for it, according to the historian Lord Macaulay, 'out of the spoils of Spanish galleons from the Indies'.

The TV sports presenter **Steve Ryder** lives in a riverside cottage at Hurley, although he asks visitors not to be specific about its location for fear his family may be overwhelmed by rubber-neckers. He loves the place:

> It's got the great advantage of having terrific communications with
> London and yet, not being a through route, the village is
> comparatively quiet and you don't have traffic destroying the place.
> There is a wonderful community life here which can absorb every
> hour of the week if you let it.

On the Buckinghamshire bank, opposite Hurley Lock, is **Harleyford Manor**, red brick and plain but handsome, four-square with bays, built in 1755. It is one

DANESFIELD

Beyond Hurley, the white and slightly supercilious-looking mansion of Danesfield, built in the 19th and 20th centuries, stands on the Buckinghamshire chalk bluffs above the river. It is now a posh country house hotel (tel: 01628 891010) for well-heeled nobs and nobesses. Carol Shearman, Danesfield's ever-so-helpful marketing manager, told me something of its history:

A man called **Robert 'Soapy' Hudson** built the present Danesfield House at the turn of the 19th and 20th centuries. He was the son of the 'Sunlight' soap magnate, Robert Spear Hudson. 'Soapy' knocked the old place down, built a new one with such disregard for expense that it became, and still is, an architectural Italian Renaissance show piece.

The Royal Air Force (Reconnaissance and Photography Section) occupied the house from 1941 to 1977 when the Grand Banqueting Hall must have been the most luxurious officers' mess in the country, possibly the world.

In keeping with its status, there is, of course, a ghost, a 'grey lady' who walks through the grounds of the hotel every night at twilight.

of the houses claimed to be the model for Toad Hall in *Wind in the Willows*. The house is now host and clubhouse for **Hurley Marina**, and the adjacent sprawl of a caravan park (see *Visitor information* below) is anything but pretty. The Thamesider artist G D Leslie, in his 1881 evocation *Our River*, wrote:

No house on the river has a sweeter situation [than Harleyford Manor]; here are cannonballs and fortifications (against whom intended I do not know), neatly kept landing places, the usual trespassers' boards, and some lovely backwaters, in one of which is a very fine boathouse with the stream running through it, near which a beautiful plane tree overhangs the water, beneath which tree the late **Emperor of the French** was very fond of lying in his boat when on a visit here in bygone days.

Just imagine! The Emperor of the French boating on the river! Now, that would have been something to see.

Visitor information There are 350 pitches for tents at Hurley Riverside Park, which is close to the Thames Path. To book, contact the estate office (Hurley Farm, Hurley, Berks SL6 5NE; tel: 01628 823501). Facilities include WCs, showers, wash basins, shaver points, Elsan disposal, fishing pitches, boat-launching slip, shop, launderette and disabled amenities. Open Mar 1–Oct 31. Pitch prices from £7 per night for two people, additional persons £1.50 each .

A mile after Danesfield (see box opposite) are **Black Boy Islands**, where the river bends like a shepherd's crook southwest into Berkshire, then northwest back into Buckinghamshire. The islands are named after **King Charles II**, who was so dark-skinned that his mother, **Henrietta Maria**, declared he was 'a black baby'.

MEDMENHAM

A short distance upstream, on the Buckinghamshire bank, is sepulchre-white **Medmenham Abbey**, beautiful, notorious, sinister and 18th-century Gothic. Behind, hugged by trees, is a 15th-century manor house. In front is a lawn running to the river's edge.

Seen from the Thames Path, through willow fronds hanging like harp strings above the water, the abbey makes as tranquil a picture as any since the beginnings of freshwater Teddington. But wash the abbey's salt-white arches in moonlight, add wisps of mist rolling from the river to drift like wraiths through the moonlit trees . . . then tell me there are no such thing as ghosts!

The place should be full of them, at least a baker's dozen, all howling and repenting their sins, for it was here the notorious **Sir Francis Dashwood** brought his twelve Hell Fire Club members in the 18th century. These, and Sir Francis, became the psychopathic self-styled 'Monks of St Francis' who enjoyed nothing better than a hearty sexual debauchery or two, and a lot more if they could get them.

Dashwood, later England's only chancellor to admit he was drunk while presenting the budget speech, dedicated his youth, and not a little of the rest of his life, to vice and sex and all manner of wonderfully disgraceful things. He founded the Hell Fire Club at Medmenham in 1745, filling the abbey with phallic symbols and pornographic statues and paintings. The club's motto was 'do what thou wilt' and, true to their membership oath, the members 'wilted' a good deal. There were special 'nun's cells' set aside for romps with their fastidiously chosen lady friends. The orgies were 'nameless' according to chronicles of the time – but precise details of what went on are few, as members were sworn to secrecy and little was ever published about their actual goings on. We do know, though, that Medmenham's Hell Fire Club went out of business when a baboon dressed as the devil was secreted into the abbey and so  successfully convinced members it was Old Nick himself that no meetings were ever held here again.

It's a pity the Thames Path is on the Berks rather than the Bucks bank because things on the Buckinghamshire side of the river are much more interesting hereabouts. **Medmenham Village**, for instance, is meticulously tended, comfortable and straggly, a goodly spot to bide a while. Parts of it – the late 14th-/early 15th-century church, and the 14th-century **Dog and Badger** pub – have featured in TV's *Vicar of Dibley*. The pub is also reputed to have been much used by members of the Hell Fire Cub (see above), and I can't believe it wasn't.

Ferry Lane leads from beside the church to the river where the old Medmenham ferry used to pick up and drop its fares. On the upstream side of the lane is a bronze plaque, which reads:

> This monument was erected to commemorate the successful action
> fought by Hudson Ewebank Kearley, first Viscount Devonport P C,
> which resulted in the Court of Appeal deciding on the 18th March,
> 1899, that Medmenham ferry is public.

The case was brought by local landowner Kearney to prevent an inn-keeper from claiming the ferry for his own and closing it down if passengers refused to pay a heavy crossing toll. The action was complex, long and expensive, but Kearney won and he erected the monument to ensure that no-one ever forgot the outcome. Ironically, though the monument remains, the ferry has gone.

'From Medmenham to sweet Hambleden Lock the river is peaceful beauty', wrote Jerome in *Three Men in a Boat*. It still is, a pastoral seclusion, one hundred and more years on. For the next two and a half miles nothing interrupts the unspoiled loveliness of the river and the landscape, except for a cottage close to **Magpie Island**, and that fits the landscape perfectly, a Gothic retreat with quatrefoil windows.

Shortly after, on a rise above the Thames Path, stands the sturdy, five-bay, neo-classical pedimented brick mansion of **Culham Court**, built in 1770, a little like Harleyford Manor, but better. **King George III** was entertained here, right royally too. His host arranged that hot rolls from the king's favourite London baker, Gunther, were brought every day wrapped in hot flannels. They were galloped to Culham Court by relays of horsemen, and arrived in time for breakfast. The king expressed no surprise, merely exclaiming, 'Ah . . . Gunther's rolls. Capital! Nothing like Gunther.'

ASTON

Beyond Culham Court the Thames Path leaves the river to follow a narrow lane downhill into Aston and the Victorian red-bricked **Flowerpot** (built 1890), which used to be an 'inn' but is now a 'hotel'. On the outside front wall is the legend, 'Good accommodation for boating and fishing parties'. Inside is one of the largest collections of stuffed fish in the country. The American writer-artist team, **Elizabeth** and **Joseph**

Pennell – she wrote and he illustrated – called at the 'terracotta' Flowerpot the year it opened. From the entrance to the Flowerpot, wrote Elizabeth,

> we looked on elms, the loveliest in the whole length and breadth of
> England . . . which met over the narrow lanes bordered with fields of
> fiery poppies, while near by there were to be seen old-fashioned
> gardens full of early sunflowers waiting to count the steps of the sun
> that would not shine.

The elms are gone (isn't that sad?), killed by a blight we are still unable to control. But there are always summer poppies in the fields surrounding the pub, which doesn't please the farmer, and one of the nearby cottagers was growing sunflowers, whoppers, the last time I called. The sun wasn't shining that day, either.

HAMBLEDEN

Upstream of Aston, the Thames Path rejoins the river and half a mile later reaches Hambleden Lock, weir, mill, and village. It is a place you will never forget. From walkways over the great weirs, a footpath goes to the white weatherboarded mill, now converted into very upmarket apartments but still looking for all the world like an old mill, then a mile north to pretty Hambleden, one of the most attractive villages in the whole of Buckinghamshire.

Set at the base of a Chiltern valley, surrounded by plump wooded hills, Hambleden is in a perfect setting, squat as a broody hen, with blithe cottages lining the roads fanning north and south from the village square. Most of the

Hambleden Mill

cottages are tiny, book-ended snug and warm in brick and flint terraces. By contrast, the 17th-century **Manor House** seems gigantic, a much-gabled Jacobean building where **Lord Cardigan**, of Light Brigade (see page 95) and cardie fame, was born. It lies at the edge of the village, opposite the church. Cardigan's sea chest, which accompanied him to the Crimea, is preserved in the beautiful old church. The 12th-century **St Mary the Virgin** at Hambleden is flint and chalk with stone dressings under an ancient tiled roof. The square tower, heightened in the early 1880s, contains eight bells, one of which was rung at the time of England's victory over the French at Agincourt. There is an extraordinary monument, and a very odd relic, inside the church. The monument is the **d'Oyley family** tomb, said by experts in tomb furniture (yes, they do exist) to be one of the finest alabaster monuments anywhere in England; it portrays the kneeling figures of Sir Cope d'Oyley, his wife and ten children. That's the 'extraordinary'. The 'odd' is part of a bed, said to have been **Cardinal Wolsey**'s, built into the south transept altar; the carving bears Wolsey's hat and coat of arms.

Major George Howson, MC, lies in Hambleden churchyard. He organised the poppy factory for the Royal British Legion.

We return on the footpath by which we came in order to rejoin the Thames Path at **Hambleden Lock** – it is worth a second look anyway. **Hambleden Mill**, even though it stopped milling in the mid-1950s, driven by water-turbine, is a famous calendar subject. So is the 'Hambleden Lasher' (where the river pours into a crash of frenzied froth at the foot of the weir), where canoeists have a regular slalom course.

Hambleden Lock's best-remembered keeper is **Caleb Gould**. He kept the lock for an astonishing 59 years, from 1777 until he died aged 92 in 1836. Not much is recorded about him other than that he refused to acknowledge 'modern' fashions, invariably wore an ankle-long, early-18th-century coat with capes and silver buttons, and ate a plate of onion porridge every night of his life. He sold bread to bargemen, which he baked in a large open-air oven behind his cottage. He is buried up-river in Remenham churchyard. His grave carries the famous epitaph by poet **John Gay**:

> The world's a jest, and all things show it.
> I thought so once, and now I know it.

Above Hambleden Lock the landscape becomes more sophisticated, estate-formal with decorative trees. Large houses and isolated cottages are on the Buckinghamshire bank where the landscape eases seamlessly into the Cotswold country of Oxfordshire.

One of the houses looking down on the Buckinghamshire Thames is **Greenlands**, described in *Three Men in a Boat* as

> the rather uninteresting-looking river residence of my newsagent – a quiet, unassuming old gentleman, who may often be met with about these regions, during the summer months, sculling himself along in easy vigorous style, or chatting genially to some old lock-keeper, as he passes through.

The reference to 'my newsagent' puzzled me for years. I hadn't realised this was one of Jerome's funnies. The newsagent was **William Henry Smith** (1851–91), W H Smith, founder of the famous chain of bookshops (now high-street emporiums selling books, magazines and stationery items). His 'empire' began in 1852 when he started a chain of railway station bookstores selling 'railway novels', one-or-two-shilling 'yellowbacks' which became established reading for train travellers. He entered politics, and was subsequently appointed First Lord of the Admiralty by Disraeli. It was a promotion regarded as so bizarre in light of Smith's limited knowledge of the sea and ships that W S Gilbert lampooned him as 'Sir Joseph Porter' in HMS *Pinafore*; Prime Minister **Benjamin Disraeli** henceforth called his First Lord 'Pinafore Smith'. In 1896, W H Smith all but killed off **Thomas Hardy** by refusing to stock *Jude the Obscure*.

Greenlands today, the house and a pickle of add-ons in the grounds, is occupied by **Henley Management College**.

Visitor information The house is not, officially, open to occasional callers, but the administrator, business development manager Lyn Stone, has been known to treat enquiring visitors kindly, providing they telephone first (01491 571454).

Just up-stream of Greenlands is **Regatta – or Temple – Island**, with an 18th-century classical temple perched on its banks. It is topped by a cupola sheltering a naked lady, who has unsurpassed views of the dead-straight two-mile regatta course ending below Henley Bridge. The island marks the starting point for **Henley Regatta** rowing course – the same course over which Oxford rowed the first university boat race against Cambridge, and won by five or six lengths, in 1829. Nearly 20,000 watched the race. 'Every inn and public house was crammed to excess,' reported the *Oxford Herald*. 'Provisions of every sort were soon exhausted.'

The 'temple' is really a fishing lodge, designed by **James Wyatt** (1746–1813) when he was only 25 and had already made a name as a neo-classical architect. Wyatt painted frescos, nice ones I am told, inside the chapel, which was built in 1771 for the wealthy **Freeman family** living at **Fawley Court**, the house overlooking the island. Fawley Court was designed, first time round, by **Sir Christopher Wren**, was remodelled in classical style by James Wyatt, and had Victorian bits and pieces stuck on later, not to mention an Ionic colonnade by **Capability Brown**. As a consequence, the house is a bit of a hotchpotch, but quite handsome for all that, and unique as a surviving example of a Wren country house.

It was lucky to survive at all, especially during the English Civil War when **Cromwell** held nearby Henley and Fawley got knocked about a bit. I was told about the civil war conflict and its effect on Fawley Court by **Chris Jackson**, at Henley Tourist Information Centre, who is the most helpful, friendly, and knowledgeable TIC person I have ever met. This is what he said:

> Fawley Court in the days of the civil war was owned by **Sir Bulstrode Whitlock**, an all-round Henley bigwig, a lawyer and well-to-do, a typical squire-type of person. He was a strong Parliamentarian and Fawley Court was occupied by Cromwell's forces. The neighbouring house down-river, Greenlands, was occupied by a king's man, a good friend of Sir Bulstrode's despite their differences. His house was occupied by Cavaliers. The two neighbours agreed that they would disagree and do as little damage to each other's houses as possible, merely toss a few cannonballs into the gardens, that sort of thing. The Greenlands' man must have reneged on the deal, however, because Fawley got damaged a lot and a letter by Sir Bulstrode (now in Henley's River and Rowing Museum) records that the Cavalier soldiers 'did all the mischief and spoil that malice and enmity could provide barbarian mercenaries to commit.'

In a way, Sir Bulstrode got his own back on Greenlands by eloping with the daughter of the house, **Frances Willoughby**, to the consecrated chapel at Fawley Court where the 'mixed marriage took place swiftly and quietly'. Despite his support for parliament, Sir Bulstrode was not executed when Charles II got the throne back, but was fined a hefty £90,000, which even the mortgage of Fawley Court could not provide. As a result, Charles II reduced the fine to £60,000 and Sir Bulstrode paid up.

Visitor information Fawley Court and gardens are open to the public between March and October (Wed, Thu and Sat, 14.00–17.00). Closed Easter and Whit Sunday. Admission adult £4, OAP £3, child £1.50. There is a gift shop and café serving light refreshments.

FAWLEY VILLAGE

People make pilgrimages to Fawley Village because of its **Thomas Hardy** (1840–1928) connections. His grandmother, **Mary Hardy**, born 1772, lived with her aunt in Fawley for the first 13 years of her life. She didn't like it and would never speak about it. Perhaps it was this which coloured Hardy's own opinions of the village, for he chose it, renamed 'Marygreen', as the setting for the tragic *Jude the Obscure* because it struck him as a suitably gloomy place for the ill-fated Jude Fawley to live. Hardy experts believe that the little school where Sue Bridehead worked with her hated husband Philotson is modelled on the still-standing old school at Fawley.

Hardy almost certainly visited the village several times and at least one occasion, in 1885 or 1886, when he visited the churchyard as the church was about to be pulled down, is recorded in his journal:

> I entered a ploughed field which might have been called the Valley of
> Brown Melancholy, where the silence was remarkable.

The old church has long gone, but the melancholic churchyard is still there, much neglected. Jude described the new church of St Mary as 'of modern Gothic design, unfamiliar to English eyes', and the German-born British art historian, **Nicholaus Pevsner** (1902–83) called it a 'serious, almost forbidding church' (in his 50-volume *The Buildings of England*). Its saving grace is one of the stained-glass windows by the craftsman, artist and poet **William Morris** (1834–96).

From Fawley it is possible to follow Jude's route towards Oxford – or 'Christminster', as Hardy renamed it – and across the ancient Ridgeway path.

REMENHAM

Other than its chocolate-box setting, there's not a lot going for the village of Remenham, lying close to the river, half a mile east of Henley. It's a scrappy sort of a place, scattered along the Berkshire south bank, backed by the wooded **Remenham Hill**. Even its church, **St Nicholas's**, well-snugged in a cosy setting, has not enjoyed a good press, being tabbed 'self-consciously quaint' by architectural photographer-writer, and one-time editor of the authoritative *Architects' Journal*, **Eric de Maré** (1910–2002). He wrote the enjoyable *Time on the Thames* after a long and slow voyage up the river in the late 1940s/early 1950s. The actress **Jenny Agutter** was married in the church. The grave of the Hambleden lock-keeper, Caleb Gould (see page 156), is by the south door.

Henley-on-Thames

Everyone should try to reach Henley-on-Thames in time for tea – proper tea, an English sort of tea, in a real English teashop where they have bone china and serve hot buttered crumpets and toast. Henley is a very English sort of town, a bright, happy sort of town, a timeless, Edwardian-elegant sort of town, a big-little sort of town, small and intimate in winter and spring, with teashops to cope. But its international renown is so big, and the streets can be so over-crowded in midsummer that wise travellers only go there outside 'regatta' time.

Henley was a fashionable place in the 1750s, an inland port and an important staging post for Oxford–London coaches, which accounts for its wealth of Georgian buildings. It is still an entrancing place.

HENLEY REGATTA

Most people like Henley – except during regatta (first week in July), when it is jam-packed with several nice folk and a lot of pompous-ass people, with more money than manners, who have come (the spectators not the rowers) to be seen and to feed their faces on free nosh and booze. The town has always been packed at regatta time. In the 1890 edition of his *Dictionary of the Thames*, **Charles Dickens Jr** complained:

> [T]he river is so inconveniently crowded with steam launches, houseboats, skiffs, gigs, punts, dinghies, canoes and every other conceivable and inconceivable variety of craft, that the racing boats have sometimes great difficulty in threading a way through the crowd.

Much of the old regatta elegance has gone, replaced by fibreglass gin palaces whose occupants preen for admiring glances from the shore, while former rowing men, landlubbered by boardroom bellies, swagger and bray, one to the other, with fog-horn voices. In the beginning the regatta was purely an Oxford and Cambridge affair, with a handful of public-school hangers-on, a very English 'do', and an aristocratic one. Foreigners and artisans were tolerated, just, as spectators, but they certainly weren't allowed to compete. It became a 'Royal' regatta in 1851 when **Prince Albert**, Queen Victoria's Prince Consort, travelled up-river by boat to attend that year's high jinks. In 1872 an American was graciously permitted

to enter for the Diamond Sculls, but he had the good grace, and sense, not to win. Everything went downhill in 1906 when a foreign entrant, a Belgian, did, winning the Grand Challenge Cup, then went on to win it the following year and the year after that. The swaggerers and the brayers didn't like it, nor do they truly like 'foreigners' winning to this day – which they do, often.

Although Henley Royal Regatta is now an international, professional rowing competition, it still remains primarily an aristocratic, bumptious few days of wealth and booze, the lawns a kaleidoscope of razzle-dazzle: striped tents the colour of Joseph's coat, blazers and caps, white flannels, summer dresses and hats. And the river is a pageant of modern gin palaces, elderly steam launches, rowing boats and skiffs, punts and canoes.

For all its pomposity and overcrowding it remains something to be seen and wondered at.

THE TOWN

The best of Henley, during regatta and other times, lies near the river. The bridge, built 1787, stone with balustrades and five arches, is one of the most graceful on the Thames. It was designed by a Shrewsbury man, **William Hayward**, who died before it was finished; nobody I spoke with knew anything about him. But they knew about the lady who carved the flamboyant keystone heads on either side of the central arch. She was **Anne Damer** (1748/9–1828), of nearby Park Place, who sculpted the heads of Thames and Isis, best seen from the bank, at some time in the 18th century. She mingled with the good and the great, carving the likenesses of **George III**, **Nelson** and the actress **Mrs Siddons**, and was a close friend of **Napoleon's wife**, as in 'not tonight Josephine'. She was a cousin of **Horace Walpole**, who bequeathed his home at Strawberry Hill to her after his death. She lived the last years of her life at Strawberry Hill and was buried with her tools, her apron, and the ashes of her dog.

On one side of the bridge is a post-modern extravaganza housing **Henley Royal Regatta Headquarters**, on the other the **Leander Club** on less extravagant lines. Members of the Leander Club wear pink, as **John Betjeman**'s 'Henley Regatta 1902' observes:

HENLEY-ON-THAMES

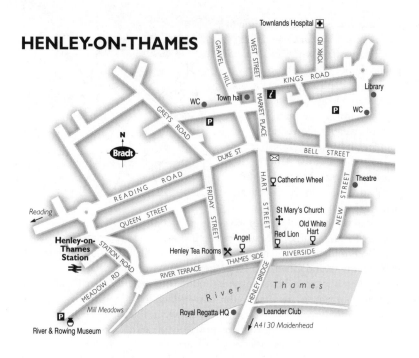

Underneath a light straw boater
In his pink Leander tie
Ev'ry ripple in the water caught the Captain in the eye.

St Mary's Church, in Hart Street, beside the bridge, is chiefly 16th-century, unspoiled and gloomy. To the west of the churchyard is a row of **almshouses** which look older than they are (endowed 1547, rebuilt 1830). The south end of the row adjoins a handsome early Georgian brick house facing Hart Street.

To see Henley's best features, head for **Hart Street**, **Market Place**, **Friday Street**, **New Street**, and **Bell Street**, which is the main shopping centre.

Henley's pubs

If you like ancient pubs then you are in your element. One of them, although writer **John Mortimer** never identified which, was portrayed as the 'Swan's Nest' in his novel *Paradise Postponed*, where Henley

becomes Hartscombe and young Leslie Titmuss is pushed, 'his arms and legs waving helplessly, into the dark, brackish water of the Thames'. The Swan's Nest could be any one of many lovely Thameside pubs between here and Maidenhead:

> [A] pleasant, low, brick and weather-boarded building by the river. Its untended garden stretches down to the water, where a few punts and rowing boats are moored for the pleasure of visitors, and swans glide in a ghostly fashion over the dark water. In the twenties and thirties the name of the Swan's Nest was synonymous with adultery and illicit weekends. It figured in society divorce cases and it achieved that somewhat raffish reputation, which it cannot shake off, although the Guards officers and debutantes, the dubious foreign Counts and undependable married ladies no longer trail their fingers in the water from its punts or order champagne in its bedrooms.

There are over 20 pubs in Henley; many are lovely, duck-your-head-and-crouch ones, so old they still have their original bull- and bear-baiting yards. Beyond the church is the red-brick **Red Lion**, overlooking the river, where the **Duke of Marlborough** permanently rented and furnished a room so that he had somewhere to rest on his journeys between London and Blenheim. **Charles I** stayed at the Red Lion in 1632, and again in 1642. **Emperor Alexander of Russia** popped by in 1814, after having his carriage pulled through Henley's streets by a team of enthusiastic townsfolk instead of horses. There is a window in the pub scratched with verse by the poet **William Shenstone** (1714–63) when he stopped for a noggin and was offered a free night's lodging in exchange for the rhyme:

> Whoe'er has travelled life's dull round;
> Where'er his stages may have been;
> May sigh to think he still has found
> The warmest welcome at an inn.

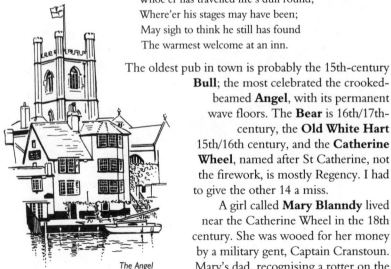

The oldest pub in town is probably the 15th-century **Bull**; the most celebrated the crooked-beamed **Angel**, with its permanent wave floors. The **Bear** is 16th/17th-century, the **Old White Hart** 15th/16th century, and the **Catherine Wheel**, named after St Catherine, not the firework, is mostly Regency. I had to give the other 14 a miss.

A girl called **Mary Blanndy** lived near the Catherine Wheel in the 18th century. She was wooed for her money by a military gent, Captain Cranstoun. Mary's dad, recognising a rotter on the

The Angel

make, forbade the romance and so Cranstoun sent the girl a packet of 'love powder' with instructions to dose her father in order to make him look favourably upon their union. The powder was arsenic, the father died, and the girl was tried and hanged at Oxford in 1752. Her ghost, riding a white horse, haunts the street close to the Catherine Wheel.

The River and Rowing Museum

I've saved one of the best bits of Henley till last. It's the **River and Rowing Museum** on the lawns of Mill Meadows which the Thames Path skirts as we head out of town. It won an award for its architecture soon after it opened in 1998. The exterior is, indeed, stunning, but it deserves an award for what's inside as well because the museum's contents are even better than the outside. It is unique in the world for its interactive galleries devoted to rowing, the Thames and the town of Henley.

Visitor information The first thing you do should be to visit the TIC (tel: 01491 412703) in the Market Place at the top end of Hart Street because it is the best-peopled tourist information centre in all the Thames Valley.

The River and Rowing Museum (Mill Meadows, Henley-on-Thames, RG9 1BF; tel: 01491 415600; email: museum@rrm.co.uk; web: www.rrm.co.uk) is open May 1–Aug 31 (10.00–17.30 Mon–Sun) and Sep 1–Apr 30 (10.00–17.00 Mon–Sun). Closed Christmas Eve, Christmas Day, New Year's Eve and New Year's Day. Admission: £4.95 adults, £3.75 concessions and children (5–16 years). Facilities include car park, WCs, café, gift shop and baby facilities. There is excellent access for wheelchair users.

There's a campsite at Henley (tel: 01491 573419), about 400 yards from the Thames Path, with 120 pitches. Open Mar 1–Oct 31. Facilities include WCs, showers, wash basins, launderette, clubhouse, swimming pool, and fishing. Cost per night is £4 per person, plus £2 for electricity, and a £1 tent-pitching charge.

Henley to Reading

Distances From Henley Bridge: Marsh Lock 0.95 miles (1.5km), Wargrave 3.05 miles (4.88km), Shiplake Railway Bridge 3.33 miles (5.3km), Sonning Bridge 6.16 miles (9.85km), River Kennet 8.33 miles, (13.3km) Reading Bridge 9.25 miles (14.9km)

'The river up to Sonning winds in and out through many islands, and is very placid, hushed and lonely,' wrote Jerome K Jerome. It still is. After Henley, the river passes **Rod Eyot** islets on its way south to **Marsh Lock Island**, slap-bang in the middle of the Thames.

MARSH LOCK

It is only a mile out of town, yet cows lumber down to the river to drink. In *Three Men in a Boat*, Jerome wrote, 'It is a part of the river in which to dream of bygone days . . . and things that might have been, but are not, confound them'. The island lock, complete with picture-book keeper's cottage, giant trees and a prize-winning garden, is approached by a long wooden bridge over the weir.

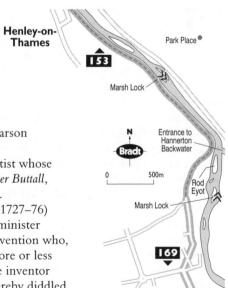

The lock, the weir and the bridge were designed by an extraordinary man, a country parson whose brother was **Thomas Gainsborough**, the English artist whose most famous portrait is of *Master Buttall*, better known as the 'Blue Boy'. **Humphrey Gainsborough** (c1727–76) was a non-conformist Henley minister with a genius for design and invention who, for some reason, history has more or less forgot. Was it, perhaps, because inventor rivals pinched his ideas and thereby diddled him out of royalties and recognition? Chris Jackson, at the Henley TIC, thinks it might be. So did a 19th-century lady, **Emily Climenson**, author of the 1896 *Guide to Henley-on-Thames*:

> Humphrey Gainsborough made a sundial capable of pointing the
> hour to the second. It stands on three legs and has the words
> 'Humphrey Gainsborough' deeply cut in it. [This is now in the
> British Museum, but not on display, and no-one I asked seemed
> keen on digging it out for my benefit – *Ed*] . . . He made a working
> model of a steam engine and invented a separate steam condensor;
> unfortunately he showed this to a stranger . . . and this man, an
> engineer who was on chummy terms with [James] Watt, told him
> about Gainsborough's idea of a separate steam chamber. Watt's
> engine [incorporating Gainsborough's steam chamber] was brought
> out in 1769.

Humphrey Gainsborough never received recognition for his contribution to Watt's steam engine. He was discovered dead on the river bank on August 23 1776. The *Gentleman's Magazine* subsequently referred to him as 'one of the most ingenious men that ever lived and one of the best that ever died'.

Just upstream of Marsh Lock is a **Victorian boathouse** tucked into the Berkshire bank. Behind it, peering over a golf course which now surrounds it, is **Park Place**, an indifferent French Renaissance-style Victorian house of the 1870s. The original house was built for the **Duke of Hamilton** and was, for a time, like Cliveden (see page 132), the home of **Frederick, Prince of Wales**, father of George III. Park Place was purchased from the executors of Frederick by **General Henry Conway**, an 18th-century governor of Jersey who, together with Humphrey Gainsborough, shares the honour of being the only Henley residents painted by Thomas Gainsborough. In the grounds of Park Place is a complete megalithic chambered tomb, a monument unique in southern England. It was brought from Jersey by General Conway in 1785, carried stone by stone on barges up the river to be re-erected where it stands today.

Soon after Marsh Lock, the river passes the entrance to the long and lonely **Hannerton Backwater** on the opposite bank, beautiful, overhung by trees, its loneliness worth exploring, slowly, by punt or rowing boat. It rejoins the Thames a mile upstream at Willow Marina.

Meanwhile, the Thames Path bears away from the river, leaving the spindle-tree eyots of **Ferry**, **Poplar** and **Handback** behind, heading slightly inland to the river-garden houses of **Lower Shiplake**; in one of them, Thames-Side Court, there is an astonishing narrow-gauge railway wriggling its way through an eight-acre garden.

Upstream of the Wargrave bend, the river runs under a truly ugly railway bridge where the River Loddon flows into the pasture-fringed Thames below **Shiplake Lock**.

WARGRAVE

Wargrave is pleasant, long, and largely Georgian, tucked into trees. It used to be worth £27 6s 8d – the value the Domesday Book put on the place in 1086 when it was one of the richest and most populous villages in East Berkshire. It was once a royal stronghold. **Emma**, 'Fair Maid of Normandy' (AD990–1052), twice queen of England (once wife of Aethelred and then of Cnut or Canute), lived here as the first holder of Wargrave Manor. Her son **Edward the Confessor** was born here. Whatever was left of the royal palace, in Church Street, was demolished by Victorian vandals in 1827.

The green in the centre of the village is called **Mill Green**. On one side is the 15th-century **Wargrave Court** manor house (with timber-work exposed during Victorian and Edwardian alterations). On the west side of the green is **St Mary's Church**. The original Norman-Saxon church was rebuilt after it had been burned to the ground in 1914 by suffragettes, led by **Emmeline Pankhurst**, because, so the tale goes, the vicar refused to take the word 'obey' out of the marriage service. Inside is the tomb of **Madame Marie Tussaud**, of waxworks fame; she lived somewhere close by – although no-one could tell me where – until she died, aged 90, in 1850.

In the heart of the village are timber-framed houses, two 17th-century pubs, and a Queen Anne vicarage. One of the pubs, the **St George and Dragon** on the Henley Road, has an interesting story which the Thamesider artist **George Leslie** recounted in his 1888 book on the Thames, *Our River*:

> It was during our stay at Wargrave . . . that my friend Mr Hodgson and I repainted Mrs Wyatt's signboard for her. . . I painted my side first, a regular orthodox St George on a white horse, spearing the Dragon. Hodgson was so taken with the idea of painting a signboard that he asked . . . to be allowed to do the other side. . . [I]t occupied him little more than a couple of hours. . .; the picture represented St George, having vanquished the dragon and dismounted from his horse, quenching his thirst in a large beaker of ale.

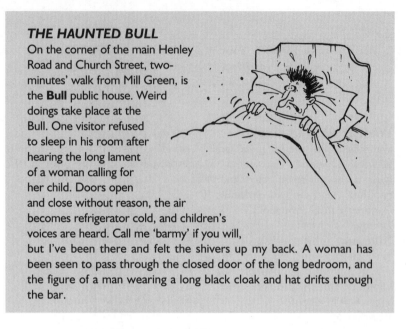

THE HAUNTED BULL
On the corner of the main Henley Road and Church Street, two-minutes' walk from Mill Green, is the **Bull** public house. Weird doings take place at the Bull. One visitor refused to sleep in his room after hearing the long lament of a woman calling for her child. Doors open and close without reason, the air becomes refrigerator cold, and children's voices are heard. Call me 'barmy' if you will, but I've been there and felt the shivers up my back. A woman has been seen to pass through the closed door of the long bedroom, and the figure of a man wearing a long black cloak and hat drifts through the bar.

Today this famous old sign hangs indoors behind glass beside the bar, while its place outside has been taken by a copy. Ukelele-playing, tomb-stone-grinning **George Formby** filmed one of his slapsticks, *Keep Fit*, in and about the pub in the 1930s. Nowadays the George and Dragon (tel: 0118 940 5021) is a child-friendly Harvester restaurant and pub.

Wargrave's **almshouses**, as well as the village's recreation ground, allotments, and Mission Hall on Crazies Hill, were all the gifts of a single benefactor. She was a cousin of Florence Nightingale, **Harriette Smith**, who lived in a house called Woodclyffe where the parson-novelist **Henry Kingsley** (1819–75) stayed while he was writing *Westward Ho!* in the 1850s and *The Water Gipsies* in the 1860s. **Florence Nightingale** visited twice.

SHIPLAKE

Shiplake is in two parts, the old and the new, the upper and the lower. One part is huddled round the church of **St Peter and St Paul**, the other clustered about the railway station. There's a good up-hill bridle-path walk from the lock to the commuter-desirable, but not inspiring, village, one and a half miles distant. The views from the top of **Shiplake Knoll**, near the church, are good. Queen Victoria's poet laureate **Alfred, Lord Tennyson**, (1809–92), married **Emily Smallwood** here, in the church which was subsequently brutalised by restoration but is almost redeemed by ancient and brilliant coloured windows of French or Belgian glass of extraordinary beauty.

I had often wondered why the couple were wedded in what was a tiny, out-of-the-way Oxfordshire village where no-one went. A lady arranging flowers in Shiplake's church told me:

They met in 1836, fell deeply in love, but were unable to marry because Tennyson was poor. Tennyson came from Lincolnshire. Emily came of a landed Berkshire family who had lost their money. It wasn't until the success of his *In Memoriam*, nearly 15 years after they first met, that the poet felt able to ask Emily to become his bride when they met again, almost by chance, at her cousin's house in Shiplake. They took out a special licence and were married one month later in Shiplake Church. The first night of their honeymoon was spent in Pangbourne.

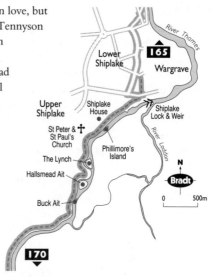

Tennyson, a shrewd businessman, didn't pay the parson for conducting the marriage ceremony. Instead he composed a bad poem and made a present of it to the church:

> Vicar of this pleasant spot,
> Where it was my chance to marry,
> Happy, happy be your lot,
> In the vicarage by the quarry.

Ah, well, perhaps marriage had temporarily deranged Tennyson's poetical abilities.

'They were very much devoted to the Thames and Thameside villages,' the lady in Shiplake church told me. When they settled, for a time, in Sussex, Tennyson told a friend he liked his house and that 'It wants nothing but the great river Thames looping along through the midst of it'. He no doubt also had the upper Thames in mind for the opening lines of *The Lady of Shalott*:

> On either side of the river lie
> Long fields of barley and of rye.

Another poet and a famous author also have connections with Shiplake. **Algernon Charles Swinburne** (1837–1909) used to visit his parents at their 'Holmwood' Georgian country home, a mile northwest of the village, in order to dry out after one of his many drinking sprees. The author, **George Orwell**, real name Eric Blair (1903–50), lived as a child in a house called 'Roselawn' in Station Road, on the corner with Quarry Lane.

SONNING

From Shiplake, two miles of leisurely walking carries Thames Pathers through a tree-lined avenue, with pleasure boats tethered to both banks of the ever-slimming river. It passes four small islands – **The Lynch**, **Hallsmead**, **Buck** and **Long** – to **Sonning Bridge**, where the Thames Path crosses over the 18th-century, hump-backed bridge, from Oxfordshire to Berkshire, and then into Sonning, 'the most fairy-like nook on the whole river', according to Jerome K Jerome.

There's a palatial house, designed to look like the White House in Washington DC, complete with its own helicopter pad, on the bend of the river at Sonning. 'Don't mention its name, don't describe it too well,' begged its owner, the spoon-bending **Uri Geller**, who was about to put the house and grounds on the market for a princely £10 million. There are eight bedrooms, five bathrooms, seven acres of grounds with a swimming pool and tennis court – 'a very special house,' said Mr Geller, who bought the property mainly because of its river views. The wooden enclosure around the house protects his privacy. 'Boats pass by but they can't see me swimming.'

Arguably the prettiest of all Thameside villages, Sonning appears to have everything going for it: a river-hollow setting, thatched and timber-framed cottages, a web of narrow streets, a long history. But it is all a bit unreal, more like a carefully orchestrated film set than a village of people and bricks and mortar. Every cottage, each one a smother of roses, honeysuckle, clematis, jasmine, is desperately preserved, lived in by the quietly wealthy who anxiously avoid and studiously hate the summer-time queue of cars containing rubber-necking gawpers. It is best, if you have the choice, to pass through before cock crow when the web of streets still savour of freshness rather than the fumes of motor cars. Walk from the bridge up Thames Street (look for The Deanery, which was designed by **Edwin Lutyens**, with gardens by **Gertrude Jekyll**, and was lived in once by **Edward Hudson**, founder of *Country Life*), into Pearson Street where there is the imposing Dower House, and then into the high street, where you will find the famous **Bull** inn and the church.

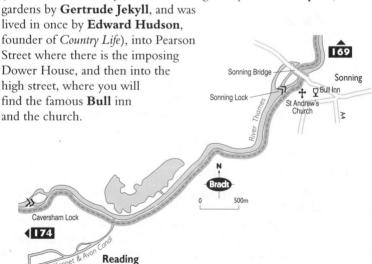

A 19th-century Sonning lock-keeper, **James Sadler**, a poet, wrote affectionately about his village:

> Is there a spot more lovely than the rest,
> By art improved, by nature truly blest?
> A noble river at its base is running,
> It is a little village known as Sonning.

The **Reverend Sydney Smith** (1771–1845), clergyman, famous essayist and wit, lived here for a while, in a cottage off the main street, although no-one I met could point me towards the correct one. Smith described his life in Sonning as 'a kind of healthy grave', and when asked to define heaven, replied: 'Eating paté de foie gras to the sound of trumpets'.

    St Andrew's Church, close by the Bull inn – 'low quaint rooms and latticed windows' (*Three Men in a Boat*) – is not much changed from the Reverend Smith's day. It is remarkable for its monuments; there are, for example, excellent Tudor brasses, a carved oak screen, and a Saxon coffin lid. St Andrew's is Norman, with interesting memorials. There's a wonderful brass on the chancel floor, dedicated to **Sir Laurence Fyton** – 38 inches tall, dressed in armour, his hands clasped in prayer, and a sickle-shaped speech bubble curving over his head. Another memorial, 'The Rich', in the tower, is 'the vilest paganism imaginable', according to the art historian Pevsner. Clearly, then, it should feature on everyone's itinerary. Jane Austen's uncle, **Reverend Edward Cooper**, was made rector of the church in 1784 and she may have visited him here, although no records of her coming have been found. The churchyard, soft-brick walled, peaceful, leads down to the river and the Thames Path which runs along the southern bank into Reading.

    The **lock gardens** at Sonning are a lovely sight in summer. Almost lost in the trees on the opposite side of the river, in **Sonning Eye**, is a restored mill, mentioned in the Domesday Book, now converted into an out-of-town theatre with restaurant, but the mill-race still roars. Top-name stars often perform here.

    It's a 1.69-mile (2.46km) walk from Sonning Bridge to **Blake's Lock**, where the Thames is joined by the Kennet, a famous chalk stream where wealthy folk fish for stew-pond trout. The Kennet is inextricably linked to the **Kennet and Avon Canal**, whose entire 87 miles (140km) can be explored, via Bath and Bristol, to the Bristol Channel.

    The Thames Path crosses the canal entrance via **Horseshoe Bridge**, attached to the 1839 Brunel Great Western Railway Bridge. Just under a mile further on, past a supermarket where customers can, and occasionally do, arrive by water, is **Caversham Lock**, with **Reading Bridge** upstream of that.

READING

Jerome K Jerome considered the riverside of Reading 'dirty and dismal'. It has improved since his day and now provides a more or less pleasant riverside walk through the town. I wouldn't linger long, though, because there are much nicer things beyond – lovely Mapledurham, for example, where the Thames entirely regains its countrified heart, while from Mapledurham up to Streatley and Pangbourne, and far beyond, the river is glorious, just glorious.

There are, though, some nice things to be found in Reading. There is a grand museum, on the corner of Blagrave Street and Valpy Street, displaying all manner of things to do, and not to do, with the history of the town.

> *Visitor information* Reading Museum (tel: 0118 939 9800; email: info@readingmuseum.org.uk) is in the town hall in Blagrave Street at the centre of the town. Open Tue–Sat 10.00–16.00 (Thu 10.00–19.00), Sun and bank holidays 14.00–16.00. Admission free.

Gloomy **Reading Gaol** glares over the ruins of **Reading Abbey** in the southeast corner of **Forbury Gardens**. It is not half as intriguing a building as **Kenneth Grahame** made it sound in *Wind in the Willows*:

> . . . across the hollow-sounding drawbridge, below the spiky portcullis, under the frowning archway of the grim old castle, whose ancient towers soared high overhead, past guardrooms. . .
>
> The gaoler nodded grimly, laying his withered hand on the shoulder of the miserable Toad. The rusty key creaked in the Lock,

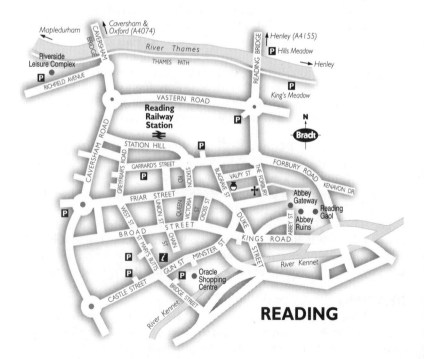

READING

> the great door clanged behind them; and Toad was a helpless prisoner
> in the remotest dungeon of the best-guarded keep of the stoutest
> castle in all the length and breadth of Merry England.

The gaol would hardly be worth a second look if it hadn't once contained Mr Toad and, of course, Oscar Wilde.

Oscar Wilde was gaoled here, with hard labour, between 1895 and 1897, for 'ambiguous sexuality and practices'. His labour, as it happens, wasn't so hard; he worked in the garden and the prison library. Even so, life was onerous for one who confessed to being overcome with 'distress without end or limit'. Shortly after his release in 1897, Wilde fled to France, and later, inspired by the fate of a fellow prisoner, Charles Woolridge, who was hanged at Reading Gaol on July 7 1986 for cutting the throat of his unfaithful wife, wrote *The Ballad of Reading Gaol*:

> Yet each man kills the thing he loves,
> By each let this be heard,
> Some do it with a bitter look,
> Some with a flattering word.
> The coward does it with a kiss,
> The brave man with a sword.

There's a **Jane Austen** remnant in Reading as well, but that's not worth much of a look either. In fact there's very little of it left. It's at the **Abbey Gateway**, on Abbot's Walk, where Jane and her sister Cassandra went to Mrs La Tournele's boarding school in 1785. The original house, in the gatehouse of Reading's ruined abbey, was rebuilt in 1861 after collapsing, but not before Miss Austen's school was photographed by the English pioneer of photography, **William Henry Fox Talbot** (1800–77). The photograph, I am told, is on exhibition with other examples of Talbot's work at the Laycock Abbey National Trust museum in Wiltshire.

On the north wall of the ruined abbey chapter house is a plaque inscribed with the four-part harmony, words and music, of 'Somer is icumen in', the c1250 pop song hit which was used by **Benjamin Britten** in his 1949 'Spring Symphony'. It was discovered in Reading, hidden in the pages of the early-13th-century abbey journal.

Enough of towns. Let's head on up the river.

Reading to Wallingford

17

Distances From Reading Bridge: Caversham Bridge 0.51 miles
(0.816km), Mapledurham Lock 4.23 miles (6.8km), Whitchurch Lock
6.41 miles (6.25km), Goring Bridge 10.51 miles (16.8km), Moulsford
Railway Bridge 13.16 miles (21km), Wallingford Bridge 16.46 miles
(26.3km)

On the short reach between Reading and Caversham bridges is **Fry's Island**,
unique as the location of the only bowls club in Britain reached by ferry.
Locals call it 'Montfort Island' after a duel fought there in 1163 between
Simon de Montfort and another nobleman who had been accused of
dropping the royal standard during a battle with the Welsh. It must have been
quite a gala occasion because **King Henry II** came along to watch de Montfort
beat the other chap up.

MAPLEDURHAM

After Reading, the Thames Path runs through the dreary suburbs of
Caversham (on the north bank) and **Tilehurst** (on the south). If it were not
that lovely Mapledurham House and Mill and hamlet are only two miles away
then they would be dull miles indeed. Caversham, wrote **Henry James**,
sprawls like 'an amorphous invertebrate'. It is a place of soulless villas. Soon,
though, open meadows on the Oxfordshire bank
help the river regain its spirits. After a brief
diversion through the

straggling A329 'village' of Purley-on-Thames, there are glimpses of the ancient earth-red walls of the classically beautiful manor, mill, and hamlet of Mapledurham, all on the far side of the lock. Sadly, none of this wonder can be reached from the Thames Path, but, if you wish, it is possible to travel from Reading to Mapledurham on the launch *Caversham Lady*, which leaves Caversham Bridge when the mill and house are open (see *Visitor Information* box, page 176).

Mapledurham House

Mapledurham Lock inspired **E H Shepard**'s drawings for Kenneth Grahame's *Wind in the Willows*, while **Mapledurham House** is said to be a model for Toad Hall (as is Hardwick Hall – see page 177 – and a number of other Thameside mansions). Peculiarly, Shepard is always remembered by his initials, 'E H'. I looked him up in a biographical dictionary and found that his forenames were Ernest Howard.

John Galsworthy changed the name of Mapledurham House to 'The Shelter', and housed Soames Forsyte there in the closing pages of the *Forsyte Saga*. Soames is supposedly buried under a crab-apple tree in the churchyard within sight and hearing of the river that to Galsworthy was 'the emblem of essential change'.

But these are fictional. The reality of Mapledurham is good, even better – an extraordinary relic of feudal England bypassed by time and the A4074 – and certainly the best-preserved of any riverside village below Kelmscot (see page 214). There is no shop, no pub and no post office; just the house, the church, the mill, two cottages, and a single street ending in a cluster of almshouses built in 1614. You can draw breath here and listen to the river's sighs.

Mapledurham House is still the home of the **Blounts** despite the passing of four centuries. It was built by the family, at the time of the Spanish Armada, in the shape of an 'E' for 'Elizabeth', the queen. It has mullioned windows, pointed gables, high chimneys, ornamental turrets, and bricks so weathered that the light turns them sometimes rose-red, sometimes pink, sometimes deep orange. Open to visitors from Easter until the end of September, the house also has some finely decorated rooms and an 18th-century chapel attached. There is a priest-hole and a secret passage, giving weight to stories that the Catholic Blounts were often persecuted by the English Church, and would hide fleeing priests. The Mapledurham estate was the setting for the film *The Eagle Has Landed* and, in more recent times, for TV films starring John Thaw as Inspector Morse and the Joanna Lumley series *Class Act*.

The diminutive **church**, distinctive with a square tower and a pyramid roof, lies within yards of the house. Its most remarkable feature is the Blount aisle

POPE AND MAPLEDURHAM HOUSE

The poet Alexander Pope, whose love for the Blount sisters was a great romance, often visited Mapledurham House. **Martha** was 17, and **Teresa** 19. They were undeterred by Pope's lack of inches (four feet and six inches – 1.3m), his deformed spine, and his ponderous limp. He was 19 when he was attracted, first by Martha, then by Teresa whom he called 'Patty', and then by Martha again. As venomous as a viper in old age, Pope's Mapledurham youth was by all accounts a happy one. In later life, when he was rich and famous and of acid tongue, he gave Teresa an annuity of £40 on condition that she did not marry anybody else for six years. Nor did she. But he still loved Martha best, nevertheless . . .

which belongs not to the church, which is Anglican, but to the Blounts, who aren't. This is an anomaly which upset a 19th-century vicar so greatly that he argued to a higher authority that the aisle should be returned to the church. However, he lost on the grounds that the Blounts had enjoyed its exclusive use for centuries, looked after the place and, in any case, kept the church locked shut and wouldn't let anybody else have a key.

One of the vicars was **Edward Coleridge**, nephew of the poet. Another was **Lord Augustus Fitz-Clarence**, fifth of **William IV**'s ten children by the king's actress-mistress, Mrs Jordan. Goodness knows why Augustus, 24, chose to become vicar of this tiny and isolated parish – unless he had most unusual good taste for a Hanoverian, and hankered for a rural and simple life. He had a tough time wresting the job away from the previous vicar, who only went when the king gave him the bishopric of Chester. The Reverend Fitz-Clarence had the privilege of preaching to his own father on the morning of William's accession to the throne.

The weatherboarded **Mapledurham Mill**, fringed by trees and a picturesque weir at its feet, was converted to electric power in the early years of this century. Corn is still ground here occasionally. It is neither the biggest nor the most impressive mill on the Thames, but it is one of the prettiest.

Visitor information Mapledurham House and grounds are open Easter–Sep (Sat, Sun and bank holidays 14.00–17.00). Mapledurham Watermill is open (same times, same days, same period of the year as the house). For further details, tel: 0118 972 3350.

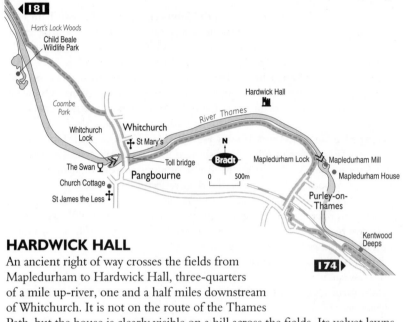

HARDWICK HALL

An ancient right of way crosses the fields from
Mapledurham to Hardwick Hall, three-quarters
of a mile up-river, one and a half miles downstream
of Whitchurch. It is not on the route of the Thames
Path, but the house is clearly visible on a hill across the fields. Its velvet lawns
and dark shrubberies stretch almost to the edge of the river. **Elizabeth I**
stayed here on one of her progresses. **Charles I**
popped by when he was a prisoner on a
closely escorted day out to play bowls on
the hill behind the house in July
1647. After the game he
was given refreshments
by the lady of the house,
whose portrait now
hangs in the hall.

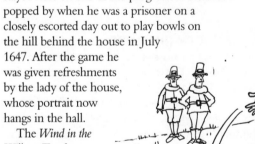

The *Wind in the
Willows* Toad
actually lived here
– at least Sir Charles
Rose, MP, did in the
late 19th and early 20th centuries, and he is said to have been the model for
Toad. Shepard certainly used parts of Hardwick in his drawings of Toad Hall.
Pleasantly irregular and two storeys high, the house stands at the foot of the
Chiltern Hills. A roseate mansion with clusters of gables and chimneys, it was
built for lords during the reign of Richard II, when equality was nothing and
wealth and power everything. It was partly rebuilt after Parliamentarian
vandals knocked it about a bit during the English Civil War. A room on the
first floor is rich in late-16th-century decoration, the whole more impressive
than beautiful.

PANGBOURNE

Let's return to the Thames Path on the southern bank of Mapledurham Lock from where the river curves a majestic sweep two miles to Pangbourne and its poorer, but nicer, cross-river neighbour, Whitchurch-on-Thames, on the northern shore. Writing in 1939, **Robert Gibbings**, in his *Sweet Thames Run Softly*, described the reaches to Pangbourne as so crowded with views, they 'might have dropped from the gold frames of the Royal Academy'. One well-known river artist, **George Vicat Cole**, often painted from his steam launch *Blanche* on these very reaches, sometimes rafting alongside fellow artists **George Leslie** in his punt, **Keeley Halswelle** in *Kelpie*, and **S P Jackson** and his companion dogs in *Ethel*. Cole showed pictures of the *Sunset Afterglow on the Thames near Pangbourne* at the Royal Academy's exhibition of 1866, the bank-side woods blue with mist, the river reflecting fiery skies.

The towpath walk into Pangbourne is far the nicest way to approach the town, with open country nearly all the way – a *Wind in the Willows* riverscape, as drawn by Shepard who came here to sketch – then a graceful, near seamless, entry into the riverside twinships of Pangbourne and Whitchurch. Here you find affluent Victorian villas, neat-clipped lawns, steps down to the water's edge awash with mauve and yellow and scarlet aubrietia and geraniums, gleam-varnished launches slumbering beside moss-green jetties. These are sleepy places.

Berkshire's Pangbourne and Oxfordshire's Whitchurch are divided by a private toll bridge where the Thames Path crosses from Berkshire into Oxfordshire. Both townships make quiet resting places for wealthy

PANGBOURNE AND KENNETH GRAHAME

Kenneth Grahame retired to Pangbourne after his son was killed in a railway accident. He lived at **Church Cottage**, next to the church, until his death in 1932 at the age of 73. Behind a high fence, the handsome but modest house looks much the same as it did when he lived here, and the old village lock-up in the garden (where drunks were incarcerated until they dried up) is still the tool shed. The owners have been known to let callers look inside the cottage, providing they ask nicely, but I consider it an impertinence.

Grahame was well liked, but didn't take much part in local affairs. His wife Elspeth did, and is still remembered by long-time Pangbourne residents as being 'nice but batty'. An elderly gent, who was a boy when the Grahames lived here, told me that his mum used to say the Grahames were 'careful with their cash', had no servants, and were often seen sitting together in the front porch 'pecking at their lunch from a paper bag'. Neither Grahame nor Elspeth ever recovered from the death of their son, who was found dead on the railway line near Oxford's Port Meadow in 1920, struck by a train. The coroner recorded accidental death, but people to this day suspect suicide. Elspeth sold her son's clothes at a jumble sale.

commuters. Pangbourne, in particular, retains traces of its former Edwardian elegance – despite the main Reading–Oxford road which pierces its heart.

The **Swan Inn** – Jerome K Jerome's 'quaint little Swan Inn, as familiar to the habitués of the Art Exhibitions as it is to its own inhabitants' – is no longer so much the haunt of artists but of sightseeing visitors and local residents able to afford the price of these affluent regions. The 'three men in a boat' crept stealthily away from the river at the Swan, after returning here in a downpour, and slipped quietly back to town – 'three men well out of a boat,' said Harris on the final page.

As well as Kenneth Grahame (see box below), other famous people have lived in or close by Pangbourne: D H Lawrence, Lytton Strachey and D H Evans all spring to mind. **D H Lawrence** lived at a house called 'Kylemore' (next to the public footpath, more or less opposite a house called 'Wild Wood' on the A329 Reading–Oxford road). **Lytton Strachey** lived at 'Mill House' in Sulham Road, Tidmarsh, a mile from Pangbourne on the A340, when he was correcting proofs of his *Eminent Victorians* and when he began work on his biography of Queen Victoria in 1917, and at various other times between then and 1924. **D H Evans**, founder of the famous shopping chain, lived at 'Shooters Hill House' (now the masonic hall). In 1896 he built the seven houses facing the river just upstream of the Swan; Edwardian locals called the houses the 'seven deadly sins' because, they maintained, Evans kept mistresses in each and every one of them, including the society hostess **Lady Cunard**.

The **Church of St James the Less** is not old, but the pulpit is Jacobean and there is a fine tomb to **Sir John Davies** and his two wives, with

Grahame had begun his tales of the riverbank as a bedtime story on Alastair's fourth birthday in 1904. The boy had asked for a story about a mole, a giraffe and a rat. After several nights the giraffe became a toad and *Wind in the Willows* was born on the reaches of the river Thames between Pangbourne and Cookham.

The great mansions of Mapledurham, Harleyford and Hardwick, and no doubt others as well, all near the river, suggested Toad Hall, and the sinister Quarry Wood gave birth to the Wild Wood (see also pages 139 and 143). Three years later, Grahame was persuaded to turn the tale into a book. It was published in 1908. The snooty critic at *The Times* dismissed it as a 'negligible contribution to natural history'. What a nerd he must have been! The book sold well in any case, and was reprinted three times in the following year.

Wind in the Willows became so famous that when Grahame died on July 5 1932, schoolchildren decorated Pangbourne's St James the Less church (see text above) with willows gathered from the riverbank. He was buried not here but in St Cross churchyard, near the river Cherwell in Oxford, in the same grave as his son. At the north end of Pangbourne's main street he is commemorated by a sign shared, curiously, with King Berhtulf of Mercia, who gave the town its charter in the 9th century AD.

recumbent effigies and the figures of two little children kneeling, half-hidden behind the organ. Sir John was present at the capture of Cadiz in 1596, and was knighted on the battlefield by the Earl of Essex. He bought the manor of Pangbourne in 1613, but died six years later. The church houses a rare collection of seven 'hatchments' – large diamond-shaped boards painted with the coat of arms of the local **Breedon family**, who were lords of the manor. The boards were paraded at the funeral of each deceased Breedon, and the one on the north wall has a skull replacing the family crest, denoting the last of the Breedon line.

The stern but imposing building on the Berkshire hills overlooking the river is **Pangbourne College**, founded in 1917 for the training of boys for the Royal Navy and the merchant service.

WHITCHURCH

The Thames Path changes banks now, crossing the unlovely private toll bridge from Pangbourne to Whitchurch, from Berkshire into Oxfordshire. The bridge is one of only two on the non-tidal Thames charging tolls. When it was opened in 1902, pedestrians, sheep, boars and pigs were all charged the same: 1/2d each. Carriages were 2d 'for each and every wheel'. Since decimalisation, there is no toll for walkers. Look up-river as you cross, for it provides one of the best of all picture-book views of the Thames: tall, overhanging trees, with the gates of **Whitchurch Lock** creating a white foil to the dark green of the river and its banks. The little **River Pang**, after a placid voyage through Berkshire fields and woods, joins the Thames beside the lock; stuffed full of trout, or so they say, it must be paradise to fly-fishers.

The village of Whitchurch-on-Thames is a prettier place than Pangbourne; indeed, it surpasses its pushier and bigger sister altogether. There's a backwater, a mill (mentioned in the Domesday Book), a church, a few red-bricked houses and cottages scattered snug beneath the steep Chiltern Hills. It is quieter, more withdrawn than sophisticated Pangbourne, and has been allowed to grow old gracefully.

Whitchurch

Although most of **St Mary's Church** was rebuilt in 1858, it still retains a Norman doorway and its 15th-century porch. Inside are good Victorian stained glass and a monument to **Richard Lybbe** (died 1599) who was a founding lord of the manor of Hardwick. There's a brass as well, to **Thomas Walysh**, a 'trayer' or 'wine taster' to the royals of the 15th century.

From Whitchurch, the Thames Path takes a Chiltern interlude, a diversion just under two miles long up the B471 hill out of the village. It then bears left (signed to Long Acre Farm and Goring) across the fields alongside Coombe Park, where there was once a grand 18th-century mansion, although now only a single wing remains. Before dropping back to the river opposite **Child Beale Wildlife Park** (where there are ponds and a collection of birds), the path runs along the edge of a sheer-drop chalk pit with stunning views of the Thames. Soon, 82 miles (131km) from London Bridge, the river enters one of its most scenic stretches as it reaches towards dramatic Goring through **Hartslock** beech woods. There used to be a lock here, Hart's Lock, named after a family of lock-keepers. It was removed in 1910.

On the other side of the river, among the Berkshire woods, the limestone mansion of **Basildon Park** is just visible. It was built in 1767, more for show than domestic convenience, by **John Carr**, a good architect but one over-burdened by strict classical rules. **Alexander Pope** decried the building as 'silly':

> 'Tis very fine,
> But where d'ye sleep, or where d'ye dine.
> I see by all you've been telling,
> This tis a house, but not a dwelling.

Not far from the river's edge on the opposite Berkshire shore, a quarter of a mile short of another of Brunel's Great Western Railway bridge masterworks, is the little 13th-century flint church of **Basildon** nestling close to a farmstead. A local man, the agriculturist **Jethro Tull**, lies buried there. He was born in 1674, son of a Berkshire squire, grew up, went to London, didn't like the place, and returned home to invent, in 1701, his seed-drill. He was convinced that the creation of a good seed bed was the basis of good husbandry but was ridiculed by his hide-bound neighbours. Tull stuck to his guns and proved his argument and his seed-drill so successfully that he was able to rename his own farm 'Prosperous'. He was buried in Basildon churchyard on March 9 1740. Also in the church is a sculpture of two boys bathing on a rushy riverbank – a sad memorial to brothers **Edward** and **Ernest Deverell**, aged 15 and 16, who drowned while bathing close by here in 1866.

THE GORING GAP

Beyond Brunel's brick railway bridge, the river sweeps right towards the Goring Gap, which ends at the upstream side of Streatley and Goring at **Cleeve Lock**. First, though, we pass a house called '**The Grott**' on the Berkshire bank. It acquired the name because it was built, in 1810, on the spot where **Lady Jane** of Basildon Park had earlier erected her 'devine grot'. This was one of those peculiar arrangements embellished with shells and corals that sprouted here and there along the Thames when Pope was busy making his own in Twickenham.

Now, we enter the famous Goring Gap. Elsewhere, the Thames is beautiful, stunning, serene. Here it is sheer drama, the result of chaos surging from the inner earth: first, rivers of scalding lava, followed by ice, thus gouging out the ravine of Goring. Now it is beautiful, mellowed by years and turned fruitful by man, shouldered by beechwoods, chestnuts and maples, too.

GORING AND STREATLEY

The Thames Path reaches Goring first, then crosses the long bridge into Streatley, from Oxfordshire into Berkshire where Wessex used to cross into Mercia. This is the end of 'sophisticated' Thames, the final outpost of London commuter country. Look from the bridge, up-river or down, and be thankful for so much beauty: the old mill streams (Streatley Mill has gone, but the Goring Mill remains), the long weir and foaming lasher, two church towers, the tidy lock, and giant trees everywhere (even the eyots are clad in them).

Goring is very Edwardian, with lots of luxury villas and balconied boathouses. Streatley is prettier, although, as **Jerome K Jerome** pointed out, Goring 'is nearer the railway in case you want to slip off without paying your hotel bill'.

Oscar Wilde arrived by train to spend the entire summer of 1893 at 'Ferry Cottage' in Goring's Ferry Lane, where he wrote bits of *An Ideal Husband* and used the name of the village for the play's viscount and Basildon for the countess. **Ferry Cottage**, now much grander than it was in Wilde's day, was enlarged when **Sir Arthur 'Bomber' Harris** (1892–1984) – commander-in-chief of RAF Bomber Command during World War II – spent the final years of his life here.

Chunky-towered **Goring Church**, very English-country, is a wild mix of Gothic styles, even more so than most country churches. It was built at the end of the 11th century, became a convent in the reign of **Henry II**, was remodelled about 1300, and fiddled with again, by the Victorians, who added the apse. The over-preserved church contains one of the oldest bells in England, summoning the faithful for near 700 years, and can even be heard,

STREATLEY & GORING

STREATLEY

GORING

River Thames

The Swan

Goring Lock

RIVER BRIDGE

HIGH STREET

HIGH STREET

Youth hostel

The Bull

A329

READING ROAD

Miller of Mansfield

Goring & Streatley Station

WALLINGFORD ROAD

N

Bradt

sometimes, above the unbearable roar of summertime traffic. (Come to Goring early or late in the day, or out of season, otherwise not at all – that's my advice.) The rood screen is made from wood taken out of HMS *Thunderer*, one of **Nelson**'s ships-of-the-line.

The village has several worthy buildings: near the church are two almshouses dating back to 1786, and a 17th-century vicarage in Manor Road. The **Miller of Mansfield** hotel in Station Road is mainly Georgian, with a 17th-century wing of flint and brick relieved by small Gothic windows, but very 20th-century grim in its bars.

Streatley, also with a chunky church, is more soothing, less swanky, more rural. There is also the famous riverside terrace of the **Swan Hotel**. When I last came this way the only remaining **Oxford College Barge** was moored close by the inn; it may be there still. In the 1880s, according to **Arthur Pask**'s *A Playful Guide to the Thames*, the corridors of the Swan were 'so narrow and wooden that you fancy yourself inside a prison hulk'. In the same decade, the artist **G D Leslie** published his lovely book *Our River*, in which he joked, 'the little coffee room at the Swan has easels and artists' traps in every corner', and the village of Streatley 'swarms with [painter] geniuses and their aesthetically dressed wives'.

In the 1890s, a famous and regular contributor to *Punch* – **Mr Ashby-Sterry**, signing himself the 'Lazy Minstrel' – observed:

> I'd rather much sit here and laze,
> Than scale the hill at Streatley . . .

'POTWELL INN'

I fell in love with **H G Wells**'s Mister Polly when I was a schoolboy, and had imagined one day drinking a mug of ale in the riverside, willow-shaded garden of his 'Potwell Inn' some two miles up-stream of Streatley. How devastating was the reality. This was the Polly's pub I was looking forward to:

> The nearer he came to the place the more he liked it. The windows on the ground floor were long and low, and they had pleasing red blinds. The green tables outside were agreeably ringed with memories of former drinks, and an extensive grapevine spread level branches across the whole front of the place. Against the wall was a broken oar, two boat-hooks, and the stained and faded red cushions of a pleasureboat. One went up three steps to the glass-panelled door and peeped into a broad, low room with a bar and a beer engine, behind which were many bright and helpful-looking bottles against mirrors, and great and little pewter measures, and bottles fastened in brass wire upside down, with their corks replaced by taps, and a white china cask labelled 'Shrub,' and cigar boxes, and boxes of cigarettes, and a couple of Toby jugs and a beautifully coloured hunting scene framed and glazed, showing the most elegant people taking Piper's Cherry Brandy . . .

> (Her) hands are brown, her eyes are grey,
> And trim her nautical array –
> Alas! she swiftly sculls away
> And leaves the Swan at Streatley.

Kenneth Grahame borrowed a friend's cottage in the main street of Streatley (although I cannot tell you which one) for a holiday walking tour of the Thames and the Berkshire Downs. Sidney Ward, a colleague from the bank, recalled a weekend spent with Grahame:

> [At] Streatley . . . we had a grand twenty-mile walk along the Ridgeway [the ancient track along the Chilterns and the Downs – *Ed*]. [We] came home happy and tired, bought some chops and fetched a huge jug of beer from the pub. . . Then great chunks of cheese, new bread, great swills of beer, pipes, bed and heavenly sleep.

Grahame was a great walker, and loved the hills of Berkshire, its woods, meadows, pathways and the Thames. His *The Romance of the Road*, published in 1891, tells of the pleasure of the ancient Ridgeway Path which comes down to the Thames at Streatley and where you may well meet fellow walkers crossing your path:

> The best example I know of an approach to this excellent vitality in roads is the Ridgeway of the North Berkshire Downs. Join it at Streatley, the point where it crosses the Thames: at once it strikes you

All right, so I knew it was fiction, that reality would be different. It was. But I cannot tell you what little likeness today's posh road-house **Beetle and Wedge** bears to Wells's comfortable Potwell, for it saddens me too much. This is not, nor surely ever could have been, the 'quaint, three-gabled old place, overgrown with ivy and shaded by clumps of luxuriant elms', promised by *The Royal River* (various authors) of 1886, '. . . its brick-floored parlour a cool retreat from the glare of the outer world'? Surely this could not have been the idyllic riverside pub where the fastidious playwright **George Bernard Shaw** once stayed, and where the landlord ran a lazy cross-river ferry from here to there? Could today's Beetle and Wedge ever have been the way Wells discovered it as he strolled the riverbank, 'serenely luminous', 'atmospherically still', the river 'at its best'?

I am told that there is an oil painting hanging in the bar, dating from 1830, which shows the sort of riverside the 'three men in a boat' would have known; but I didn't go inside. In fact I couldn't leave fast enough, even though the next two-and-a-bit miles meant a plod up the lane away from the river, then along the traffic-bruised A329 through Moulsford, before the Thames Path rejoined the river at the end of a lane called Papist Way.

out and away from the habitable world in a splendid purposeful
manner, running along the highest ridge of the Downs, a broad green
ribbon of turf. . . [S]uch a track is in some sort humanly
companionable; it really seems to lead you by the hand.

Towards the end of his life, the poet **Laurence Binyon** (1864–1943) lived in Streatley. He is best remembered for the poem 'For the Fallen', which has become an inseparable part of Remembrance Sunday: 'They shall grow not old . . . as we that are left grow old'.

A long hill-climb out of Streatley provides another panoramic view of the Thames Valley: distant hills, farmland, parks and woods, the river a thread of silver fringed by willow trees and poplars. Ashby-Sterry again (great poetry it's not, but ain't it fun!):

I am not certain what's o'clock,
And so I won't go through the lock;
But wisely steer the *Shuttlecock*
Beside the 'Swan' at Streatley!

And when you're here, I'm told that you
Should mount the Hill and see the view;
And gaze in wonder, if you'd do
Its merits most completely:
The air is clear, the sky is fine,

The prospect is, I know, divine –
But most distinctly I decline
To climb the Hill at Streatley

But from the Hill I understand
You gaze across rich pasture land,
And fancy you see Oxford and
P'raps Wallingford and Wheatley:
Upon the winding Thames you gaze.
And though the view's beyond all praise,
I'd rather much sit here and laze
Than scale the Hill at Streatley!

The famous **Bull** pub is at the bottom of Streatley Hill (just a short step from the YHA hostel).

[O]ne of the pleasantest houses of all on the Thames. The exterior is picturesque and antiquated, the interior is comfortable and quaint.

The description was written by **A S Krausse** in his *Pictorial History of the Thames* well over a hundred years ago, but it's still an accurate one. Jerome K Jerome and his companions 'lunched at the Bull'. There is an ancient yew tree in the garden, said to be the burial place of a nun and a monk executed in 1440 'for misconduct'.

I was looking forward to leaving Streatley, not because I didn't like the village (which I did), but because the Beetle and Wedge pub – 'The Potwell Inn' of **H G Wells**'s 1910 novel, *The History of Mr Polly* – was no more than two miles distant (see box, page 184). First, a mile and a bit above Cleeve Lock, we pass on the far bank another famous and extremely ancient pub, **The Leatherne Bottle**. It was here, and thriving, in the 16th and 17th centuries, providing spring water 'very good for the ache of Corns', according to King Charles II's Dr Plor. The pub is now a noted restaurant where diners have included **Emma Thompson**, **Kenneth Branagh**, **Rula Lenska**, **George Cole**, **Willie Carson** and **Keith Floyd**. It no doubt serves wonderful food, but I did not even dare investigate the menu! Its garden supplies herbs and vegetables.

MOULSFORD AND SOUTH AND NORTH STOKE

Moulsford, and South and North Stoke on the opposite shore, are all three fair-to-middling sorts of places. They are hardly worth a special visit, however, even though the contralto who wowed an earlier generation, **Dame Clara Butt**, lived at South Stoke's Brook Lodge until she died (to be buried in the churchyard) in 1936, or because **Michael Caine** lived in the 12th-century Rectory Farmhouse at North Stoke until quite recently.

It took me three miles, and a bit more, to get over my dudgeon about the Beetle and Wedge. But I did. By the time I reached the bridge at Wallingford I felt quite chipper again. Wallingford is a great restorative.

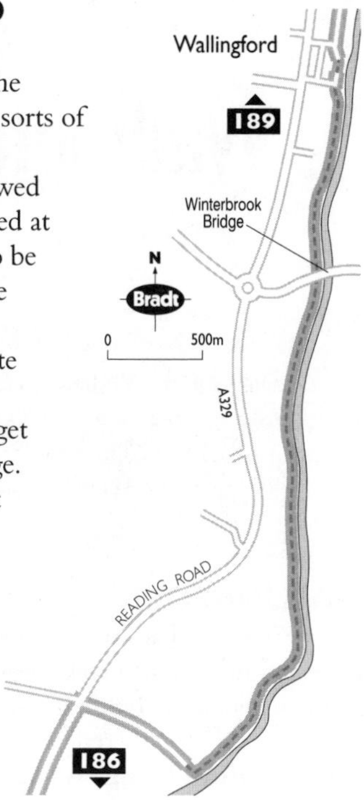

Wallingford

189

Winterbrook Bridge

N

Bradt

0   500m

A329

READING ROAD

186

Wallingford to Abingdon

Distances From Wallingford Bridge: Benson Lock 1.24 miles (1.98km), Shillingford Bridge 2.49 miles (3.98km), Day's Lock 5.20 miles (8.3km), Clifton Hampden Bridge 7.73 (12.36km), Culham Lock 10.99 miles (17.58km), Abingdon Bridge 13.57 miles (21.7km)

WALLINGFORD

On the Thames Path approach to Wallingford Bridge, the gardens of imposing Georgian houses drift elegantly down to the river on a swathe of lawns and a froth of blossom. Behind, the quaint candle-snuffer steeple of **St Peter's Church** provides a serene backdrop.

Wallingford Bridge is fine, exactly the sort of structure that should herald the approach to an ancient town: 17 arches, six spanning the river and the other eleven carrying the road over a flood plain, the whole a comforting medley of bits from the 13th century and more from the 16th, the 18th and the 19th centuries. The bridge was widened in the early years of the 1800s, which is why the arches on the upstream side are rounded and the downstream ones, the originals, are pointed.

William the Conqueror crossed the Thames here after giving Harold one in the eye – a strange route, you might think, from Hastings to London. He may have crossed by ford, or perhaps by a wooden bridge which possibly supplemented the old ford of Walling in 1066. In any case, William obviously didn't like the crossing because he immediately told **Robert d'Oyley** to erect a stone bridge and, later, to build a castle to watch over the river. Wallingford is a comfortable sort of town and an attractive one. Its criss-cross clutter of narrow back-streets is a pleasure to explore. It's a good place for

Wallingford

replenishing stores, too. There's a **Market Place** (where a market is still held every Friday, as it has been since 1155) overlooked by a pillar-propped, Jacobean town hall (1670) which leaves me and other visitors agape with pleasure. The town hall has for some time been too small to cope with bureaucratic needs and now houses a nice little gallery of paintings upstairs and a tourist information centre (tel: 01491 826972) beneath.

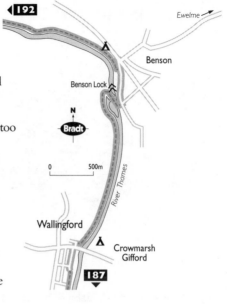

Next to the town hall is the **Corn Exchange** (1856), now a theatre and cinema (which is what people tend to do with corn exchanges these days, before wondering what next to do with them when fewer and fewer people turn up to watch the films and the plays). There is a snug little **Town Museum** (tel: 01491 835065) where I got talking to a local resident called Arnie about famous Wallingfordians. I hardly knew anything about Wallingford or its people when I arrived in town, but Arnie did. He was an overwhelming source of knowledge.

He told me that if I went to the ancient **George and Dragon** pub (at least 500 years old ... and counting) halfway up the high street, which is the long road leading up from the bridge, I would see an outline of tears scratched on the wall. These marks were made by a landlord's daughter, long ago, after she had witnessed her Royalist fiancé being stabbed to death in the bar. **Dick Turpin** is reputed to have often stayed at the George, but Arnie didn't really believe that and I didn't believe the story about the tears so I didn't go to see if they were there.

He then rattled off a stack of other Wallingford facts, with the speed of a Gatling gun; I shall repeat only some of them, not strictly in his words, but in the order he told them:

The most famous Wallingfordian of all is **Sir William Blackstone**, who lived in the 18th century and wrote *Commentaries on the Laws of England*, which influenced the American Declaration of Independence. I found out, subsequently, that Blackstone was born in 1723, died in 1780, is buried in the grounds of St Peter's, and lived at 'Castle Priory', a spacious house between St Peter's Church and the river. His *Commentaries* are still so highly regarded that they are required reading for lawyers.

The castle, now a ruin with not much to see beyond a mound and a derelict wall, was the last Royalist stronghold to surrender, after a 16-week siege. It was destroyed by the Commonwealth victors in 1652.

WALLINGFORD

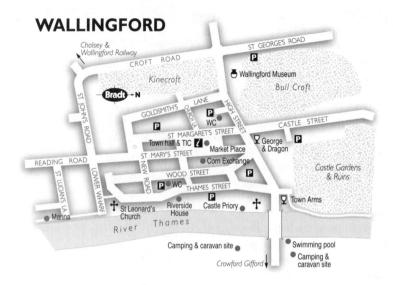

The crime writer **Agatha Christie** (1890–1976) lived for 35 years at 'Winterbrook', a Queen Anne house about a mile out of town overlooking the river, where she brought her second husband, the archaeologist **Max Mallowan**, in 1941. It was at Winterbrook that she wrote a few Poirot novels and a radio play called *The Moustrap*, later adapted for its astounding, record-breaking run on the stage, set in the Great Hall of Berkshire's Monkswell Manor.

The artist-craftsman **William Morris** stayed at the **Town Arms** pub-cum-inn-cum-hotel (like the George and Dragon, it is in the high street) in 1880 during his famous trip up-river from the family's town house in Hammersmith to their country one at Kelmscot, which we shall visit later (see page 214).

The artist **George Dunlop Leslie** lived at a house called the 'Riverside' in Thames Street from 1884 to 1907.

When the Domesday Book was compiled, Wallingford was the largest borough in Berkshire (it is now in Oxfordshire), and more important than Chester, Cambridge, Exeter, Ipswich or Colchester. At one time it had 14 churches, now there are three: St Mary's the More, St Peter's (disused), and St Leonard's. The latter is the oldest and the most interesting because, although mucked about in the 1850s, it was allowed to retain two good Norman arches covered with a diaper pattern, while the whole of the north wall, with herringbone work, is original. The painting over the altar is by **G D Leslie**.

The actress **Sheila Hancock**, wife of the recently deceased *Inspector Morse* star, **John Thaw**, was taught to swim in the Thames at Wallingford when she was a wartime evacuee here.

A curfew bell still sounds at 21.00 every evening from the tower of St Mary's.

An hour and more later, over-Arnied with facts, I tottered back to the Thames Path; he was a nice man, but I wouldn't invite him for a long weekend. Come to think of it, I'd be in two minds about a short weekend as well. On the opposite side of the river, beyond the bridge-site caravan and camping grounds, is the village of **Crowmarsh Gifford**, which sounds like the name of a country dude in a Jilly Cooper brick of a 'bonkbuster' (Ideally, he would be a fat one as gifford is an old English word meaning 'bloated'.) It was once a leper colony, and has a small Norman church with a massive vestry door of oak, formerly in the west wall, which bears the marks of Roundhead bullets.

Visitor information Wallingford Town Museum is open all year (Tue–Fri 14.00–17.00, Sat 10.30–17.00; Sun and bank holidays during Jun–Aug 14.00–17.00). Admission adult £2.50, child (under 16) free.

BENSON

The summertime Thames Path walk from Wallingford to Benson Lock is a profusion of willow-herb, purple loosestrife, vetch and sun-burned grass. When I last came this way, brown-backed swifts and blue-green swallows were skimming the surface of the river, and a dragonfly, striped like a tiger, patrolled the sedge grasses.

The path changes sides at Benson Lock, over the gates and across the weir. There is a Riverside Café, not far from a way-marker recording the distances from London Bridge, 82 miles behind, and Cricklade, 63 more miles to come. Whew!

I remember Benson for its delphiniums and lupins (the village is full of them in memory, their mauve and gold heads sun-cocked behind every wall; or is that, perhaps, just my imagination?) but not for its footfalls of the famous, for there don't seem to have been any. History book people who came this way – and there must have been stacks of them – obviously whisked through so quick they barely left a shadow let alone a footprint. The exceptions are **William Dines** (see below) and **King Charles I**, who paused long enough for a quick Privy Council at the Red Lion pub (now 'Monarch Court House') during the civil war. Benson's heart is at the crossroads, where I wouldn't think the buildings have changed in two hundred, perhaps three hundred, years. There are three

Benson

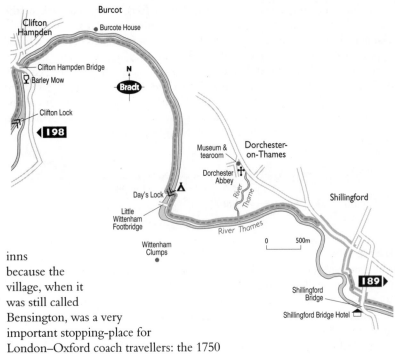

inns because the village, when it was still called Bensington, was a very important stopping-place for London–Oxford coach travellers: the 1750 **Castle Inn**, the nearby **White Hart**, which is Regency, and the **Crown**, dated 1709, in the high street.

The flint-and-stone **St Helen's Church**, much restored, has a Georgian tower. In its churchyard lies William Dines who was a 19th-century would-be spaceman. Lacking the advantages of rocket science, he flew kites and balloons carrying instruments to record conditions in inner space from his home in nearby **Pyrton Hall**.

EWELME

A pleasant lane leads two and a half miles (4km) from Benson to Ewelme (pronounced 'u-elm'), a diversion from the Thames Path but one worth taking for it takes you to the best-preserved 15th-century village in England and Jerome K Jerome's grave.

Ewelme is the most beautiful of all the villages on or near the Thames – and the most richly endowed with ancient buildings; most are old, many very old. Here, local legend has it, **Henry VIII** spent his honeymoon with **Catherine Howard**, and here **Anne Boleyn** pushed him into the King's Pool, which has been known by that name ever since.

Jerome K Jerome is buried in the shadow of the 15th-century **All Saint's Church**. While he was on a motoring tour of England in 1927 he was taken ill and died suddenly. His ashes were brought to All Saint's Church at Ewelme for burial because that's what he had requested; I have not been able to discover what his connections with the village were, or why he chose it for his final resting place. His gravestone is plain and the inscription simple:

> In loving remembrance of Jerome Klapka Jerome. Died June 14th 1927. Aged 68 years. 'For we are labourers together with God.'

During his lifetime he wrote lots of books. Three achieved special fame: *Idle Thoughts of an Idle Fellow*, *Three Men in a Boat*, and *Three Men on the Bummel*. They are funny books, but the funniest, *Three Men in a Boat*, wasn't meant to be funny at all:

> I did not intend to write a funny book at first. I did not know I was a humourist . . . [T]here was to be 'humorous relief', but the book was to have been 'The Story of the Thames', its scenery and history. Somehow it would not come . . . I decided to write the 'humorous relief' first, to get it off my chest, so to speak. After which, in sober frame of mind, I could tackle the scenery and history. I never got there.

Thank goodness he didn't. Thank goodness, too, that his editor made sure he didn't by blue-pencilling slabs of Jerome's purple prose which could well have turned the book into the most put-downable one in the English language – no, that's the English translation of Tolstoy's *War and Peace* (I have a friend who claims to have read it from cover to cover, but I do not believe her). He wrote *Three Men in a Boat* at a time when the delights of the Thames were being 'discovered' by a book-reading public. The year when he put on his candy-striped blazer and took his companions, George Wingrave and Carl Hentschel, afloat on the Thames (there was no dog, despite the subtitle: 'to say nothing of the DOG'), there were 8,000 small craft registered on the river, a year later 12,000.

There are two especially extraordinary things about the book; firstly, that some readers, the lucky ones, come close to hysterical collapse at the funny bits (trying to giggle silently on a crowded bus or train is not a comfortable experience; take it from me), and, secondly, that the lost world of 1888, which the book describes, is not quite lost at all. Jerome's 'fairyland' of Cliveden is still there, as is all the 'loveliness' of most of the river above Reading, and especially the bits we haven't yet done, up to Oxford and the 'stripling' Thames beyond.

'Most of my life, I have dwelt in the neighbourhood of the river,' wrote Jerome in his memoirs.

> I thank old Father Thames for many happy days. We spent our honeymoon, my wife and I, in a little boat. I knew the river well, its deep pools and hidden ways, its quiet backwaters, its sleepy towns and ancient villages.

There are none of them sleepier than Ewelme. Perhaps that's why he chose it for his resting place. The interior of the church is beautiful: carved roof-work and corbel carvings, an octagonal 15th-century font with a contemporary cover carved in wood, over ten feet high and surmounted by a figure of St Michael considered to be the finest of its kind in the county by those who consider such things. The alabaster monumental tomb of Alice Chaucer, grand-daughter of the poet Geoffrey Chaucer, is extraordinary; three-tiered and vast, it was made soon after her death in 1475, an elaborate canopy surmounted by winged figures and sheltering the recumbent effigy of Alice. She was a busy woman, marrying four times, each time bettering herself until she made duchess rank. **Chaucer**, the poet, visited her often here and, it is said, had the village's famous spring in mind when he wrote:

> In world none more clere in hewe,
> Its water ever fresh and newe. . .
> That whelmeth up in wavis breighte,
> Its mountenance of two fingers heighte.

Joined to the church by a covered stairway, worn thin by pilgrims' feet, is **Ewelme's almshouse**, dated 1437, red-bricked apartments wrapped round immaculate lawns. They used to house 13 'distressed men' who were required to attend church five times a day. Now modernised, the houses are still in use. An adjoining school, more like a manor house than a school, claims to be the oldest of its kind in Europe.

The mile walk from **Benson** to **Shillingford Bridge** is as good as everything else about this neighbourhood of the Thames Valley. There are wide open fields on one side, tiny cliffs on the other, a final glimpse of the Chilterns astern, and ahead of us the two famous spinney-topped rounded hills, the '**Wittenham Clumps**'. Locally, the 'Clumps' are better known as the 'Bubs' because they are like breasts, or 'Mother Dunch's Buttocks' because they are like the backside of the wife of the unpopular squire who was Cromwell's uncle. The westernmost hill, **Harp**, is 400 feet above sea level and slightly higher than neighbouring **Sinodun**. Both form conspicuous landmarks, from as far away as Oxford in the north and a scarp of the Chilterns 20 miles distant in the south.

From here to Oxford the Thames twists and turns so much, so often, that now you see the 'Clumps', now you don't, now they are in front, now behind; at times it seems you must be going backwards.

The artist **Paul Nash** (1899–1946), best known for his Battle of Britain war paintings, drew the twin hills in 1912, and then did so again and again. He appears to have become vaguely obsessed with them, and his later oil version, *Landscape of the Vernal Equinox*, was in the late Queen Mother's collection at Clarence House.

The 1827 balustraded Shillingford Bridge, with the wide lawns of sophisticated **Shillingford Bridge Hotel** swooping down to the far bank, looks well. Some say it is one of the finest bridges on the river. I don't, but they do. It lies exactly halfway between Reading and Oxford. From the Thames Path bank there are fine views upstream, and good ones down as well: hotel, ancient bridge, trees, lazy river, meadows and hills – magic!

Here the Thames Path meanders past commemorative plates recording historic floods – the highest, in 1809, level with my head. Soon we cross the meandering River Thame, draining down from the Vale of Aylesbury to join its parent stream.

An 18th-century visitor from Germany, **Pastor Carl Philip Moritz**, chronicled his walk along these reaches in *Journey of a German in England* in 1782:

> The country became so beautiful that I had no wish to go further, but
> lay down on the green turf and feasted my eyes on the view as if
> enchanted. . . [T]he hills by the Thames revealed their many shades
> of green – bright green, dark green, pale green – with the tufted tops
> of trees here and there among them.

One day I came this way when bees were bumbling among the tall grasses and the sky was still the cobweb-blue of early morning, promising soon to turn to the hard enamel of high summer. Mist was rolling over the river and a wood pigeon cooed high in the branches of a giant ash. I sat on the riverbank and dabbled my toes in the last wisps of sunrise mist rising from the river. Perfect!

DORCHESTER

On the far side of the little Thame, a footpath runs inland to nearby Dorchester-on-Thames, while the Thames Path continues on towards Day's Lock. A brief diversion to traffic-free Dorchester's half-timbered houses and thatched cottages is worth the mile diversion there and back. It is a heartening little village, honest, thorn-worn and old, yet, like Harris tweed, with lots more life in it yet so long as do-gooders do not crush it for love or building developers overwhelm it for gold.

Until 1092 it was the thrusting, flourishing capital of Wessex and the centre of an enormous episcopal see. A cathedral was built here in the 7th century, but was torn down after the Norman Conquest and a new abbey church erected in its place. Happily, the magnificent **Dorchester Abbey Church** survived the dissolution and, although the Victorians meant to 'restore' it, there wasn't enough money in the kitty and so most of the 'improvements' were left undone.

There are lots of treasures inside, but one is outstanding: the famous **Jesse window** in the north wall of the sanctuary, a dazzling array of figures in stained glass framed by medieval tracery and sculpted stone. This 14th-century masterpiece records a legend from the Book of Isaiah: 'And there shall come forth a rod out of the stem of Jesse, and a branch shall grow out of his roots . . .'. Another star attraction is the effigy of an unknown knight in the Lady Chapel; its remarkable curves are said to have influenced **Henry Moore**.

The 14th-century pilgrim's guesthouse, beside the path to the church, is now a tearoom (open Wednesday, Thursday and weekend afternoons), where visitors sit round a communal table and mumble to each other in tones mostly reserved for church and conversations in public about sex. The lady serving teas would have none of these sheepish mutterings. 'Pass the cups!' she ordered, and, into the faces of shy arrivals (my wife and I), boomed 'Come in, come in! We're all friends here!' As we shuffled to our seats one of the ladies already at the table snorted into her teacup, which made her neighbour giggle and soon everybody was giggling as well. 'You see! You see! Now we're all friends!' squalled the woman.

Next door, in a one-time schoolroom, is a museum portraying the history of the abbey, the village and the neighbourhood.

Visitor information Dorchester Museum is open every Easter and then from May to September (Tue–Sat 11.00-17.00, Sun 14.00–17.00, bank holidays 11.00–17.00). Admission free.

Somewhere near Day's Lock, where the Thames Path crosses the lock and weir to the other bank, the River Thames becomes Oxford's 'Isis'; I'm not going to attempt an explanation why, however, because nobody I asked was able to give me a convincing reason. Nor where the change of name actually takes place.

There's a nice church at **Little Wittenham**, not strictly on the Thames Path but no distance away either. **Robert Gibbings**, artist and author of *Sweet Thames Run Softly*, which recalls a languorous voyage down-river in a home-made punt, lived here in 'Footbridge Cottage' until his death in 1958. He wrote of the Thames:

> Every mile of water has its own character, every bridge too, every village, and every farm whose meadows are enriched by the silt of winter floods.

It's a lovely book, written so naturally that it seems not to have been written at all.

The 'Wittenham Clumps' (see pages 194 and 195), worthy of climbing unless a long day on the Thames Path has left you short of puff, are in reach by footpath from Little Wittenham. From their beech-copse summits the reward is huge, a vast and panoramic view of southern England from Wallingford to the south and east and the distant wooded hills beyond the ribbon-river to the north.

BURCOT

A mile and a half up-river from Day's Lock, on the far bank of the bight in the great Clifton Hampden horseshoe bend, is the hamlet of Burcot, tucked half-hidden behind the gardens of elegant river-backed villas. In one, 'Burcote Brook', the poet laureate and novelist **John Edward Masefield** lived from 1932 until his death, aged 89, in 1967. He was 'a teller of tales', poetic and prose. His house, now a rest home, has a small boathouse sprouting from a coppice. The teller of tales wrote to a friend that it was,

> a tangled woodland, with a rookery, willows where kingfishers flashed
> and thickets where nightingales nested. . . We look out on the river
> and on Wittenham Clumps. . .

Masefield's estate covered 15 acres. His best-known poems were, probably, 'Sea Fever' ('I must go down to the sea again') and the narrative 'Reynard the Fox'; his best story was the one he wrote for children, *The Midnight Folk*. He wanted his ashes scattered beside the river; instead they were taken out of the sunshine and buried in the gloom of Poet's Corner, Westminster Abbey, which is disgraceful.

CLIFTON HAMPDEN

In summer, the two-and-a-half-mile walk from Day's Lock to majestic Clifton Hampden Bridge is fragrant with the scent of meadow sweet. The bridge, with six red-bricked arches, was built in 1864, replacing a ferry. It was designed by **Sir George Gilbert Scott** who sketched it first on a shirt cuff, complete with the narrow pathway which exempted pedestrians from the toll levied on vehicles. Now it is too narrow to cope with modern traffic. The village, looking even more like a stage set than Sonning does, is memorable for its 16th- and 17th-century thatched rose-pink cottages – like 'tea cosies', declared the architectural historian Pevsner. They are all, each and every one of them, so chocolate-box, so perfectly picture-postcard, that it would be no surprise to trip over Jane Austen heroines strolling among the gardens' hollyhocks.

The church of **St Michael and All Angels** is perched, tastefully as is right and proper, on a little cliff from where there are good views. Inside are two notable memorials, one to **Mrs Sarah Fletcher** who died in 1799, aged 29, an

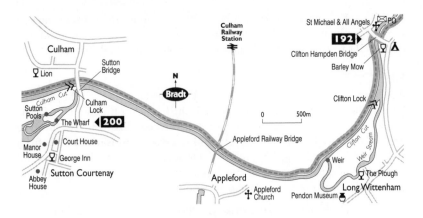

artless Beauty, innocence of Mind, and gentle Manners... But when
Nerves were too delicately spun to bear the rude Shakes and Jostlings...
Nature gave way; she sunk and died a Martyr to Excessive Sensibility.

Poor soul, poor relations; what a burden she must have been on her near and
dear. The second is to **Sergeant William Dyke**, who may have fired the first
shot at the Battle of Waterloo, shouldn't have and probably didn't, but was
reduced to the ranks for doing so anyway. That's what the locals tell you, just
as they also insist that Dyke was later pardoned by the Duke of Wellington
during a flying visit to the neighbourhood. But there is nothing in the history
books about such things. Still, if the local folk believe them then I shall as well.

A short walk upstream of the bridge is the **Barley Mow** pub, the *Three Men
in a Boat*'s

> quaintest, most old-world inn up the river. Its low-pitched gables and
> thatched roof and lattice windows give it a story book appearance,
> while inside it is even still more once-upon-a-timeyfied...

It is said that Jerome wrote some
of *Three Men in a Boat* here, but
that is wrong. **Arthur T Pask**,
whose *Playful Guide to the Thames*
pre-dated *Three Men in a Boat* by
some years, praised the Barley
Mow as likely to appeal to those
who admired 'old-fashioned
places and enjoyed bumping
their heads against ceilings'. He
went on to deplore those
Thames innkeepers who

> keep pace with the times and have his place chock-full of cads and
> rowdies. They are sticking up brand-new beer-machines, and gas-
> fittings and suchlike all along the river now, and seem to forget that

half the charm of doing the river is resting in the queer old shanties
that have held their own for three or four centuries.

The original inn was damaged by fire in 1975
but has been faithfully restored. People –
those of the clever-clogs variety –
sneer at the place and say that it is
nowhere near as good as it once
was, but I like it and I think
Jerome K Jerome would have. I
don't see why you wouldn't as
well.

In one of his more reader-
friendly essays, the writer-critic-
artist-intellectual **John Ruskin**
(1819–1900) recalled standing by
the river at Clifton Hampden,

> wrapt in a poetic dream while the sunset dyed the waters to an ever
> deeper and deeper red, then faded to nothingness as a small boy hurried
> from one side of the bridge to the other, just in time to spit on an
> unlucky oarsman passing underneath.

Sadly, oarsmen are to be found in far fewer numbers these days and cruiser
captains are, more often than not, protected by wheelhouse roofs.

SUTTON COURTENAY

The three-mile Thames Path walk from Clifton Hampden to the simple stone
bridge of Sutton Courtenay, after passing under an ugly iron railway viaduct
near Appleford, is a disappointment, the landscape dull and flat on both sides
of the river. I've walked this walk several times. On one occasion the day was
lovely, once it was middling to dull, and once as long and as boring as a post-
office queue. But there are nice things to be seen at Sutton Courtenay, which
makes it all worthwhile. Although it requires a detour to the other side of the
Thames, then over a series of weir bridges, you really should visit this lovely
village and its tranquil backwater called **Sutton Pools**.

Sutton Courtenay is idyllic. A link path from the Thames Path leads
through the trees to Sutton Weir Pools and the main river, an unspoiled
riverside wonderland. Here a lasher catches the water from the weirs among
magnificent giant willows which fringe the banks from here to the
backwater's top-end join with **Culham Cut**. The sound of rushing water
mingled with birdsong makes this a walk into a sort of Middle-Earth
dreamland of tranquillity which would never have existed were it not for a
greedy miller who charged so much for vessels to pass through the mill-pool
that the Victorians decided to bypass his tolls entirely and build Culham Cut.

The **Old Wharf**, on the tree-canopied backwater of Sutton Pools, was the
home of the last Liberal prime minister, **Herbert Henry Asquith**

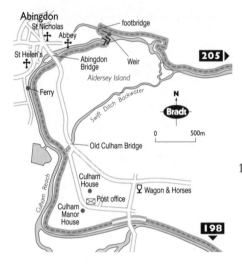

(1852–1928; served as PM between 1908 and 1916), first Earl of Oxford and Asquith. He regarded the neighbourhood of Sutton Courtenay as the 'real essence of England', and is buried in the village churchyard. Near to his grave are those of **George Orwell** (real name Eric Blair; 1903–50), author of *Animal Farm* and *1984*, near the far corner of the churchyard, and **Martha Pye**, who died in 1832 aged 117. There is also a yew tree believed to be 300 years old. The church, facing the village green, contains styles that range from Norman to Tudor times. The tower, with a one-handed clock, is Norman, the brick porch with a parvis, or living-room, above is Tudor, and the chancel and nave date from some time between the two. There are a hexagonal Jacobean pulpit, box pews, and an elegant rood screen, but my personal favourites are the open timber roof and the royal coat of arms of Charles II painted large and bold over the chancel arch.

Sutton Courtenay has a feel of the Middle Ages about it. The grass-verged main street, spacious and timeless, is especially good. So are the buildings. There's the **Court House** near the church, stone-built with narrow lancet windows, and one of the oldest inhabited houses in the county; inside, I am told, there is an open timber roof with carving. The gabled **Courtenay Manor House**, built around about the 1200s, is opposite the **George Inn**; it was once the home of the Courtenais, who were granted the manor by Henry I in 1161, and is now owned by **David Astor**, former editor and director of the *Observer*. The house called **The Abbey**, largely 14th-century, was a cell or grange belonging to the monks of Abingdon.

And so . . . back over Sutton Bridge and past Culham Lock on the Thames Path, with the spire of Abingdon's St Helen's Church in the distance. After the Cut, the path turns sharply to the right along the bank of **Culham Reach**, sometimes called 'Regatta Reach' and a favourite sailing ground for dinghies, then over the timber footbridge spanning the old, now-disused, **Swift Ditch** (meaning 'short cut'), which was the main navigation channel until 1790. The island created by Swift Ditch is **Aldersey Island**. Its open meadows provide a soothing contrast to the tight-knit build of Abingdon opposite, the old weathered bricks and tiles of early-18th-century almshouses dominated by the stone spire of St Helen's Church, which is one of the poet John Masefield's three steeples:

Gleaming with swinging wind-cocks on their perches. . .
And three giant glares making the heavens dun,
Oxford and Wallingford and Abingdon.

The view from the river is perhaps the best country-townscape of the whole Thames.

ABINGDON

The best time to come to Abingdon is at the going down of the sun, when the beech leaves have turned gold, the crowds have mostly returned home, and the town is once again **John Ruskin**'s 'Queen of the Thames'. He lived here for nearly a year, at the **Crown and Thistle Inn** in Bridge Street, while he was the first Slade Professor of Art at Oxford in 1871. There is a sketch of his, entitled simply *Abingdon*, in the ownership of the Brankwood Trust at Coniston in the Lake District; that is unfortunately about all I could find about Ruskin's stay in the town. In fact I couldn't find much about the connections of anyone famous, which is strange for such an old and big-little town. I did find out that **Thomas Trapham**, a Cromwellian who sewed Charles I's head back to its body after the king's execution, lies in **St Helen's Church**, but you wouldn't exactly call him famous, would you? Ditto **Kit Kempster**, who helped build St Paul's Cathedral in London and designed Abingdon's County Hall – but Kempster isn't famous enough to be listed in the *Chambers*

ABINGDON

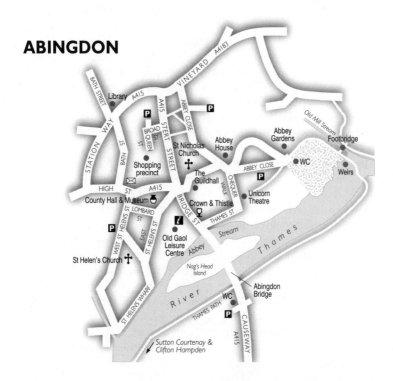

Biographical Dictionary either. Nor are **John** and **Jane Blacknall**, buried in the 12th-century **St Nicholas Church**, who, under the terms of their wills, have bread for the poor placed on their tombs every month.

The painter **Joseph Mallard William Turner** – now that's a name everyone recognises – must have visited Abingdon because he did a watercolour entitled *The Remains of Abingdon Abbey*, and another called *Abingdon Bridge* (now in London's Tate Britain). Other than the paintings, however, I could find no record of his coming or his going but I bet he did.

Abingdon

Still, Abingdon is a town worth visiting, as the nice people who man ('woman' would be more accurate) the TIC desk at 25 Bridge Street (tel: 01235 522711) will tell you. The 'tourist-trail' sights of Abingdon take a day to find and explore and that still leaves a lot unseen.

To my mind, the very best of the town is to be found in the Lady Chapel of St Helen's Church. Here there is a 600-year-old ceiling painting, a medieval masterpiece, recently restored; it has 52 panels on the subject of the *Tree of Jesse*, the same subject as portrayed in the window of Dorchester Abbey Church. There's a chained bible, one of the first examples of **Archbishop William Laud**'s (1573–1645) authorised version. There's a striking 18th-century monument to a family called **Hawkins**, 'crowded', according to **Charles Dickens Jr**, with 'busts of fat naked children weeping tears of colossal size'.

Abingdon Abbey, on the right of the bridge as you enter the town, remains magnificent, even in decay. Founded in AD675, it became the most splendid monastic establishment in Europe, covering three miles in circumference, and was still flourishing up to the Dissolution in 1538. Regrettably, little is left of the **Abbey Buildings** (open daily Apr–end Oct 14.00–16.00, closed remainder of the year and Good Friday; admission £0.60; tel: 01235 533701) at the end of Thames Street. You will find the 15th-century gate near the spacious, tree-girdled Market Place; the Long Gallery (first used for abbey clerks, then as a dormitory for travellers), with a timber gallery on the first floor of the same period; and the 13th-century Prior's House, with its so-called 'Checker' (an exchequer or counting house, which became a granary and then a house of correction in the 19th century, and is now the Unicorn Theatre). Fragments of the abbey also survive in the form of winding paths and rockeries.

The **Old Mill** and its leat, dreamlike and ancient only yards from the rumble of 21st-century traffic, is worth visiting, too. So is the **Tudor Grammar School**, founded for 63 boys of the town by an Abingdon man in the 63rd year of his life during the 63rd year of his century.

Abingdon was the county town of Berkshire for 300 years until it lost its borough status and became part of Oxfordshire in 1974. That's why there's a **county hall** here. Its cellars used to be warehouses, the ground floor a market and the first floor a court room. There is now a **small museum** (open daily 10.40–16.00; closed Christmas Day, Boxing Day and bank holidays; admission free; tel: 01235 523703). The balconied roof is the scene of Abingdon's famous bun-throwing on royal occasions, as it has been ever since the coronation of George III, when free buns were first dropped on to the heads of grateful peasants.

I can only stay for so long in towns before their excessive bustle begins to make me fret. So let's leave and wander further up-river to the place where **Lewis Carroll** said his last goodbyes to Alice. There, how's that for an exit line?

Abingdon to Oxford

Distances From Abingdon Lock: Black Bridge 1.37 miles (2.2km), Nuneham Park 2 miles (3.2km), Nuneham House 2.93 miles (4.68km), Sandford Lock and lasher 4.58 miles (7,3km), Kennington 5.68 miles (9km), Iffley Lock 6.26 miles (10km), River Cherwell (mouth) 7.26 miles (11.6km), Folly Bridge 7.71 miles (12.3km)

NUNEHAM PARK

Nuneham Park, humped within woods above the river on the left-bank (the right and facing one as we walk upstream), is two miles (3.2km) upstream of **Abingdon Lock**. It's an attractive riverscape, marred only by an eyesore railway bridge called Black Bridge. **Lock Wood Island** is passed soon after the bridge. A hundred years ago and more, the garden of a decaying thatched cottage on the island, linked to the far bank by a rustic bridge, was by all accounts a happy gathering place for picnickers. **D S MacColl**'s *The Thames from Source to Sea*, written around 1890, records:

> By the landing place is a cottage with exaggerated thatch. Here they make tea. They make most not for the University picnics that the summer term brings to these hospitable woods, but when the revolt of the town sets in with the long vacation. The river is as populous as ever then with dashing young fellows in flannels, and enchanting young ladies dressed in the depth of fashion. Great and many barges are towed down to Nuneham, and there merry people dance . . . and float up again . . . in the heavy purple dusk, trolling snatches of song.

The **real 'Alice'** (on whom the famous books were to be based), named Alice Liddell and then Alice

Hargreaves, visited Lock Wood Island with **Lewis Carroll**, the cleric and Oxford don (he lectured in mathematics) whose real name was (Reverend) **Charles Dodgson**. Alice was to recall, long after her childhood had gone and she had married and changed her name to Hargreaves, one such visit on June 17 1862:

> When we went on the river . . . with Mr Dodgson which happened at most four or five times every summer term, he always bought out with him a large basket full of cakes, a kettle, which we used to boil under a haycock, if we could find one. On rare occasions we went out for a whole day with him, and then took a large basket with luncheon – cold chicken, and salad and all sorts of good things. One of our favourite whole-day excursions was to row down to Nuneham and picnic in the woods there, in one of the huts specially provided by Mr Harcourt for picnickers. . .
>
> To us the hut might have been a Fairy King's palace, and the picnic a bouquet in our honour. Sometimes we were told stories after luncheon that transported us into Fairyland.

We are coming closer to the very 'wonderland' which Lewis Carroll invented for Alice. Here, though, it is not 'wonderland' but 'through the looking-glass', right here, within the fields and wooded banks of the river, although the Thames is never mentioned in either story. We shall come to 'wonderland' soon after Oxford (see page 210).

Dodgson began to rough out *Through the Looking-Glass* (as a follow-up to *Alice's Adventures in Wonderland*) not long after a boating picnic with Alice to Lock Wood Island when she was 11. However, it was not published until the real Alice was almost grown up and the magic rapport that Dodgson had enjoyed with her, and other young girls, was all but gone.

The white king in *Through the Looking-Glass* is Dodgson; he had always regarded himself as a chivalrous knight escorting Alice until she grew out of childhood. It was at the edge of Nuneham Park woods, over there, beyond and just upstream of Lock Wood Island, where the white knight took his farewell of Alice. And it is because the child Alice was growing up that Dodgson's retrospective farewell is all the more poignant:

> 'You've only a few yards to go,' he said, 'down the hill and over the little brook, and then you'll be a Queen – But you'll stay and see me off first?' he added as Alice turned with an eager look in the direction to which he pointed. 'I shan't be long. You'll wait and wave your handkerchief when I get to that turn in the road! I think you'll encourage me, you see.'

The lonely '**Old Boathouse**' residence above the island is the original late-19th-century Radley College Dry Boathouse. Soon, on the opposite bank, sometimes obscured by trees, is **Nuneham House**, and, prominent on a wooded hill, the Jacobean **Carfax Tower**, which is a folly, transferred here in the 1780s from Oxford – where it wasn't a folly but a redundant part of the city's water-supply system. This 'conduit' was presented to the Earl of Harcourt after it had become a nuisance to coaches when it was slap bang in the middle of Oxford's soon-to-be-widened 'High' in 1787. It is an elaborate affair, carved in the Jacobean manner by one **Otho Nicholson**, whose initials are included upon it; there are mermaids, dragons, unicorns and heaven knows what other devices.

Nuneham House, park and entire village (1,200 acres/480 hectares in all) was bought by the Lord High Chancellor of England, **Viscount Harcourt**, in 1710 when he got fed up with his ancestral seat at Stanton Harcourt, 20 miles up-river. He moved himself, lock, stock and barrel, to Nuneham Courtenay, which he thought much nicer, if a trifle squashed. Indeed, half a century later he decided the house was too squashed, and the views from his front window not what he wanted, and had the old place knocked down and replaced with today's bigger,

grander, Palladian mansion. Not only that, but because the old village of Nuneham was spoiling his view, he had it moved, giving the dispossessed new homes – pairs of identical 18th-century cottages facing each other on the Oxford Road (now the A4074). He built the villagers a new church as well, retaining the original one for his own personal use.

This high-handed action, not uncommon in the 18th century, when power, arrogance and wealth ruled, was attacked by the Irish novelist, playwright and poet **Oliver Goldsmith** (1728–74) in his famous 'The Deserted Village' (1770):

> The man of wealth and pride,
> Takes up a space that many poor supplied. . .

Goldsmith mentions an old widow who moaned so much and well about her impending move that she was allowed to end her days in her clay hovel. There was such a widow at Nuneham. Her name was **Barbara Wyatt**, and there is a memorial to her on the terrace of the park.

Nuneham House and park now belong to Oxford University, from whom permission to visit needs to be obtained. There's not a lot worth saying about the house; it's really quite boring. The setting, though, isn't bad. As that man of letters and collector of the 'gothik devine', **Horace Walpole**, remarked after a visit in 1773:

> Nuneham astonished me with the first *coup d'oeil* of its ugliness, and
> the next day it charmed me. It is as rough as a bear, but capable of
> being made a most agreeable scene. . . Nuneham is not superb, but so
> calm, riant and comfortable, so live-at-able; one wakes in the morning
> on a whole picture of beauty.

Presumably **Queen Victoria** agreed because she chose to spend her honeymoon here. The magazine *Country Life* liked it too, describing it in the 1970s as a

> wide amphitheatre of stately trees, with the house, as it were, in the
> centre of the dress-circle, and the river the orchestra.

Facing the northern boundary of Nuneham Park, alongside the Thames Path, is the new **Radley College Boathouse**. The college, founded in 1847, is a mile west of the river. It rivals Eton as a rowing school and you may well see the college crews training. A mile from Radley is **Sandford Lock** and lasher, where a footbridge crosses the wide weir channel towards a colourful little group of cottages and a small church beyond the newer and duller houses on the other side of the lock. Although of no special interest in itself, the church

THE DROWNING OF PETER PAN

On the evening of Thursday May 19 1921, the author of the play *Peter Pan*, **J M Barrie** (Sir James Matthew Barrie, 1860–1937), left his London flat to post a letter. He was stopped by a reporter and asked if he would provide some background facts to the drowning. 'What drowning?' asked Barrie. The reporter realised that Barrie knew nothing of the incident involving his adopted son, Michael Llewelyn Davies (regarded by most as the model for Peter Pan), who had been drowned earlier that day while bathing in the River Thames at Sandford Pool. Barrie knew that Michael could not swim a stroke, suspected secretly he had committed suicide, and never recovered from the shock.

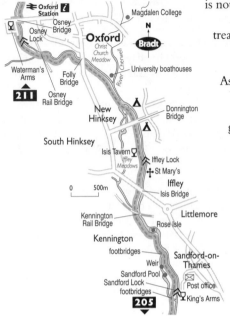

is notable because it contains, almost unheralded, one of the greatest treasures of the entire river. This is a beautiful piece of alabaster carving representing the Assumption of the Virgin, upheld by angels with a reliquary at the base on which are traces of gilding and colour. It was found buried for preservation in the church porch.

People still bathe in the **Sandford Lasher**, astonishing given its thunderous fury and the memorial beside it to Christ Church College graduates who have been drowned here. One was the original **Peter Pan** (see box, page 207). Above Sandford Lock is **Kennington** on this bank, **Littlemore** on the other . . . and the first grubby hints of industrial Oxford ahead. **Bagley Wood**, to the far west of Kennington, is referred to by **Matthew Arnold** in 'The Scholar Gipsy'.

LITTLEMORE

Littlemore was the home and retreat of **John Henry Newman** (1801–90), a prelate and theologian pursued by the press the way pop idols and media personalities are hounded today. He had sought renascence of the Church of Rome within the Church of England establishment in the days when such matters were regarded as grave and important. He failed and was forced to retreat from Oxford, where he was vicar of the university church of St Mary, to Littlemore where, he complained,

> I cannot walk into or out of my house, but curious eyes are upon me.
> I had thought that an Englishman's house was his castle, but the
> newspapers thought otherwise. . .

Newman had wanted to work and die in the University of Oxford but he entered it only once again, after an absence of 30 years. He wrote:

> There used to be much snap-dragon growing on the walls of my
> freshman's rooms there, and I had for years taken it as an emblem of
> my perpetual residence even unto the death in my university.

Newman's village and house is now buried and lost in a wilderness of Littlemore villas. I wouldn't bother to look for either if I were you, but walk on beneath the traffic-growling **Isis Bridge** to the 812-acre (33-hectare) **Iffley Meadow**, where rare fritillary blooms are a mass of purple in the spring.

IFFLEY

The 12th-century **St Mary's Church** in Iffley's suburbs can be reached via the rustic footbridge over the weir. It is worth the diversion: an 800-year-old church almost unchanged since the day it was built, and one of the best-preserved Norman churches in the whole of England. There's a doorway with flowers just like those carved in the cathedral porch at Spain's Santiago di Compostela, and others with fishes and animals and birds. There are no transepts, aisles or chapels, but a Norman nave and round arches highly decorated with zigzags, grotesques, centaurs and mounted knights. The black marble font is contemporary, as is the coloured window, but both are good.

As recently as the middle of the 20th century, funeral processions came by river from Oxford to the church. However, it was decreed that bodies could no longer be carried over the lock (one of the oldest pound locks on the river, built in 1632 and rebuilt in 1923 with rollers for punts) for fear of 'creating a right of way'. I don't understand why it matters that an occasional funeral would cause a 'right-of-way' pause in the workings of the lock, but that is what I was told.

There are no road links with the **Isis Tavern**, ensuring that trade comes purely from the river and the Thames Path. It used to be a farmhouse, but has been a pub since 1842. Until 1979, beer was delivered by punt. There are oars and photographs of stern-faced rowers decorating the bars. I knew the pub before my first visit, or at least I knew its setting, because of a painting, showing Iffley church in the background, by **Peter de Wint** (1784–1849). He was among the finest English watercolour painters ever and another of the Thamesider artists who rowed and roamed the reaches of the upper river. He captured the riverscape scene from Eton to Oxford, and of the London river as well, with a richness rivalled only by Turner, and was greatly praised by Ruskin and Thackeray. The 'nature poet' **John Clare** wrote of him:

> The only artist who produces the real English scenery in which
> Britain's landscapes are seen and felt upon paper with all their poetry
> and exullerating [sic] expression of beauty. . .

The river approach into Oxford is wonderfully unspoiled. At the end of Iffley Meadow it runs under **Donnington Bridge**, half a mile later past the entrance to the River Cherwell, and then, after another half a mile, reaches **Folly Bridge**.

Oxford to the River's Source

Distances From Folly Bridge: Godstow Lock 3.27 miles (5.23km), Eynsham Lock 7.11 miles (11.37km), Bablockhythe Ferry 10.91 (17.5 km), Newbridge 14.92 (23.8), Kelmscott Manor 24.97 miles (39.95km), St John's Bridge 30.46 (48.74km), Halfpenny Bridge, Lechlade (31.11 miles (49.77km), Inglesham 32.11 miles (51.37km), Cricklade 42.19 miles (67.5km), the Source 54.44 miles (87km)

OXFORD

Mile for mile, the number of famous footprints marking the remaining 53 miles (84.9km) from Oxford's Folly Bridge to the source of the baby Thames, in a remote Gloucestershire field, are far fewer than those we have traced in the more urban, crowded stretches of the middle and lower Thames. As a result, despite the distance still to be walked, this is the shortest section of the book. It could be a lot longer, mind, if we were to cram in all the doings and achievements and writings and sayings of the many great Oxford men and women who have walked or voyaged by water from Folly Bridge to the Trout Inn at Godstow. We can't; there isn't the space. But one author, one writing, I can and must include.

Godstow and *Alice's Adventures in Wonderland*

Along these early stretches of the 'stripling Thames', through Binsey and Port Meadow to Godstow, the world of *Alice's Adventures in Wonderland* was created. It was a world of fantasy dreamt up and first told in a rowing skiff taking the **Reverend Charles Lutwidge Dodgson** and friends to a Godstow picnic:

> All in the golden afternoon
> Full leisurely we glide
> For both our oars, with little skill
> By little arms are plied,
> While little hands make vain pretence
> Our wanderings to guide.

Dodgson, tutor of mathematics at Oxford, was, of course, **Lewis Carroll**, a name he came to use in order to hide his growing fame. Dodgson had invited a university associate friend, Robinson Duckworth, and the three daughters of

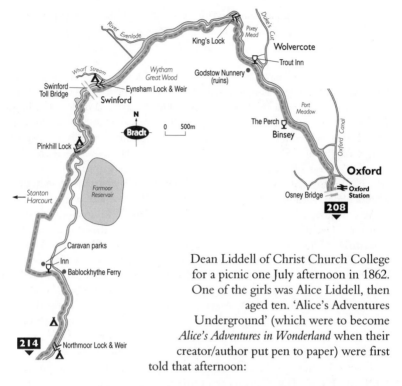

Dean Liddell of Christ Church College for a picnic one July afternoon in 1862. One of the girls was Alice Liddell, then aged ten. 'Alice's Adventures Underground' (which were to become *Alice's Adventures in Wonderland* when their creator/author put pen to paper) were first told that afternoon:

> Alice was beginning to get very tired of sitting by her sister on the bank and of having nothing to do. . . So she was considering, in her own mind (as well as she could, for the hot day made her feel very sleepy and stupid), whether the pleasure of making a daisy-chain would be worth the trouble of getting up and picking the daisies, when suddenly a White Rabbit with pink eyes ran close by her. . .

And those words, of course, were the start of it and the beginnings of a great episode in publishing history.

As an adult, Alice Liddell was to give details of the picnics on the river she enjoyed with Dodgson:

> Mr Dodgson always wore black clergyman's clothes in Oxford, but when he took us out on the river, used to wear white flannel trousers. He also replaced his black top-hat by a hard white straw hat – but of course he retained his black boots, because in those days white tennis shoes had never been heard of. He always carried himself upright, almost more than upright, as if he had swallowed a poker. . .

They boarded their light rowing boat at Folly Bridge. Duckworth rowed stroke. As they went up the river towards Godstow, Dodgson at bow began to tell a story. Robinson Duckworth later recalled:

> I remember turning round and saying, 'Dodgson, is this an extempore
> romance of yours?' And he replied, 'Yes, I'm inventing as we go
> along.'

At Godstow, when a haycock beside the ruins of a nunnery in a meadow had
been found, the tale was continued. As the world now knows, Alice's early
adventures involved a duck (which was Duckworth), a dodo (which was
Dodgson), a lory (which was Lorina Liddell, Alice's elder sister), and an eaglet
(which was her younger sister, Edith). Alice, of course, was Alice. And the
source of the tale? Shakespeare's *A Midsummer Night's Dream*, perhaps, for it
was the white rabbit with pink eyes from Landseer's painting of *The Dream*
which, Dodgson later told a group of friends, 'sent my heroine straight down
a rabbit-hole, without the least idea what was to happen afterwards'.

At Godstow's famous, stone-built **Trout Inn**, and at Godstow Lock,
there are last glimpses of Oxford's spires pricking the sky across **Port
Meadow**. The poet and Oxford man, **Gerald Manley Hopkins**
(1844–89), described this very view as the 'Towered city and branchy
between towers'. Others have praised Oxford with as much extravagant
eloquence. The writer and man-of-letters, **Arthur Quiller-Couch**
(pseudonym 'Q'; 1863–1944) exclaimed, 'Oxford; more beautiful than . . .
dreams!' Much of that beauty has been marred beyond mending. But from
Godstow the warts cannot be seen. **Godstow Nunnery**, and the meadow
where Alice picnicked, are to the left of the lock; the ruins are few, just a
precinct wall and the skeleton of a small chapel where 'Fair Rosamund of
Clifford', **Henry II**'s mistress, was buried.

King Henry, 'a man of low stature and fat of body, of a fresh colour, and
of good expression in his speech', first saw Rosamund walking close by this
very nunnery. The king 'became enamoured, declared his passion and
triumphed over her honour'. He whipped her off to his palace at Woodstock
close by, and hid her from his wife in a 'bower protected by a maze of arches
and winding walls of stone'. She remained hidden for years, but one day the
jealous queen found a way through the maze, following an unravelled ball of
silk dropped by Rosamund, and gave poison to the king's mistress.
Rosamund's body was carried to the choir of Godstow Nunnery and buried
there 'within a sumptuous and wonderfully contrived tomb'. This was in
spite of the zealot Bishop of Lincoln demanding, 'Take the Harlot from
hence and bury her without the church!' The Thames poet **Thomas Love
Peacock** (1785–1866) wrote about the incident in his poem 'The Genius of
the Thames' after a river excursion from Marlow through Oxford towards
the source. He was accompanied by his pale friend, **Percy Bysshe Shelley**
(1792–1822), whom we have met before and shall meet again (see pages
148–9 and 217–18).

The Trout Inn, now the place where dawn bacon-and-egg breakfasts are
served after all-night commemoration balls, was once the guesthouse of
Godstow Nunnery. It's a lovely spot, with generous terrace from which
undergraduates set trout leaping by feeding them with titbits; if you haven't been

to the inn before you may nevertheless recognise it, because the terrace appeared in goodness knows how many episodes of ITV's *Morse*, starring John Thaw.

Not so long ago, as recently as the 1950s, the Trout was tucked hard into the country; now it is almost in Oxford suburbia, just off the ring road, near two large motels. Behind us, across Oxford Canal's Wolvercote Cut, are the final glimpses of the smelly, industrial parts of Oxford. Wonderful, greener things, historic spots, famous yesterday's people, await us as we travel upstream.

From Godstow, the Thames changes its character. It grows suddenly narrower, more intimate, twisting suprisingly, and, until Lechlade, with not a single town or village touching its banks. This is the changeless, 'medieval Thames', as **John Buchan** called it. For the next few miles there are no houses, no roads, no railways, no pubs. Would you believe that, not so very long ago, some guidebooks did not describe the river above Oxford 'because the Upper Thames is so little known'. Let's leap-frog, seeking more footsteps of the famous further on up-river.

Swinford Bridge, by **Eynsham Lock**, was built in 1771 by the Earl of Abingdon, 'whose liberality and public spirit have . . . been amply repaid by the revenue derived from this undertaking', a contemporary commented. It wasn't so long ago that the toll was still one penny per wheel; it's a good deal more these days, £1 when I last crossed this way.

BABLOCKHYTHE

There used to be another river crossing for highway vehicles, at Bablockhythe. A handful of road miles from Oxford, it is a looping, twisting 12 miles (19.2km) by river; but such green, pleasant miles they are, where the only sounds come from the tub-tub-tub of motor-cruisers, the summer drone from bankside grasses, and the whisper of damselflies over the surface of the water.

Matthew Arnold, accompanied by his 'Scholar Gipsy', roamed the river banks at Bab-lock-hithe, as the old folk used to spell out the name, when it was served by a wide-beamed ferry-punt and a famous and important station on the Upper Thames. Comparatively recently (when I crossed this way in the 1960s, or was it the 1970s? – I can't remember), a car ferry worked by chains still served the river here, a descendant of a line of ferries that went back to the 13th century. Now it has gone, replaced by a younger vessel which will come when it is hailed from the shore. Gone, too, is the ancient inn where the ferryman lived, replaced by a modern nasty. Travelling man and writer, **William Senior**, wrote of the old inn in his *Royal River* of the 1880s:

> one of the small old-fashioned inns of the humblest sort, where the rooms are low, the beams big and solid, the floors ragged, and the apartments fitted up with all manner of three-corner cupboards and antique settles.

Long departed is Bablockhythe's once-vaunted loveliness. Matthew Arnold's 'Scholar Gipsy', who crossed the 'stripling Thames' here, would barely recognise this nowadays caravan-cluttered hamlet:

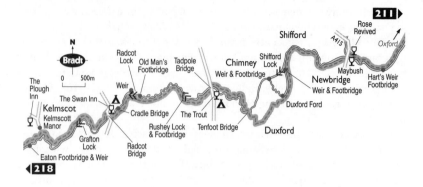

> In hat of antique shape, and cloak of grey
> Crossing the stripling Thames at Bab-lock-hithe
> Trailing in the cool stream they fingers wet
> As the slow punt swings round . . .

The wonder is that the soft green hills overlooking the Thames above Bablockhythe remain the 'warm, green-muffled Cumnor Hills' wandered by the 'Scholar-Gipsy':

> O born in days when wits were fresh and clear
> And life ran gaily as the sparkling Thames,
> Before this strange disease of modern life. . .

NEWBRIDGE AND KELMSCOT

Oxfordshire's Newbridge, beside the mouth of the River Windrush, was 'new' when it was built because all the bridges up-river were older; it is, nevertheless, old enough, dating back to about 1250. There are two pubs here: the **Maybush**, snuggled close to the bridge, and the **Rose Revived** opposite, overlooking the river, once voted the most beautifully named inn in Britain. I have paused at Newbridge not because there are any especially famous footsteps to be traced here, but because I need a drink. Craftsman, poet and artist **William Morris** (1834–96) moored his boat here in 1880. He was travelling upstream from Kelmscott, his house in Hammersmith (see page 43), in his 'houseboat' – which was like a commodious and ornate cricket pavilion on a punt propelled by oars. His destination was another house called Kelmscott, this one a country retreat of his which we shall visit next (see opposite).

His daughter, **May**, described their boat as 'a sort of insane gondola', Morris called it 'old but delightful':

> [I]magine a biggish company boat with a small omnibus on board,
> fitted up luxuriously inside with shelves and a glass-rack, and a sort of
> boot behind this; room for two rowers in front, and I must say for
> not many more except in the cabin or omnibus. Still what a joy, to a
> little mind, to see a landscape out of a square pane of glass, and sleep
> at nights with the stream rushing two inches past one's ear.

CUMNOR VILLAGE AND SIR WALTER SCOTT

Cumnor Village is one mile from the Thames Path, but recommended for those with energy to spare. This pretty Berkshire village, with grey-stone cottages and magnificent rose gardens, is the place of Amy Robart's mysterious death in **Sir Walter Scott**'s (1771–1832) historical romance, *Kenilworth*. The story is, perhaps, based on fact. The real Amy was, indeed, discovered dead at the foot of stairs in Cumnor Place, an Elizabethan mansion demolished in 1811. Married to Robert Dudley, Earl of Leicester, she had been murdered, her neck broken from a fall down stairs. Rumour had it that she had been killed by her husband, or that he had ordered his steward, Anthony Forster, to commit the deed. There was an inquest. One witness said she had heard Amy praying for deliverance from an undefined 'desperation'. But the verdict was accidental death. Rumours to the contrary have persisted ever since, Walter Scott believed them and wove the tale into his romance.

The voyage, from Hammersmith to Kelmscot (the village has one *t*, Morris's manor home has two) took several days; some say it took only two, but I do not believe that such an unwieldy craft could be rowed the distance in such time.

Kelmscott Manor, on the Oxfordshire bank (Gloucestershire is on the other), half a mile upstream from **Radcot Bridge**, is easy to miss because it is half-screened by trees. Secluded, divided from the Thames by rough grazing pasture and half-hidden by a high garden wall, it is almost a secret, and certainly doesn't flaunt its charms. It is four-square, sober and moderate, set in the heart of stone country where, Morris stressed, 'every house must either be built . . . of grey stone, or be a blot on the landscape'. There is not a single 'blot' within a ten-mile (16km) radius – perhaps a good deal more – of Kelmscott Manor.

Morris's manor stands in a perfect river setting. A door in the garden wall opens on to a view of the kind of river Morris (like me) favoured most:

> [T]he smallness of the scale of everything, the short reaches and the
> speedy change of the banks, gives one a feeling of going somewhere,
> of coming to something strange, a feeling of adventure I have not felt
> in bigger waters.

It is not an easy place to find; it is a hard place to leave, 'a heaven on earth,' according to Morris, 'an old stone Elizabethan house, and such a garden close down on the river, a boat house, and all things handy'.

Today, most people think of Morris as the designer of beautiful cottons and wallpapers. But he was already an established writer, artist, designer, interior decorator, printer and businessman when he came by road from London to discover the house in 1871. He was accompanied by his beautiful wife, Janey, and their friend, laudanum-sick, poet-artist and founder member of the pre-Raphaelite brotherhood, **Dante Gabriel Rossetti**. Morris described their first visit:

> We crossed the road, and my hand raised the latch of a door in the
> wall, and we stood presently on a stone path which led up to the old
> house. The garden between the wall and the house was redolent of
> the June flowers, and the roses were rolling over one another with
> that delicious superabundance of small well-tended gardens which at
> first sight takes away all thought save that of beauty. The blackbirds
> were singing their loudest, the doves were cooing on the roof ridge,
> the rooks in the high elm-trees beyond were garrulous among the
> young leaves, and the swifts wheeled whining about the gables.

Rossetti and he took out a joint tenancy. It was a mistake, given that Rossetti
became obsessed with Janey, possibly even fell in love with her although their
relationship has never been chronicled or understood. It is known that after a
time Morris longed for Rossetti to leave. Indeed, it is astonishing that Rossetti
remained so long given that he found life here, beyond the delicious Janey,
unbearably dull, the countryside 'deadly flat', the river walks 'monotonous'
and the village of Kelmscot 'the doziest clump of old beehives . . . you could
find anywhere'. Finally, though, he left after complaining of Morris 'bugging
and blaspheming in a boat', and was so ill with mercury-poisoned delusions of
horror and persecution (brought on by too many swigs of laudanum.

According to its present-day guardians, 16th-century Kelmscott Manor is
little changed since Morris left it for the last time in 1886. It remains soft and
grey and yellow-stoned, a zigzag of gables and angles, with lots of stairs going
up and lots coming down again, and small rooms tumbling one from the
other. But I cannot accept that the interior is unchanged. Most of the
wallpapers are modern, although gorgeous. There are paintings by Rossetti
which would not have been on the walls in Morris's day (including one of
Janey, *Mrs Morris in a Blue Dress*), nor would the tiles by William de Morgan,
wall hangings by Morris himself, or so many of the richly bound books from
the great man's own Kelmscott Press. The furniture is hand-made, the
furnishings hand-woven. Everything is sumptuous.

This is surely not the home it was when Morris and Janey lived there? After
all, when **George Bernard Shaw** and **W B Yeats** came to visit they said it
was 'sketchily furnished, draughty and damp, spartan'. Morris's close friend,
the painter **Edward Burne-Jones** (1833–98), found the place so
uncomfortable that he never stayed too long or too often. Even Janey, in a
letter to the poet and traveller **Wilfred Scawen Blunt** (1840–1922), called her
days at Kelmscott 'a half-savage life'.

It is a privilege to walk in Morris's house, in his garden, in the same
Thameside meadows where he walked. As the poet **Edward Thomas**
observed in his *Literary Pilgrim in England*:

> Morris loved the earth; she was his delight, his joy, his refuge, his
> home; the companion of his uncompanionable thoughts. . . No one
> has praised her better; and the poetry of Nature reveals how close,
> how passionate, he was in his worship.

Shall we move on?

ST JOHN'S BRIDGE TO LECHLADE

One of Morris's favourite walks was to St John's Bridge, then Lechlade and back. Let's follow in his footsteps.

The River Lech falls into the Thames beside the Trout Inn, close by St John's Bridge and St John's Lock. There is a famous Victorian statue of 'Father Thames' here (originally shown at the 1854 Great Exhibition, and subsequently at the source of the Thames until it got so beaten up by vandals that it had to be moved to the safety of St John's in 1973). This was originally a 'flash' lock or 'staunch', a dammed weir through which, in Georgian and Victorian times, craft were sent whooshing downstream on a white-water 'flash' or 'flush' created by lifting boards or 'paddles' jammed across the weir. The historian-novelist **C S Forester** (1899–1966) provides a vivid description of  shooting this very 'flash' lock when he places his naval hero Captain Horatio Hornblower, RN, at the helm of an express barge bound from the Thames and Severn Canal, through Lechlade, to London:

> To him it appeared a wildly reckless thing to do . . . and then it was too late to do anything. . . Hornblower steered for the centre; he could feel the altered trim of the boat as her bows sank and her stern rose on the slop. How they were flying down, down. . . The bows hit the turbulent water with a jar and a splash; the boat lurched in the eddy. . . Two seconds careful steering and they were through . . . gliding over a smooth surface once more, foam-streaked but smooth, and Hornblower was laughing out loud. . .

Do others, I wonder, experience the small *frisson* of excitement I feel on the edge of St John's Lock (or, better still, passing through today's staid pound lock by boat) in recalling that Hornblower – C S Forester's second self, the naval hero of my boyhood – shot this very lock? Silly, isn't it? As a five-star bonus, the poets **Shelley** and **Thomas Love Peacock**, and Shelley's lover (and later wife) **Mary Godwin**, creator and author (as Mary Wollstonecraft Shelley) of *Frankenstein*, hauled themselves up by boat through the same staunch when they

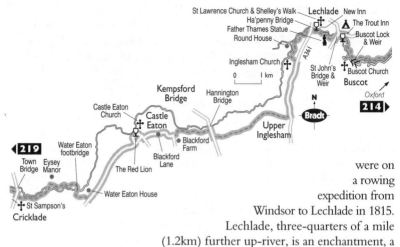

were on
a rowing
expedition from
Windsor to Lechlade in 1815.
Lechlade, three-quarters of a mile
(1.2km) further up-river, is an enchantment, a
comfortable-sized Gloucestershire town, six miles (9.6km) upstream
from Radcot Bridge. Earth-snug and limestone-mellow, this Thames-huddled
township was the destination of Shelley and his companions when they rowed
the 33 miles from Windsor to the 'dim and distant spire' of Lechlade's church.

Upstream navigation for cabin cruisers ends at Lechlade's ancient bow-backed
bridge, called 'Halfpenny Bridge' because half a penny was the price for
pedestrians to cross until the toll was done away with in 1839. Shelley and his
fellow oarsmen, who in those days called themselves 'rowists', meant to go
further – to Cricklade, at least – but a bread-and-butter wearied Shelley was
forced to rest for the night at the 18th-century **New Inn** beside the church. It's
still there, still provides liquid refreshment, meals and accommodation, and still
has lawns down to the river. However, it does not, I think, still serve the 'three
mutton chops, well peppered' which so revived Shelley's strength that he
immediately announced plans to row the length and breadth of the British Isles.
He never did; in fact, once he and his companions had discovered it would cost
them £20 to proceed on to the adjoining Thames and Severn Canal, just
downstream of Inglesham hamlet, they aborted their voyage and returned to
Lechlade. Here, that evening, Shelley wandered into the churchyard and
composed his 'A Summer Evening Churchyard'. A plaque set into the
churchyard wall, at the beginning of what is now called 'Shelley's Walk', quotes
the poem:

> Clothing in hues of heaven thy dim and distant spire,
> Around whose lessening and invisible height
> Gather among the stars the clouds of night.

INGLESHAM

Inglesham is 2.5 miles (4km) south of Lechlade. It has a little **church**, a very
special one, on the riverbank. Mostly 13th-century, it escaped the lunatic
restoration of many Victorian architects but, instead, received the loving care

of **William Morris**, who was commissioned to watch over its gentle restoration. Despite the simple austerity of its exterior, it is a church that cannot be matched by any other in the whole of England. There's a nave, a bellcote above the west gable, north and south aisles, a chancel, a south chapel, and a south porch; all, apart from the porch, are original, and date to about 1200. It is the interior, though, which makes Inglesham so special – a festival of architectural intricacies emerging waist-high above box pews, which spill from the nave into the chancel. The walls are coloured in creams and blotchy greys, crumbling pinks and browns, overlaid here and there by fragments of texts. There is a Saxon sculpture of the 'Virgin and Child' in the south aisle, a 14th-century reredos, 15th-century screens, a 16th-century pulpit, 17th-century squire's and vicar's pews, and 18th- and 19th-century congregational pews. You can reach out and almost touch times past within the shadows of Inglesham Church.

THE RIVER'S SOURCE

Our journey is almost done. It needs another 23 miles (37km) before we reach the source of the Thames in a remote Gloucestershire meadow. We pass on our way the sleepy village of **Kempsford**, which boasts a history older than the Norman Conquest, with the remains of a castle and another fine church. **William Cobbett** (1763–1835) found it 'Very ancient and capacious' when encountering it on one of his rides. We come then to **Castle Eaton**, **Cricklade**, **Ashton Keynes** – where the river, 'far-off, lonely mother of the Thames', is no more than nine feet wide and trickles between tiny stone bridges providing access to the houses – followed by **Somerford Keynes**, and then . . . the source of the River Thames? 'Is this little wet ditch the Historical Thames?" asks an **H G Wells** character. The source is not always easy to find; indeed, during a long and dry summer it would be impossible to find were it not for a reassuring stone sign at Thames Head, a mile from the village of Kemble, three miles west of Cirencester, near the Fosse Way, in the tree-circled dip of a remote hips-and-valley field called **Trewsbury Mead**. There is also an ancient ash tree inscribed with the letters 'T H' for Thames Head. The steep bank behind is the former Thames and Severn Canal, long since abandoned.

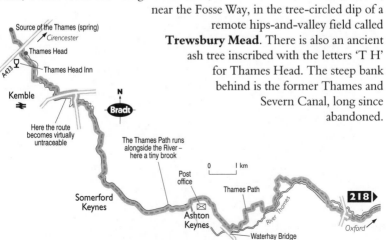

And so our long walk is done. I'm off to the pub, the **Thames Head Inn**, a mile or so (1.6km) back the way we have come (a mile west down the A433 which the Thames Path crossed earlier). The landlord there is accustomed to ordering transport for weary Thames-Path walkers seeking the nearest railway station at Kemble Village.

BRADT ECCENTRICS

Eccentric Britain

The Bradt Guide to Britain's Follies and
Foibles
Benedict le Vay
'Benedict le Vay's splendid indulgence is
occasionally a bit of an eye-popper but mostly a
chuckle, and his obvious affection for the odd
and oddball shines through.' *Observer*

Eccentric London

The Bradt Guide to Britain's Crazy and Curious
Capital
Benedict le Vay
London-born Benedict le Vay revisits his
childhood stomping grounds and devises
district-by-district guides to everything
compelling, curious, bizarre, absurd or hilarious.
Plus the oddest shops, museums, jobs, pubs
and people you could possibly imagine.

Eccentric America

The Bradt Guide to All That's Weird and Wacky
in the USA
Jan Friedman
'Some travel guides are such fun they are worth
reading in their own right; this is, quite definitely,
one of them.' Amazon.com

'Read the first couple of pages of this book and
you'll realise just how much of the great US of A
you've been missing.' *The Sunday Times*

Bradt Guides are available from all good bookshops,
or by post, fax, phone or internet direct from

Bradt Travel Guides Ltd

19 High Street, Chalfont St Peter, Bucks SL9 9QE, England
Tel: 01753 893444 Fax: 01753 892333
Email: info@bradt-travelguides.com Web: www.bradt-travelguides.com

ENGLISH HERITAGE

English Heritage is the independent but government sponsored organisation responsible for the historic environment of England. Its aim is to protect England's unique architectural and archaeological heritage for the benefit and enjoyment of people now and in the future.

Properties

The most visible aspect of its work is the 400-plus sites and monuments in its care, most of which are open to the public, many of them free of charge. They are to be found all over England, and range from World Heritage Sites Stonehenge and Hadrian's Wall, through grand houses like Audley End and Osborne House – favourite home of Queen Victoria – to the ruins of great medieval abbeys and castles, megaliths and ruined chapels. From the castles of Pendennis and St Mawes at the tip of Cornwall, built by Henry VIII after his split from the Pope to counter the possibility of invasion by the forces of Catholic Europe, to Carlisle and Aydon Castles on the Scottish borders, much earlier fortifications against the ever-present threat from the marauding Scots, all of history is here. But not just history: the fact that our heritage is all around us and part of daily life is exemplified by Aydon Castle in its other guise as a working farm right up to 1966.

London properties

In and around London, English Heritage properties range from a length of the wall that protected Roman London, to the Jewel Tower, part of the original Palace of Westminster, and to the grandeur of Kenwood, standing in magnificent grounds beside Hampstead Heath, with its splendid Adam interiors now housing a fine art collection, including a Vermeer and a Rembrandt. Marble Hill House, Chiswick House and Ranger's House are all splendid buildings, and Rangers House now houses part of the amazing Wernher Collection of European art.

A different kind of experience is to be found at two of English Heritage's properties in south-east London. Eltham Palace was one of the major royal medieval palaces, used as a regular home by kings and queens from Edward I to Henry VIII, who grew up there. The magnificent Great Hall was built by Edward IV. But even more remarkable is the Art Deco home grafted into the medieval remains by Stephen and Virginia Courtauld in the 1930s. Their spectacular designs, which included a centrally-heated cage for their pet lemur, Mah-Jongg, have recently been completely restored. Another kind of experience again is to be found at Down House, home of the great Victorian scientist and creator of the Theory of Evolution, Charles Darwin. It was in his study here that he worked on the scientific theories that first scandalised and then revolutionised the world, culminating in the publication of the hugely significant *On the Origin of Species by Means of Natural Selection* in 1859.

Protecting the heritage

But English Heritage does much more than manage the historic properties in its care. As England's principal centre of expertise on all aspects of the historic environment, its advice leads to the protection of the best of the past – some of it surprising! As you look around you while following the walks in this book, you will see hundreds of buildings listed as being of vital historic importance, and therefore preserved for the future. The great buildings that saw history happening are of course on the lists; but so are scores of 'ordinary' buildings down the side streets, houses that were simply homes for generations of Londoners.

The thousands of protected historic monuments include the ruined edifices of England's great industrial past and of the conflicts of the twentieth century – symbols to many of poverty, exploitation and suffering, but nevertheless important as indelible records of huge swathes of history. Conservation areas range from the glorious Georgian terraces of Bath and Stamford through chocolate-box villages to streets of Victorian and Edwardian houses. There are 43 known and researched historic battlefields on the Battlefields Register and some 15,000 historic gardens on the Parks and Gardens Register. Every aspect of England's heritage is covered.

English Heritage supports archaeological work of all kinds, from traditional excavation through geophysical survey of buried remains to the detailed analysis of standing buildings. Archaeological scientists do ground-breaking research in dating methods, artefact conservation and the study of environmental remains such as human and animal bones, pollen and seeds. The Collections and Building Conservation teams carry out wide ranges of research and practical conservation work. The Education Service is internationally acclaimed for the work it does at all levels of formal education. The National Monuments Record houses over eleven million items... One could go on!

Membership and visits

There are currently around 470,000 members of English Heritage, people who support the organisation because they believe the membership fees are a tangible and direct way of supporting its work. Membership also gets them in free to English Heritage properties, and either free or at a reduced price to the hundreds of events that take place at the properties each year. Visitors from overseas can make the most of a trip to England by buying an Overseas Visitors Pass, which will allow them free entry to all the properties for a fixed period. Details of all the possibilities and advantages of joining English Heritage or visiting its sites can be obtained from English Heritage Membership Department, PO Box 570, Swindon SN2 2UR; telephone 0870 333 1181; e-mail members@english-heritage.org.uk

Go on – treat yourselves!

Index

Page numbers in italics indicate maps